Nick Earls is the author of thirteen books, including bestselling novels such as *Zigzag Street*, *Bachelor Kisses* and *Perfect Skin*. His work has been published internationally in English and in translation.

Zigzag Street won a Betty Trask Award in the UK in 1998, and *Perfect Skin* was the only novel nominated for an Australian Comedy Award in 2003. *48 Shades of Brown* was awarded Book of the Year (older readers) by the Children's Book Council of Australia in 2000, and in the US it was a *Kirkus Reviews* selection in its books of the year for 2004.

48 Shades of Brown and *Perfect Skin* have been adapted into feature films, with *Solo un Padre*, the film adapted from the Italian edition of *Perfect Skin*, a top-ten box-office hit in Italy in 2008. *After January*, *48 Shades of Brown*, *Zigzag Street* and *Perfect Skin* have all been successfully adapted for theatre, and the *Zigzag Street* play toured nationally in 2005. *The True Story of Butterfish* is his first work simultaneously written as both a novel and a play.

NICK
EARLS

THE TRUE
STORY OF
BUTTERFISH

VINTAGE BOOKS
Australia

A Vintage book
Published by Random House Australia Pty Ltd
Level 3, 100 Pacific Highway, North Sydney NSW 2060
www.randomhouse.com.au

First published by Vintage in 2009
This edition published by Vintage in 2010

Addresses for companies within the Random House Group can be found at
www.randomhouse.com.au/offices

National Library of Australia
Cataloguing-in-Publication Entry

Earls, Nick, 1963 –.
The true story of Butterfish / Nick Earls.

ISBN 978 1 74166 634 2 (pbk.)

Man – woman relationships—Australia—Fiction.
Rock musicians—Australia—Fiction.

A823.3

Cover design by Luke Causby/Blue Cork
Cover image from Getty Images
Internal design by Midland Typesetters, Australia
Typeset in 13/16 Bembo by Midland Typesetters, Australia
Printed in Australia by Griffin Press, an accredited ISO AS/NZS 14001:2004
Environmental Management System printer

10 9 8 7 6 5 4 3 2 1

I WAS STILL ON my guard back then, when Annaliese Winter came up my driveway in her school uniform with questions to ask about her missing dog. I had stopped work for the day, or for a few hours at least, and I stood in the dark of my loungeroom with a beer I didn't need, watching her through the screen door. A tall stalk of grass was growing between the wheel ruts and she swiped at it with her right hand. I could just make out its head of seeds bobbing in her wake as she came closer.

She had ribbons in her hair, but not in a prissy way. I was sure there was some name for it, for the style. Madonna or Cyndi Lauper had done it that way in the eighties. She was in her school uniform and it was a day in the middle of the week.

Her shoes, heavy black school shoes, clunked on the wooden steps and then on the boards of the verandah. She lifted her hand to knock and saw me inside, or saw something and pressed her face against the screen, using her hands to shield her eyes from the light.

'Hello,' she said. 'Is there someone there?'

I put the beer down and said, 'Yeah,' and didn't know what to say next. 'Yeah, hello.'

She seemed to hover, silhouetted against the bright dry grass behind her and the harsh afternoon light. She was the first person who had come to the door.

'Sorry. Come in, come in,' I said, moving to the door and opening it.

She dropped her hands and stepped back and seemed to smirk.

'I was just working,' I said, though it wasn't true. 'Just doing a couple of things.' She nodded. It was definitely a smirk. She was one of the cool girls at school, she had to be. 'Even though you think I was hiding in the dark like some paranoid old lady watching you come to the door.'

'Clutching a rolling pin in case I was about to attack?' she said, and then she went 'ha' in a cool-girl this-is-all-the-laugh-I'm-giving-you kind of laugh. 'I'm not about to attack.'

She smirked with one side of her mouth and looked up at me through the black spray of her fringe. Her eyes were dark and already she was playing some kind of game with me, or that's how it seemed. Her voice was a little deeper and huskier than I might have expected, so her last line had come out with a hint of something that might have been menace or even seductiveness or just a pitch at adult banter. Whatever it was, it stuck with me and it punctuated the moment and it didn't feel quite right for a conversation with a schoolgirl on my doorstep.

'Well, that's good,' I said. 'That's a relief. I'm Curtis, by the way.'

'Yeah,' she said. 'I'm Annaliese.'

After a half pause she stuck out a hand for me to shake, and she did it with too much force, overplaying

2

confidence, like someone who wasn't actually confident but was in fact in her school uniform talking to an adult she didn't know. This – this confounding mixture – was Annaliese all over, I would realise soon enough. Maybe it's a lot of sixteen-year-old girls – an adult and someone younger both in the one body, the one complex assortment of looks and mannerisms and patterns of speech.

I shook her hand, and then leaned against the verandah rail. Inside didn't seem smart – I'd worked that out. When girls come to your door in school uniform and you're a thirty-five-year-old male in the house alone, you don't take them inside.

'Annaliese Winter,' she said. 'I live next door. I'm looking for my dog.'

'I don't think I've seen a dog,' I told her, and it seemed well short of enough. 'What's it like? What kind of dog?'

'Spaniel. Not so bright.' She smiled, and looked past my shoulder, in the direction of the house that turned out to be hers. 'I haven't seen him since yesterday morning. His name's Oscar, but he's never really got that. I could walk all over the place shouting "Oscar" . . .' She shrugged, and let it go at that.

I fetched a torch from the kitchen. We both figured Oscar had been killed by a snake, but there was no reason to say it. My long grass could have harboured anything – our houses backed onto rainforest and in this drought-stricken dry-baked late spring snakes were turning up in water tanks and cisterns. Already one dog owner had come home to a sleepy python stretched out across the dusty concrete of the garage floor with a kelpie-sized bulge in its belly. That had been in the suburban paper. And the council had been called, and relocated the snake

3

to the nearby bush where its digestive enzymes could do their quiet work.

Usually, though, the issue was venom. So we walked around my house, shining the torchlight through the slats at the bare dust, looking for a spaniel curled up and sick, and we checked around the studio and Annaliese called his name from my back door because he might at least know the sound of her voice. She cupped her hands to her mouth and called out towards the rainforest, and we listened for any sound of him but heard only the breeze and distant cars.

Some strands of her fringe were stuck to her forehead by then, and sweat ran down her neck and into her collar. I thought of offering her a drink.

'Does anyone know you're here?' I said instead.

She rolled her eyes and gave a version of her 'ha' laugh, but with her mouth closed. A 'Hmm', but with a mocking edge to it. 'Yep.' She stepped back into the shade, and looked at me. I felt fat – old and fat and failing to measure up. 'So, what's it like being back here? You've been away a while, yeah?'

'Yeah.' Sweat was ballooning from my armpits and neck across my blue T-shirt and the wind was hot as it skated in from the west and along the verandah. 'How do you know I've been away a while?'

'It's hardly a secret.'

But I was all about secrets, about privacy, about hiding out on the edge of the bush with no one knowing I was even in the country. She had me wondering if I shouldn't have come back. America would be worse though. Derek had stayed in America after the band broke up, and he was leading a mad life. I read about it

4

often enough. Dating starlets, hoovering coke, crashing cars, all in the name of working on his first solo album. He'd taken out a big mortgage on the whole rockstar cliché, if you believed the magazines, and in his case I mostly did. I also knew that the flat styleless moments in between would be killing him first, crushing him slowly as his own chaotic amines mingled with whatever he could buy to turn him into a mess that was still miles away from happy.

I wanted Annaliese to go, and I wanted my beer, which would now be annoyingly warm and wasted and putting a ring of condensation on my sideboard. I was someone with a sideboard now. Who this side of Dickens truly needed a sideboard?

That's what I was thinking when Annaliese said, 'The being away part. That was hardly a secret. But if this is supposed to be – you being back, I mean – I can keep it. One of my friends at school, her mother's the real estate agent who sold you the house. She only told me because I live next door and she knew I'd find out.'

'So is there a dog called Oscar?'

'You bastard,' she said, surprised and laughing at the same time. 'My poor dog is dead somewhere on your snake-infested land – which, by the way, I'm sure my money-grubbing little brother would be happy to mow for a fee – and this is how you respond?'

She threw her hands in the air in a gesture borrowed from television, from someone's exasperated parents on Seinfeld or perhaps something more recent.

'I'm sorry.' I laughed too, which seemed wrong. 'Though I don't think we saw any snakes when we were out patrolling.'

'No live dogs either,' she said sternly. 'You add it up, my friend.'

'I'm sorry about Oscar.' I was still stuck smiling. 'I hope he's okay. And he might be. The moment he shows up you'll be the first to know.'

Now I wanted Annaliese to stay and be some safe age, and I wanted to go to my fridge for two fresh cold Stellas. I wanted conversation, instead of rattling around the house all day, ambling from the kitchen up the garden to the studio, tinkering, tinkering, stumbling numbly between ideas and not achieving much. That had been my day, my week, more.

But this conversation was drawing to a close. Oscar would not be found, and Annaliese had a life to be getting on with in the next house down the road.

'Thanks,' she said, with next to nothing to thank me for. 'Thanks for looking anyway. Back when you believed there was a dog, at least.'

'I believe there's a dog,' I told her, and I walked her around the outside of the house to the driveway, still thinking of beer, and talk, and the cooler patch of shade going to waste on my front verandah.

She took another swipe at the same tall grass stalk on her way out. I was sure it was the same one, and again with her right hand. It occurred to me that I had last spoken face-to-face to a human more than two days before, and that had been to buy groceries. It didn't mean, though, that every last detail of the first visit to my house needed to be logged and accounted for, down to the idle battering of a slender strand of weed.

☊

THE SIDEBOARD CAME WITH the house. It was there in the pictures on the real estate website when, on a wet London day at the start of the northern autumn, I caught my first strong instinct for trying a life back here again. The house was listed as a deceased estate, so I wondered if there were plans for the furniture. The sideboard looked simple and old but not antique, at home where it stood. If there wasn't too much sentiment attached I figured it was headed for storage or a quick sale. I told the agent I'd pay a fair price for any pieces that weren't wanted, so I ended up with the sideboard in dark-stained silky oak, a similarly dark dining table with eight chairs (one with a loose leg), some unravelling cane verandah furniture for which I appeared to have paid an unfair price, and the bed the old man died in. I didn't know that part of its history for certain, but something body-sized had oozed into the mattress – not an item I'd realised I was purchasing – and the bed became the spare bed from the moment I arrived. Even with a new mattress on it, I'd kept my distance.

The hall mirror was part of the package as well. It caught me on my way into the house after Annaliese had left. It was a big mirror, but I made it look like a thin one. It was perfect for its spot on the wall – too slim for me, picking up me without the handles. I had become big on handles.

I bypassed the beer and headed straight for the studio, where I sat in the airconditioning trying to recall a dog that I was sure I'd never seen. An hour or two before, I had been playing around with adding a horn section to the track I was working on, but that now looked like a bad idea. A bad idea begat by idleness, a night of poor sleep, mistimed Stellas and one or two too many of them, and a lot of games of Space Invaders on the authentic turn-of-the-eighties machine that waited each day not more than a metre from my keyboard to lure me from my mission, my semi-serious producing debut.

Producing, I had already decided, was best not done by someone who had allowed endless tracts of time for it, as I had, but by a genius under stress facing two weeks of tension headaches and production deadlines calling for heroic feats of the kind that later became war stories. Sleepless nights, skin turned sallow, the juggernaut of failure bearing down and belching smoke.

I also knew, though, that I wouldn't end up much of a producer if that was the only way to do it. And I'd already been sallow, by my reckoning, for about two years. Others might have said longer.

We had management in London, among other places, and that was where I'd signed the deal to produce the Splades' first English-language album. I stayed with a film-director friend at Hampstead and met his new baby for the first time. It was good to be in a house people had settled into, made their mark on – a house cluttered with toys and books and pictures of holidays, and with a family of raincoats hanging on the pegs in the cloakroom just inside the front door.

I started cruising real estate websites while I was there. I skim-read my way through New York brownstones I could just afford but couldn't dare myself to buy, run-down farmhouses in France and flats in Hampstead itself, but my compass drew me south and east and back to Brisbane. From long range, from a London wrapped up in low wet cloud as the days thinned out at the end of another ambivalent summer, the images of hard blue skies and steel-and-glass million-dollar apartments on the river looked almost mythical.

I didn't buy an apartment, but I bought the sky. It was sky still as nature had made it, not a milky big-city sky fuzzed out by petrochemicals. Blue sky and a wooden house from the 1930s with a studio out the back and bush beyond – Brisbane Forest Park, acres of it. A place to hide, to think, to live quietly, to work, to start picking away at the Gordian knot I had made of my life. A foot on the earth. A foot like a brake, slowing it down, bringing some stillness. I emailed the Brisbane real estate agent then and there, and took the virtual tour.

I finished my house purchase between recording sessions with the Splades, by phone and email and fax in the office of the Vestfjord Hotel, Svolvær, three hundred kilometres inside the Arctic Circle off the coast of northern Norway. The band joined me to celebrate with a few beers around a wooden table on the dock outside, with long high racks for the drying of fish set up on the concrete nearby and floatplanes angling in from the sea to the glassy water of the harbour.

I flew out of Svolvær to find Christmas already in the shops in Brisbane, a drought set in for years and a partially furnished house waiting for me, its studio not quite what I'd imagined – a combined bedroom/loungeroom, an ensuite bathroom, a kitchenette, and cheap brown carpet on the living room floor with the footprints of absent furniture stamped in it. It was like a real-estate agent's on-site office at a new development, brought in, dropped on its twelve footings and turned into a granny flat. It was, in studio terms, best seen as a blank canvas. The only shot of it on the virtual tour had been of the outside, from the back verandah of the house, and in that it had looked generically quaint. In real life it was just generic.

The horn-section idea was definitely wrong for the track I was working on. I clicked on it, paused to be absolutely sure, and then deleted it. After years of sitting at keyboards and the occasional grand piano, I needed to have it in me to think about horns, strings and any other conceivable source of useful sounds if I was going to produce, but I wasn't proving myself by faking a horn section where it didn't fit.

It was starting to get dark outside, and I looked next door, through the trees and the parched hedge. There were lights on. A girl's raised voice – Annaliese's voice, I was sure – said something tough, and a door slammed.

I had been thinking about who might live there, and I'd had only a few clues to work with. Music and fights about music. The occasional shrieking of girls in the pool. The glow of a lit cigarette on the back verandah some nights, a spot of orange light in the distance, lifting up to mouth height and down again.

I had arrived at the house a few weeks before to find the mailbox stuffed with yellowing suburban newspapers. I took them in and read them, though they were already baked by the sun until they were almost brittle. Reading the August papers felt like opening the Dead Sea scrolls. Water restrictions were stuck on level six. A school roof that ran the risk of flaking asbestos was being replaced. Locals debated the surfacing of the last remaining gravel section of Gap Creek Road, with some saying bitumen would lead to more traffic and others saying it was long overdue. And a sleepy python had been found with a dog in its belly, and moved away into the bush.

I was still unpacking when Annaliese Winter visited that first time. The house allowed me a once-in-an-epoch bringing together of junk – boxes of things I had mailed to my brother to look after, miscellaneous furniture I kept at a storage place at Indooroopilly, and the thirty kilos or so of bare essentials I'd taken everywhere with me, my snail's shell, my port-a-home. This included a folder of my best recipes, utensils, my souped-up MacBook Pro, my external hard drive now half-full of Splades songs, the shakers and sticks and mandolin and other eclectic noise makers I might need at a moment's notice. I had ended up with less of the miscellaneous furniture than I had expected, but it was too late to complain about that now. Plus, I had the dead guy's furniture, old Mr Novak's. All that silky oak with its sombre stain and its sense of permanence. And there was just me in the house, so my furniture needs were finite and the occasional empty room could be filled when the right objects came along. For now, those rooms had boxes instead, and that was better than buying off the plan and kitting them out like a hotel, just for the sake of it.

The studio too was a work in progress, with power-boards and extension cords and a look that still said I'd just arrived. But it had airconditioning and on a couple of hot nights I'd put up with the noise of it and slept in there, waking up with a dry mouth and condensation on the windows.

There was not much but light and heat holding me to regular hours. I soon found myself watching TV well into the night, looking at the Channel Ten newsreader on the late news and saying aloud 'you are so hot' across the rise of my bare abdomen as the blue light flickered across it. Wars, drug trials, an execution pending in another country – all that went on in the background as I slumped there taken with the way she used her mouth with a mild asymmetry. Then at nine a.m. one of the Here's Humphrey presenters had me going with her rendition of Five Little Ducks. For days I had it stuck in my head, and it did me no good. And, yes, I looked for her name in the credits and I googled her, but that was as far as I took it.

♁

THE DAY AFTER ANNALIESE came to my door for the first time, I met my brother Patrick for lunch at Harveys at New Farm.

I was five minutes late, he was five minutes later and came in flapping a mobile phone and some papers. I was sure it was just for effect. He was an important man in advertising, and people were hounding him with A4, phone calls, text messages. He was wearing a see-through camouflage mesh sleeveless top and three-quarter pants, and his jet black hair was gelled like a soft-serve ice-cream. He had no need to flap to catch my eye.

He saw me sizing him up and he scowled, or at least let a well-managed wrinkle or two cross his brow. His

12

next look would be disdain – something he could communicate by instinct in a range of media – and it would coincide with a cursory scan of my inadequate dress sense, and lumbering body habitus.

'I'm sorry, is it casual Friday at your work, or nipple Friday?' I said as he sat down. Always beat your brother to the punch.

'Chubs,' he said, feigning hurt. It was his special name for me – I had never liked it and it had never been more true. 'You can't see them, can you?' He pressed his shirt flat against his chest and looked down, his face now all mock-horror at his tanned brown nipples.

'Well, you appear to have two nipple-sized, nipple-coloured things in the places where nipples might be, but feel free to seek a second opinion. Nice abs. That's what I meant to say. Obviously.'

He picked up the laminated menu and tapped it on the glass table top. 'Hey, I do a lot of crunches. These abs come at a price, and the price is extreme tedium. But they are nice abs. You're right. Might as well share them with the team on casual Friday.'

He had said to me once that he had voted against casual Friday at the management meeting. He had told them there was no casual Friday in advertising. He had told them casual Friday was on the way out all over town. He had waved his arms around dramatically but not persuasively, forecast industry-wide ridicule if not doom. But the admin staff had asked for it specially, and it would cost nothing. So Fridays turned casual, and disdain found its wardrobe. Casual Friday would, for Patrick, become parody Friday, and he would buy clothes for it that would see no wear on the week's other six days.

13

'Well, I'm sure the team appreciates the effort,' I said. 'Those abs'd break rocks. That's a lot of work you've put in with mardi gras still months away.'

He gave a flat, resigned smile and a sigh. 'I don't do mardi gras any more.'

He told me there came a time for us all when we realised we were past the mardi gras life, and it typically came around dawn as you staggered home through mascara-streaked drag queens tottering on crazy heels and the last of their chemicals, and shirtless hairless boys with plenty of gas in the tank, and you were dreaming of hours of good sleep somewhere clean and comfortable. You were old and uncool, in an instant, but it was what you were and you had no choice but to embrace it. Buy small dogs, stick to home, keep hours more like those of the styleless other world you'd spent your life backing away from. The world where your brother Chubs lived – that was his thought taken to its logical conclusion.

I was no rockstar to this man, not even a rockstar on hiatus. I was a slob who had once had a band, who had trespassed upon a cooler place, interviewed reluctantly and not well and always remained happier behind the scenes. He knew that about me. He knew I was not cool, and posters in their tens of thousands would never change that. And that was fine by me. I wasn't cool. I had a liking for music, and it had taken me places.

Patrick was the creative director at the agency, and just back from shooting a clothing ad in Finland. They were not clothes he would ever deign to buy, but I was sure he had given them a good-looking ad.

One of the staff came over to take our order. She gave me a shaky smile, tidied a strand of red-dyed hair

14

and said, in a rush, 'Hi. Are you guys ready? I should get you some water.' She stopped to renegotiate her breathing and her cheeks started to flush. 'Assuming you'd like water.'

Patrick rolled his eyes. I started to tell her water would be great, but in the same moment Patrick let his menu hit the table with a slap and then he said, 'I don't know why I'm even looking. I practically live here. I know what I want.'

He ordered a salad without dressing. I ordered a pear and walnut salad with blue cheese dressing. And then I ordered sandcrab lasagna as well.

'It'll be my main meal of the day,' I told him, and he gave me a look that spelled out that I wasn't the only one who knew it to be a lie.

'Great,' the girl taking our order said, her voice gone a little squeaky. She cleared her throat, touched it with her hand and opened her eyes wider. 'And drinks? Or just the water?'

Once she was out of earshot and he had stopped rolling his eyes again, Patrick leaned over the table to me and said, 'And would you like a paper bag with that? Or would you just prefer to keep hyperventilating? There'll be autographs before we leave this place, I just know it. All those bloody little girlie fans of yours.'

Disdain, disdain. Disdain for us all.

I was never going to persuade him that it was just my life, and not a life I'd chosen. I was in his world now – he was the Harveys regular, he should have been at least recognised and preferably fawned over. James Street was his street, all steel and glass and topiary, designer knick-knacks, six kinds of bok choy and twelve of fish roe, sleek boxy Danish furniture, bars where people sat on authentic upturned wooden packing crates and chose from cellars of three hundred wines. I supposed there had been houses here once, wooden worker's cottages, or light industry. But none of us knew, as the old James Street had made no mark on us.

The transformation, I could only assume, had been dramatic as it had passed from the calloused hands of sheet-metal workers and panel-beaters to a generation they could never have imagined. To Patrick and his partner, Blaine, to people whose sunglasses lasted a season and cost a grand, who loved to be the first to buy a new exotic ingredient, but tortured themselves over the food miles. Not that I thought Blaine would ever do that. Blaine had never been one to reflect enough, to care enough, to torture himself.

Blaine was square-jawed and difficult, and he tended to pick his opinions up flat-pack and erect them in a hurry, without much duty owed to the facts. Which was fine when he wanted to be the loudest person disparaging some new pinot gris, or grigio – I could recall that he thought he hated one and loved the other – but there had been one or two times when I had been more inclined to pick a fight.

Another staff member arrived with a bottle of water. At the table next to us, a woman with a dark bob and frameless glasses scanned some floor plans while the man she was sitting with leaned his forearms on his notes and thumbed his Blackberry. Behind him were chrome racks with bags of hand-made pasta, sachets of dukka, pots of tapenade.

Patrick's phone jiggled on the table and he looked

at it and said, 'I'm sorry, I have to take this.' He then browbeat the caller mildly and with some charm, and told them he'd be back in less than an hour – more than thirty minutes but less than an hour. 'Showing me at three would be okay,' he said, 'if you think it'll take you till three.'

He ended the call, pressed a button and watched his phone turn off, and put it in his pocket.

I asked him how his trip had been and he said, 'Fine. We cut a hole in the ice. You know how it goes. Cheesy but effective.' Then he shook off a little of his sardonic tone. 'Actually it was good. We had a great time. We've got some good pictures and we stayed up till all hours sampling the Finlandia vodka range and then ran bare-arsed in the snow. So, maybe I should reserve the right to a mardi gras comeback at some stage.'

I didn't know if he had truly run bare-arsed in the snow, and I wasn't going to ask. I wasn't going to enquire about the possible birching of his bare buttocks either, though it seemed like the next logical place to take it. He would assure me the night had gone there, and that it was just the thing for stimulating the circulation. We had enough decades behind us for me to know the trajectory of most of our conversations, even if there hadn't been as many in recent years.

We swapped notes on our visits to Scandinavia, and the work we were doing. He told me he had 'clients up to the wazoo' and I said I assumed he was wearing mesh so that people could get a good look at his crammed wazoo and not approach him with new business. He said he was not wearing mesh there, but maybe next casual Friday he should give it some thought.

17

Our meals arrived, his a plate of leaves weighed down with a few spindly low-GI roast veges, mine a sizeable slab of gourmet lasagna and a well-dressed salad, competing and mingling savoury fragrances rising from it and making my salivary glands spasm.

He looked at my plate as though it was evidence of an entry-level war crime.

'I don't know how you can eat that with no dressing,' I said, mustering some kind of pre-emptive strike. 'I assume you shit little rabbity pellets.'

'I have a family history of heart disease,' he said, and I hated him for it in a brotherly way and wanted to throw his leaves in his face. 'Sorry,' he said. 'Stupid remark. I just wish . . . I want you around, Chubs.'

He lanced some leaves with his fork. I cut a fat corner of lasagna and lifted it to my mouth.

'I'm around,' I said before posting it in there.

It had been a year and five months since our father had died of a heart attack in the early hours of the morning on the way from his bedroom to the bathroom. It was his third, and he had a seam down his chest from bypass surgery. I was fourteen when he had his operation, and fastidious management of his cholesterol and blood pressure had bought him another twenty years.

Patrick and I had played guessing games about who got which genes from where, as families do. For us it was harder than some. Patrick was inexplicably darker than the rest of us. We had both outgrown any resemblance the two of us had, though I had done so more literally, and we had no mother to measure ourselves against, since she had died when we were young. I was three, Patrick was seven. He went to her funeral but

I didn't, on the advice of a family friend who was a psychologist and said Patrick's seven-year-old grieving needs would be different to mine.

I could remember our mother, but mostly I remembered her from photographs. As time passed and the world changed – but the photos didn't – she became an abstract representation of the seventies to me. The photos stayed out on the coffee table and the bookcases and slowly grew pale, and Patrick touched them sometimes for luck, one after another. He spoke to them, and my father encouraged it.

She had a bike with a big basket with two flowers on it. That was one of the photos – her on her bike, no helmet, her hair being tossed around. She had flowing dresses, and preferred to go barefoot. She could pick things up with her toes – socks, pencils, Lego. She wore chunky wooden beads and I liked the texture. She sang in tune. I think I remember her singing Scarborough Fair. Like my father, she was a music teacher. She auditioned successfully for the state symphony orchestra as a flautist, and then she became sick. I knew that only from the chronology I'd learned. I couldn't remember her sick and I couldn't think of any flute music from my early life.

My father stayed in the house, a simple unrenovated Queenslander in an unfashionable part of town, and kept it as it was for the next thirty years.

It was a student and his mother who found him, at five minutes to ten on the first Monday of the school holidays. They had turned up for a private lesson, and saw the distorted shape of his body through the leadlight window glass of the front door. For years the prospect of my father's death, instant and non-negotiable as it would be, had scared me. I had only one parent, and needed to keep him. But his failure to die for ten years and then fifteen, and the drift of his cardiology visits to six-monthly and then annual, had me complacent. His chest seam was an old scar by then, history, a story of a bullet dodged. So the news shocked me when it came.

Patrick kept himself fastidiously lean, his diet all pulses and other cardioflatulents. I appeared to have made other choices.

'I can't believe you live at Kenmore,' he said through a mulch of rocket and bitter purple leaves. 'All that money and you live at Kenmore.'

'I'm on the Brookfield side of the road,' I told him, though I knew where the suburb line lay and I was still in Kenmore by hundreds of metres.

'Brookfield is Kenmore with ponies.' There would be little slack cut for Brookfield.

'This blue cheese dressing is amazing,' I said. 'You really should try some. Live a little.'

🎧

I LEFT LUNCH WITH Patrick with the usual feeling of incomplete satisfaction. 'All that money and you live at Kenmore.' It was very Patrick, that kind of remark. Kenmore was half an hour across town, and he had probably never been there. He lived among the clean lines and post-industrial chic of a loft-style apartment in a building that had once been a sugar refinery. He could walk to work, but tended not to because he would sweat. He had views of New Farm Park, but not really of the river, and the nearby CBD skyline sat squarely in front of his balcony, as though he had put it there, like a ficus in a pot.

I hit traffic all the way up Ann Street as he took his nipple show back to work. I looked at my watch. It was a reflex response to being stuck – I had nowhere to be and all the time in the world to get there. It was the watch my father had given me for a birthday when I was still at school. I had bought myself a sleek matt-finish German one in Berlin once, but I picked up the old watch when I came back for his funeral. A few days later I returned to the US for a party to celebrate our second album, Supernature, going platinum there, and to launch its second single.

Minutes after I arrived, the watch was slipped from my wrist by a balloon-twisting clown and then given back to me in the belly of a purple poodle before I knew it was gone. I still hadn't got the time zone right in my head and the moment felt hazy and surreal – the clown and his red nose, his unfriendly mouth set in the middle of a fat lurid smile, the people clustered around us working it out one by one and all before I did. And I was holding my balloon poodle, thanking the clown for it since it seemed to be a gift, then seeing a watch inside through the translucent purple, marvelling that the clown too might have a watch like that and then, far too late, realising I'd been had.

I pulled my sleeve up and saw my bare wrist, and that my watch, my one tangible link with my father, could have been lost so easily. The fragility of that connection was more than I could bear. I thought I would cry. I took the first jerky breath and then stopped myself. People laughed, so I made an effort to turn my lurch of breath into a laugh as well. The clown, still flat-mouthed inside his smile, was studying me closely. He went to speak, but then thought better of it. Someone popped the balloon and handed me the watch, and I put it in my pocket. I was holding a drink, so I couldn't put it on my wrist again, and I wanted it out of sight. I wanted no one but me to touch it.

'He did me earlier,' one of the music company executives said, putting his hand on my arm and giving it a squeeze. 'He's good, isn't he?' He started to steer me round to face another direction and said, 'There are some people I'd like you to meet, over by the fountain.'

My hand kept going to my pocket, checking and checking, for the rest of the night.

Patrick had been in Butterfish, in the early days. He was in the Butterfish that played friends' parties till the cops were called, that hired the cheapest rehearsal spaces in the Valley or, better still, borrowed them. The Butterfish that stuck together because the best of the music wasn't awful and the beer was free. Derek was always the exception to that, coming out of a hot afternoon's practice wired, the daylight and shoppers and the mall's benign ambling drunks unready for him. He walked as if the fans were already circling, and the rest of us just couldn't see them. LSD – lead singer's disease. It had its hooks in him even then.

Derek always used disabled toilets because he preferred the extra room. I told him it was for the wheels and he said, 'Sure, but, you know . . .' meaning he had an entitlement that couldn't be put into words, or didn't

22

need them. The people with wheels could wait their turn.

It was Patrick who gave the band its name. 'I had a friend who went to South Africa,' he said. We were sitting with a hundred bad band names scrawled across sheets of paper. 'He ate this fish and it's called a butter-fish because it's so oily you shit butter after you eat it. Seriously.'

Websites about fish don't quite support this asser-tion, but we liked the name and the job was done. Shitting butter. That was all we needed to know. The decision was made then and there in the Cosmopolitan Café, a minute's walk down the mall from the traffic I was stuck in now. Ahead I could see that a truck had lost some of its load on the way into Chinatown, and four lanes of vehicles were being painstakingly merged into two.

Patrick had been a driving force when the band started, so it was no surprise one of his names came through. He had plenty of names rejected too though. He was a great reader, or in fact mis-reader, of The Great Gatsby, and one of the band names he suggested was The Eyes of Dr TJ Eckleburg, from an advertising billboard the narrator regularly passes on his way home from the city to West Egg. His justification was that a band had just called themselves The Boo Radleys, and that name came from another twentieth-century American classic novel, though not one as sharp and wise – by his reckoning – as The Great Gatsby.

'Moving on . . .' Derek said cautiously, after a respect-ful silence, running his pen down to the next name on the list.

Try as he might, Patrick was a square peg in a room full of round holes. And he was my brother, and that didn't make it easy. His main instrument was clarinet – not one we really had much call for – his self-taught guitar playing was always marginal and, in the end, it was up to me to take him aside and point it out.

'He's got to go,' Derek said. 'Really.'

I met Patrick at his house. In the car I'd practised what I hoped was a diplomatic way of putting it, but it crumbled into something cowardly and ineffectual. I looked at the floor and talked vaguely about a new direction. I said the rest of us weren't sure about a few things.

I paused, and Patrick took my useless pause and said, curtly, 'Should we wait for your balls to drop before we have this conversation? Look, let me make it easy. I've been offered a big job in advertising, and I'm going to take it. There'll be no time for band meetings, or any of the time-wasting crap that goes on. So tell the others that. Tell them it doesn't work for me any more.'

In a life that had been characterised by false starts, accepting that job was a sure and decisive move, and ultimately a successful one. As a comedian, Patrick had been more acerbic than funny (he had always been unable to distinguish between the two). As a model his good looks had proven too straightforward. As a fashion buyer he had lasted a day and a half before realising the prospect of making a decision would paralyse him and any risk would be too much to bear. 'What if I'm the last person ever to buy low-riders?' he said. 'And what if I bought a million pairs?' Low-riders had years left to run, but he couldn't have known it.

A while before his big break in advertising, we had set up a business to record cheap jingles and on-hold information. 'Your call is important to us, and did you know we can . . .?' Insure your home contents, provide party novelties, come to your place to shampoo your dog. All of that and more.

We even got business cards printed, in a deep green that came off on your hands. Neither of us could bear to go back to complain. Patrick said we should get around it by laminating them – that could be our 'look'. I think I just put the box down on the desk and walked around the room holding my green fingers away from anything important, hoping the cards would be gone by the time I had found some way to get clean.

I stuck with Butterfish, and our lives became different. I chose sharehouses filled with guitars, and with milk crates for furniture. He bought a compact but stylish studio apartment at Teneriffe. I drove an old car then, a grime-speckled Laser from the eighties that leaked oil slowly from a site no mechanic could locate. Any time I went to Patrick's place, he would meet me at visitor parking with a sheet of cardboard at the ready.

The first post-Patrick incarnation of Butterfish held together for another year before crumbling under the weight of its non-success. I headed south out of Brisbane then. After a few weeks of running down my savings faster than I'd hoped and speaking to almost no one, I looked at a jobs board outside the shops at Jindabyne and ended up washing dishes in a Thredbo ski-lodge restaurant out of season.

The restaurant had square white plates and heavy cutlery that was shapely in a modern kind of way but, with its airport carpet and breakfast bar featuring a battery of plastic cereal dispensers and an industrial toaster, it still managed only a low-ceilinged budget before-and-après ski vibe. On Tuesday nights it hosted an informal inter-lodge darts comp, with other itinerant dishwashers and painters and cleaners drifting in to play for teams they didn't care about, and to smoke and steal drinks from behind the bar.

I played because we all played. Each time I would face down the triple twenty – the tiny, distant triple twenty – and tell myself to aim, and to try, and I would walk away with the darts splayed randomly across the board and a few points scored. And I would watch as the people who had made this their lives for twenty years bitched, drank, smoked and used whatever they could to send themselves numb.

I couldn't bear the thought of Christmas there as it approached. I swallowed whatever pride was called for, and I phoned Derek. We restarted the band with a new line-up, and I also got back with Jess, my ex-girlfriend, and thought my course was set. Which it was, for a few years at least.

We were a better band the second time around. We weren't eighteen or twenty and haggling over a name. Then, just as we seemed to find a new plateau a little higher than before, Butterfish became a different beast entirely. We played to the right people, lost track of the last of our old bad luck and picked up some good luck instead and, in 2000, in op-shop suits we had brought from home, we put our names to the kind of American contract that made the pen shake in your hand.

'It looks like we've got something over here,' I told Patrick when I emailed from LA.

He told me in his email back to be wary of the crazy promises they would make.

They kept them, for the most part.

♁

ANNALIESE'S HANDS WERE PLAYING piano as she walked along the road verge on Monday afternoon listening to her iPod. I was down at the mailbox, and I saw her before she saw me. She was in her school uniform, an over-stuffed pack on her back, her socks down, her hat tilted to keep the western sun out of her eyes. The road was otherwise empty and she was concentrating, playing precise notes. Not with great feeling, but marking them out neatly as if she might come back later and put more into it.

Then she noticed me, and her fingers sprung back from the keys and her hands turned into two fists that dropped to her sides. Her mouth opened, but no words came out. She was holding onto the very slender hope that I had seen none of it.

'Air keyboards,' I said, because I couldn't help myself. 'Cool.'

'Don't tell me you've never . . .' she started to say, and then let it go. The air keyboard player can only surrender. There is no other choice.

She looked at the mail I was holding. There was a bill for broadband installation and a bank statement – nothing to help her muster a comeback. She reached up and took her iPod ear pieces from her ears and began wrapping the white flexes around one hand.

I asked her what she was listening to, and she started to answer and then stopped and smirked. 'Asia's The Heat of the Moment,' she said.

It had been years since I'd heard the song, I was sure. I could recall a vague embarrassing liking for it, but not of the kind you could ever own up to.

'It's an interesting choice.' I was proceeding with caution.

'It's one of your favourite songs.' The tables had turned. I didn't know how, but they had.

'That's crazy.'

'Hey, I googled you,' she said, as if my credibility had been despatched and she could play an entire air orchestra in front of me with impunity. 'It's there. There's an interview. It's online.'

She was right. There was a hazy grey recollection somewhere that told me resistance was futile. 'There was a context,' I said, because I had nothing else.

'Sure there was.'

'You know there was.'

She was laughing at me now. We both knew I'd be following up my context line with something comparably pathetic.

'It was, you know, Ten Stupid Questions. One of those pieces they do. If you were a dog, what breed would you be? That kind of thing. Big-hair rock that you secretly love. And I'd heard it on the plane on the way in. Wherever it was.'

'Secretly love,' she said, in a playground teasing kind of way. 'You secretly love Asia's Heat of the Moment.'

28

She gave it a second, to let victory settle in. 'Anyway, maybe I'm listening to something much less disgraceful and I just made that up. What are *you* listening to at the moment?'

'You trying to reassert yourself after the masterful air keyboards demo.' I couldn't understand why I needed to try to be mean to a sixteen-year-old, other than that I sensed she was ready for it – almost that I was respecting her by doing it. Still, a fully-fledged reasonable adult might have just respected her by answering the question.

'I think the score's about one-all,' she said. The sun was getting under her hat now, and she lifted her hand up to shade her face. Some distance behind her, a dark blue four-wheel-drive nosed out of a lane, and its driver glanced our way before turning left and heading towards the city, leaving a drift of dust behind it.

'Asia's Heat of the Moment . . . I think you might be slightly ahead.' It was hot in the sun, and I knew I should be getting back inside. I had a call to make to Norway in a few hours, and there was some work to do before then. 'You actually play piano, don't you? That wasn't just . . . nothing.'

'Well, I learned for a few years,' she said, looking away from me and further down the road. 'I haven't had a lesson for a while, but my dad's got a piano and I was at his place on the weekend.'

I wanted to tell her she looked like she knew what she was doing, but I didn't because it could have sounded patronising, even though it was true. You don't need the keyboard to be there to have at least some idea. My father would talk through fingering on the edge of

29

the dining room table if a piece of music came up over dinner. Annaliese had small hands, which wouldn't help her, but I thought someone had drummed technique into her a while ago.

'So what *are* you listening to, when you get the chance?' she said. 'I mean, I'd love it if it was Asia, but I'm assuming not.'

'Not, sadly. Mostly the Shins' Wincing the Night Away. Rolling Stone gave it three-and-a-half stars online. Then the fans weighed in giving it five each and laying into the reviewer. And three and a half's not bad really.'

'The Shins?' The name meant something to her, clearly. 'Weren't they the band Natalie Portman's character loved in Garden State?'

'Yeah. Yeah, they were. Great movie.' I had seen it on a plane first, then bought the DVD and carried it around with me. It was somewhere in my snail's shell, my thirty kilos of life-affirming and essential matter that I needed on my back, metaphorically, wherever I went.

'It's one of my mother's favourites,' she said. 'She rents it from Blockbuster any time she's feeling particularly old.'

There was nothing to the line but innocent observation.

As she went off along the dusty road verge she put her earphones back in, but this time she kept her arms by her sides, no air keyboards, letting them swing as she walked the last few metres towards home.

🎧

THERE WAS A NOTE in the mailbox when I checked it the next day. It read: 'Hi Curtis. Welcome to the neighbourhood. Annaliese tells me you like Garden State, so that's a good start. How about coming over to dinner some time? How about tomorrow? (If this is all wrong and you want your privacy, that's fine too.) Cheers, Kate Winter.'

Kate Winter, custodian of the house of slamming doors and duelling stereos, ex-partner of the piano-owning man who was Annaliese's father.

I wanted my privacy. Patrick was the exception to that and, in close to a month, I'd seen him only twice, once either side of his trip to Finland.

I'd had years of becoming well used to saying no to things, or having people say no on my behalf, or just ignoring them, but this was no 'RSVP – acceptances only' mass mailout about an event. It was a hand-written note, just to me and from the person who happened to be my neighbour, so I decided I should write a note declining. Then I imagined the night – the most normal of all possible nights – a beer, a glass of wine, a conversation about Garden State and great music and the world that went on outside my head. And my note declining the invitation soon read, 'Dinner sounds great – how about 7.30?'

I slipped it into their mailbox and no reply came, so at 7.25 on Wednesday I walked out of my front door with a six-pack of Stella and a bottle of wine. Too much? Not enough? Not right? All those thoughts were in my head. I had no idea how to be a neighbour, a thirty-something man in the burbs, heading next door for a mid-week meal.

On my last long trip back to Brisbane – three weeks it was, I think – I stayed at my girlfriend Jess's flat and slept almost the whole time. Butterfish had just toured Europe and I kept waking at three a.m., lurching out of bed thinking I had to be somewhere, and then spending the three most alert hours of my day on the balcony reading a book and waiting for dawn. Jess had finished her physio degree not long before, and was working in a hospital. Derek and I had demos done for Supernature, and a producer and a studio booked in LA for the real thing. My life was elsewhere at the time, and not entirely like a life.

I had had higher hopes for those three weeks, too high maybe. I had convinced myself they would be a kind of highlights package of the best times Jess and I had had, but with money. We would sleep late, cook together, go to movies during the day and sneak in a perfect parallel life while around us the town went about its business. I had missed her laugh on that tour, more as it went on. I wanted it back in my life. My hopes weren't so high, really.

Should I take the beer back to my house? The wine? Did this load of booze look like I was ready to settle in for the night? Or should I have brought the beer for now and a *better* bottle of wine as a 'thank you for having me' kind of gift, a keeper? Did Kate Winter drink nothing, to set a good example to her kids? Maybe there would be other people there. I didn't know. It would have been simpler if there had been no note, none of this.

My toe caught on a rock or tree root in their rutted driveway and I almost fell, which could have ended my wine and beer dilemma then and there. I kept my eyes on the lit windows of the house and, as I got near the dark

32

front steps, a motion-activated light came on. There was music coming from inside, the Modern Lovers. I was convinced that, in some distant interview that would float forever in cyberspace, I had mentioned them. I braced myself for the prospect that the night would be a three-hour interview with a panel of middle-aged women who had all googled their hearts out and put together a play list on which every song could be met by a wry smile of recognition, since I'd mentioned it once to someone somewhere.

I stood on the verandah and listened. There was a young male voice inside, asking something in a detached tone, an older female voice giving a short reply. That was all. No panel. A rack clattered into an oven and the oven door thumped shut.

Annaliese opened the front door.

'I hadn't even knocked,' I said, my free hand in the air about to do just that. She was in a brown, patterned dress with spaghetti straps. She was barefoot.

'That's my bedroom just there,' she said, tilting her head to the right. 'The light comes in my window when something triggers it. Plus, I heard you on the stairs. Why didn't you knock? Were you checking it was the right house?'

'No, just checking I was the right person,' I said. It was supposed to be a joke. The idea had a different shape to it in my head, and it went wrong somehow on the way out.

'I don't really know what that means,' she said, with a look that suggested she already had the better of me, at not even seven thirty-one, not yet a full minute into the evening.

'Could we settle on it being enigmatic rather than weird?'

'Sure. You always were the enigmatic one.' It sounded as if we went back years. It sounded nostalgic. Then I realised it was the band's press coverage again. 'Come in,' she said. 'Come and meet the family. You be enigmatic, they'll be weird.' She turned to lead me down the hallway. Over her shoulder she said, 'Mum wanted to invite you but figured you might be a bit of a privacy freak. I said you'd be fine with it.'

The sharp edges of her shoulder blades stood out under her skin. She was wearing gold hoop earrings that swung as she walked. I hadn't seen her with earrings before, but both brief times I'd met her she had been in school uniform.

The hallway opened out into a loungeroom with two well-worn sofas, crammed bookshelves, magazines spread on the floor, a rubber plant with its lush green leaves going brown at the edges and four large, black high-top Converse shoes looking as though someone had thrown them in there with their eyes shut. The corner of the old red Persian rug was curled over onto itself and a glass of Coke, a quarter full, sat near the TV remote. It was a white body outline short of looking like a crime scene. Or three students and some milk crates short of looking like the last house I'd lived in.

'Oh, Christ,' a woman's voice said with an unhappiness that was supposed to be private, and the oven door thumped shut again.

The wall between the loungeroom and the kitchen had been renovated away, and a counter stood there now, piled with papers and phones and two lunch boxes.

'He's here,' Annaliese called out sternly.

Kate Winter appeared in oven mitts and a floral print dress. She had freckly shoulders and was curvy in a way that's sometimes unfashionable and sometimes as good as it gets. She looked fit. She wasn't one of those women you'd see lounging around in a Rubens with time on her hands. She had out-of-control blonde hair that was ineffectively clamped behind her head with combs, with wild strands breaking free and sprouting out from her head.

'Hi,' she said, and waved a mitt, which was blue and had ducks on it. 'Welcome. I'm Kate.'

'I'm Curtis,' I said. 'Thanks for inviting me.'

'Sorry, I was just swearing at the meal when you came in.'

'As long as it didn't swear back, I think we're okay.'

'You'll never hear it with the oven door shut,' she said, and smiled.

'Mum,' Annaliese said in a corrective tone. She turned to me. 'I'll put all this in the fridge, shall I?'

'Or maybe I'll drink one of the beers,' I said. 'If that's all right.'

Kate took one too and gave the top a twist with her oven mitt. It stayed put and she looked at it closely. Annaliese handed her a bottle opener and shook her head.

'A bit too deluxe for you, Mum?' she said.

'Even wine comes with a screw top these days.' Kate flipped the bottle top into the sink, then did the same with mine. Behind her, attached by magnets to the fridge, I noticed a picture of a younger Annaliese, beaming and holding a tiny puppy. Kate turned towards the wall and shouted out, 'Mark, our guest is here.'

35

There was a grunt of acknowledgement.

'That means you come out.'

This time the grunt was polysyllabic, but no clearer. There was a jangling cascade of computer noises, and the trundle of castors across a wooden floor. The bedroom door opened.

'Mark, Curtis. Curtis, Mark,' Annaliese said efficiently, looking at neither of us, as if it was a moment we simply had to get through.

Mark stood there, peach fuzz and acne and every memory I had about being fourteen or fifteen. His hair looked well slept in and the oily fringe fell down almost to his eyes. He leaned against the door frame, round-shouldered and wearing huge low-slung black shorts and a black Ramones T-shirt that had gone slack at the front. A piece of metal that looked like a nail passed through his left ear lobe.

'So, do I get a beer?' he said to Kate.

'No.'

'Special occasion.'

'Not that special.'

He shrugged, as if he hadn't cared anyway. He would have hated Butterfish on principle, I knew it. We had been way too close to pop, insufficiently evil. Fourteen-year-old black-clad boys with nails through their ears had taken it upon themselves to be our natural enemies. We should have anticipated it, but we never did. They blogged us savagely, from rooms just like Mark's, all over the world but most savagely close to home.

'So do you like the Ramones or is that just a shirt?' I said to him, figuring we were already well past hello.

'I like the Ramones.' So far he had said everything

36

in the same lifeless monotone and this was no exception, but his mouth was a different shape at the end of it. It was subtle, but it was there. It was like a crack in a window, and I realised it was his version of a smile. 'Specially the early stuff. Classic.'

'It's my T-shirt though,' Kate said, and laughed. 'He doesn't tell anyone that. He just says it's vintage.'

He glared at her, but even the glare had a kind of disengagement to it, as though he could *just* be bothered. He cleared his throat, sniffed. Something mucoid rattled in his sinuses. 'I don't have a lot of conversations about T-shirts.' Or a lot of conversations, perhaps. And I guessed that the word vintage didn't come up much.

'You certainly don't tell anyone it's mine though.'

'Obviously.'

'I can't believe it's not cool to wear your mum's clothes these days,' I said, for Kate's sake more than anything. 'What's up with you young people?'

Annaliese went 'ha'. Mark took his scowl a level deeper and in a voice as flat as ever said, 'I'm gunna change.' He half-turned towards his room, then turned back and said, 'Mum wrecked this shirt anyway. It's all stretched at the front.'

'What?' Kate scowled at him. 'That's because you sit with your knees stuck up it.'

'Sure,' he said. 'It's about the boobs, lady. Now, do I get one of those beers? Special occasion?' Kate stood there with her mouth open and her arms folded protectively across her front. Mark turned to me again. 'How many albums did you sell? The band?'

'Twenty million,' I told him. 'Ish.'

37

Kate sighed. 'All right. You can have half of mine. But just half. And it's a special occasion because Curtis is our new neighbour, not because of his album sales.'

'Whatever,' he said. 'As long as the clause kicks in.' He looked back towards me, and made his scratchy half-smile again. 'Welcome to the neighbourhood, Curtis.'

Kate poured the beer into a glass, as close to exactly half as she could manage. Mark took it, held it up to the light, and then reached out and clinked it against the neck of my stubbie.

We sat at the dining table, the four of us. There were bowls of green olives and pistachios, and a circle of rice crackers around a tub of pesto.

'So, what brought you back here?' Kate said. 'Are you working on anything?'

'Yeah, an album,' I told her. 'With a bunch of Norwegian guys. I'm sort of producing. We did some work over there to kick it off, but the stage we're at now could be done anywhere.'

Annaliese ate a rice cracker. Mark worked the pistachios like a machine, making a neat pile of shells on the table. They sat opposite me, with their backs to the loungeroom and the managed chaos of a family home. I couldn't remember when I'd last seen standard teenage mess. I got a sense of three lives densely packed, hitting each other at angles, but also sometimes fitting, or making space for one another, making allowances, teaming up. Even Mark, despite himself, gave off a hint of that. This was home and he knew every millimetre. Here he could be who he was, someone with a few more shades of grey to him than the person he *obviously* was, the classic teenager at war with his own surging adolescence, with all the surliness and misshapen clothes and the mind you know is always ticking, ticking, like a clock or like a bomb, one or the other.

🎧

'I'M NOT MUCH OF a cook,' Kate said as she came back to the table holding something that was probably a casserole. And she was right.

She lowered it onto the trivet with the duck mitts, one of which I now noticed had an old scorch mark, and she went back to the kitchen.

'Brace yourself,' Annaliese said quietly.

Kate rattled cutlery around in a drawer. 'I might be a bad cook, but I'm not a deaf bad cook.'

She returned with a bread knife, which she handed to me, and a ladle. I cut some slices from the fresh loaf of bread while she served the casserole, handing plates to the others and placing one in front of me. There were lumps of meat, quartered onions, potatoes and mushrooms, with an oily steam rising from each plate.

I asked her if it was French and she gave the one-syllable 'ha' laugh I'd heard from Annaliese and she said, 'That's very flattering, to think it might be a cuisine.'

It wasn't a cuisine. The meat was tough and the potatoes falling apart, and there wasn't much flavour to the liquid they were swimming in. The recipe was her mother's, she told me, and her father wasn't good with strong flavours and was particularly bad with garlic, which gave him a fierce pungent smell from every pore for about a day.

Annaliese pushed a piece of meat around with her fork unenthusiastically, and caught my eye. She gave me a look that said, undoubtedly, 'This is my life.'

Mark asked if there were any more pistachios, Annaliese asked what I thought of the casserole and Kate said, 'How about some cracked pepper?', all of them speaking at the same time.

So I said, 'I think some pepper would go very nicely with it, thanks.'

Kate made another trip to the kitchen and came back with a pepper grinder. She held it over my plate and was about to twist it when she changed her mind and said, 'No, you'd better do it, so you get the right amount.'

'There's a reason all those shop-a-dockets are on the fridge,' Annaliese said, as if we'd already been talking about them. 'And the reason is pizza.'

'Surely nobody pays full price for a pizza,' Kate said, missing her point and defending the wad of curling dockets that I could see magneted to the fridge door. 'They're always trying to outdo each other with deals.'

Annaliese reached out and took the pepper once I'd finished. She ground some onto her plate. 'You cook, don't you, Curtis?' she said. 'Like, properly cook.'

'Well, semi-properly. I've learned a few things over the years, I guess.' I ate another mouthful of the watery, and now peppery, casserole. The meat needed more time and the potatoes less. Kate was giving me a look that said she badly needed it to be okay.

'You're going to have to show her,' Annaliese said, sparing her mother nothing.

'Has Annaliese told you she sings?' Kate said. 'I bet she hasn't.'

Annaliese glared at her. 'So annoying,' she said.

Mark laughed through a mouthful of dinner. 'Go on, Liese. Let's hear it. How about Boys of Summer, Rock Eisteddfod style?'

Annaliese's glare turned to something more like horror. I didn't know if Mark had ever been stabbed with a fork before, but I could see it happening now.

'I remember when that was a Don Henley song,' Kate said, steering us around the impending sibling conflict. 'Do you remember that?' The question was for me – it could have been for no one else. Then, before I could answer, she said, 'Your hair's different now.'

'It was different before,' I told her. Annaliese had put her cutlery down. 'Different when I was in the band. This is it – the real thing.'

My dyed hair started with a publicist, but not in a calculated way. She used the colour herself and, one day in a hotel room, between phone interviews, when we were both verging on stir crazy, she used it on me. She called housekeeping and ordered the oldest towel they had and told them why. She said they'd have to send a new one – which they did – but no one could complain since she had effectively told them she would be trashing the towel. Somehow we splashed dye on the wall as well, on the textured regency-print wallpaper. I read in a magazine once that my change of hair colour was part of an image makeover, but there was actually nothing contrived about it. The bonus was that it sometimes worked as a disguise, now that I'd stopped dyeing it.

I told them I'd bumped into Steve Irwin once, in a recording studio where he was doing voiceovers for his TV show, and he'd said to me that that was the beauty of his khaki shirt. False teeth, a trucker's cap and a red-and-black flanno shirt gave him all the cover he could hope for. There was footage of him in the crowd at Australia Zoo, taking in a show dressed just like that, with no one around him giving him a second glance.

So, I went back to my natural hair after the band broke up, and got a bit fat. Everyone around the table was decent enough not to mention the second strategy.

Straight after dinner, Mark asked if he could be excused – the language for the request was semi-formal and clearly negotiated long ago – and he went to his room.

'Two choices now, Liesie,' Kate said. 'Dishes or homework.'

A big sigh, some eye rolling. The world, for sixteen-years-olds was a deeply, resolutely unfair place. 'What about conversation? Isn't that important as well?'

Kate just looked at her. There was a hint of an eyebrow lifting.

'I could do the dishes,' I said, and Kate said, 'Looks like it's homework.'

Annaliese threw her hands in the air, and gave me a look that said it was all my fault. 'So now I don't even get to choose.'

'You'd have to do the homework anyway.' I was standing my ground.

'Technically, yes,' she said, the dramatics in check for a moment. She gave a smile that was supposed to look begrudging. 'Okay, so you're not such a bad guy after all.'

Kate gave a shake of her head once Annaliese's door was shut, and said, 'Too much TV. Where does she get this . . .' She flailed her arms around. 'Not from me. Not from anyone I know.' She laughed. 'Endlessly entertaining. It's all melodrama around here.'

She drank the last mouthful of her Stella and then turned the stubbie around to take her first proper look at the label.

There was something close to silence for the first time since I'd arrived. The distant pounding of heavy metal, perhaps, from the headphones that were surely clamped to Mark's head as he sat in his room wargaming or cruising websites, but other than that, nothing. The CD had finished and the night was close and still.

'You don't have to do the dishes,' Kate said.

'I'd be happy to. Most nights I just clean one plate.' She almost said something, then didn't. She rearranged her cutlery so that her knife and fork lined up. 'That sounded a lot sadder than it was supposed to.'

'It didn't sound sad,' she said, too quickly. 'Well, it did. But I don't think it was meant to be sad. Okay, dig me out of this any time.'

'Let's wash the dishes.'

I washed, she handled the wiping and putting away. She asked me what I cooked, and then if I would show her something.

'But it's got to be simple,' she said. 'Something simple.'

I wondered if the decent thing would have been to compliment the casserole, but I didn't know where to start. So I said, 'Sure, recipes are for sharing.'

She picked up wet cutlery by the handful and rubbed it dry, shutting the drawer with her hip when the last forks went in. She fetched more beers from the fridge while I worked on the casserole dish. She watched as the baked black rim of gunge refused to be scoured away and she said, 'I know where the dynamite is, if you need it.' And she rolled her eyes, Annaliese-style, at the harm she could wreak on her utensils for a meal no one would love.

She wore a locket on a silver chain, and more of her hair was free now and falling to her neck in fine loose coils. Droplets of sweat were gathering above her upper lip and a strand or two of hair was stuck to her temples. She was perspiring like a Jane Austen heroine, I was hosing it out like a beast in a field. Sweat, ox sweat, spread darkly across my shirt, breaking out like a rash over my stomach.

'It's too hot for this,' she said. 'Let that soak. Let's drink these outside. It's got to be cooler there.'

We sat on the back verandah in director's chairs, with the dark of the swimming pool below us and the bush beyond. Through the trees behind Kate I could see the light on in my kitchen. I remembered looking up this way when I first arrived, and seeing the glow of a cigarette in the dark.

'Who smokes here?' I'd seen no sign of smoking all night, and the question was out of me before I'd thought of Mark and Annaliese and the trouble I might be making for one of them.

'Who smokes?' Kate said. 'No one smokes. I hope no one smokes. What makes you . . .'

'It was probably something else. Just something I saw at night when I first got back. It mightn't have even been up here at all.'

'Oh, it was though.' She had worked it out. 'But

44

you wouldn't have seen it for about two weeks and five days, I'm guessing.' She made a hmm noise and took a mouthful of beer. 'That was a guy I was seeing. And now I'm not.'

'Sorry, I . . .'

'Nothing to be sorry about. He could cook, but that was about the only thing he had in his favour. And it was mostly pasta with heavy sauces. Carbs, fat, all wrong. He had to go.' The Stella was on its way to her mouth again, but it jerked to a stop. 'Oh, shit, I hope you don't think . . .' she said, and then she stopped to get it right. 'When I asked you to show me how to cook some-thing, that was just me wanting to know how to cook something.'

'Sure.'

But she'd snapped a brake cable and her explanation was now a runaway vehicle bucking its way down a hill-side. 'This isn't a set up. I don't want you thinking that. That's partly why I didn't invite anyone else.' Heading for a big fat rock at high speed. 'I can't let my friends meet you, since they'd all be wanting me to sleep with you.'

Boom.

'Which would be a fate worse than death, obviously,' I said, offloading as calmly as I could into the inevitable awkward silence.

She moved her beer up towards the kind of grin only tetanus makes and said, in a small voice, 'Oh god.' The moment, despite her fervent desires, was refusing to open up and swallow her whole.

'Shall I, um, put on a new CD?'

I didn't wait for an answer. We could hit the pause button on the conversation and fix this, I figured. I was out of my chair and heading inside before she could speak. The loungeroom seemed brighter now. I wondered if Annaliese and Mark could have heard us talking, but the dull thud of artillery came through Mark's wall and it was clearly game on in there. With the war and the heavy metal, Kate would be okay.

There were three shelves of CDs, and I kept telling myself not to look for Butterfish, not to even think of Butterfish. People's CD racks always had me thinking that way, and I couldn't seem to stop it. I didn't want us to be there. I didn't want us not to be there. Any CD shelf anywhere was some kind of judgement about the past decade of my life. I saw Jeff Buckley's Grace and grabbed it. Fine late-night music, sensitive, no pulsating Barry White hot-lovin' agendas.

'Good,' Kate said when I stepped back out into the semi-dark of the verandah. 'That's good. About before . . .'

'There's no need to do an "about before".'

'My friends . . . I'm some kind of sport to them.' She was committed to the 'about before'. 'They've got themselves all set and from time to time I provide the entertainment. Mostly they're from a previous life.'

'Like, when you were an Egyptian princess?'

She laughed. 'No, slightly more recent. Slightly. They're from a time when I was married. And not selling cheap jewellery at Indooroopilly. But that sounds like you and washing one plate. It's not a sad situation.' She drank some beer. Her face had settled back into a more usual smile. 'Anyway, life gets complicated in ways like that. I don't think anyone can get to this end of their thirties – the middle end – without a few rough landings.

46

Anyone, with the possible exception of a couple of my friends, who seem to lead a life that's somewhere between Stepford and actually perfect. Damn them. I had a work Christmas party last year, just drinks at the Pig 'n' Whistle, and there was a live band. Someone took a photo of me from about knee-high while I was dancing. I told one of my friends about it, and I told her I looked hideously drunk and haggard. And do you know what she said? She said, "I'm sure you weren't *hideously* drunk." So, there you go. Haggard and just regular drunk. That's where she'd put me. That's the kind of back-up you want when you're thirty-seven – thirty-six then – and working hard to keep all the balls in the air.'

'I've just got a brother with six-pack abs who calls me Chubs. He doesn't let up though.'

'Six-pack abs. Does he realise how nineties he is?'

I couldn't imagine a better thing she could have said.

Inside, a door opened. Heavy feet came our way, and Mark's broad unshaped shadow cast itself onto the verandah.

'I was just wondering . . .' he said when he appeared. 'Annaliese said you might need someone to mow your lawn. And if you did, I'd probably be available for hire. And I'd happily undercut most commercial contractors.' Politeness felt wrong from a black-clad teenager with hair like a nest and a nail in his ear, but for Mark it seemed to be a tool that he could put to work whenever it might be useful. The tone was even coy, reserved.

'*Most* commercial contractors?' Kate said, picking a hole in the way a parent can. 'Do you have the overheads of *any* commercial contractors? I assume you're just planning to use our mower.'

'I'm in the neighbourhood,' he said, more to me than to her. 'And I pretty much guarantee a quick response time.' The cracked glass smile was back. I wasn't sure if it was supposed to be persuasive, or if he was just enjoying his politician's non-answer to his mother's questioning. I wondered if the smile was being pulled into its shape partly by the hot lumps of acne swelling near his mouth.

'That sounds good to me,' I told him. My grass really needed cutting, and I had no inclination to get out there myself. 'Of course I'd have to be indemnified against snake bite. Some of that grass is pretty long.'

The smile persisted. 'Well, we could talk some kind of danger money,' he said. 'Some kind of loading.'

'What?' Kate was weighing in again. 'Are you crazy? How good's an extra few dollars going to feel if a taipan bites you?'

'That won't be happening,' he said dismissively. 'You think snakes'll hang around when the mower starts? This is just a commercial arrangement.'

'Right,' she said. 'And if the worst comes to the worst I've still got Liesie to look after me in my old age.'

He gave a phlegmy unpractised laugh and said, 'Thanks, Mum. Looks like we're good to go, Curtis.' I was sensing that, while giving as little away as possible, he had loved this game, that they both had.

'Okay, it's a deal,' I said. 'I'll pay you whatever's reasonable. Come and get started as soon as you're ready to.'

'Cool,' he said, obviously fantasising about just how much he might be able to rip me off.

48

He went back to his room, his shadow swaying and following him. His door closed, and again I heard the muffled sound of loud music being compressed into willing, scheming teenage skull.

'You've clearly never done a deal with Mark before,' Kate said.

'I don't imagine the "special occasion" beer concept came out of nowhere. It sounds pretty heavily negotiated.' It wasn't the time to say that the money would be no issue, that I didn't have to think that way.

'Everything's heavily negotiated with Mark,' she said. 'I've got my limits though, and he knows it. Most of the time I've got a fair idea of where I'm going to draw the line. It's guess work to some extent, but you get a few dozen guesses a day so some of them have to work out. No, it's better than that, really. You know them, so your instincts put the lines close enough to the right place. And Mark's been a negotiator since he was about two. I've had plenty of practice. He should be drinking no beer. I know that. But I think this way he drinks less. I'm just lucky that Annaliese doesn't like the taste, or I'd be getting it in stereo. I only floss my teeth to make them floss theirs. Otherwise you get the whole "but you don't . . ." thing. So, I've flossed for years now, even though I hate it and I'd use a mouthwash even if it isn't as good. I have a friend who subscribes to Choice who told me that. Or maybe that was just her view.'

'Whereas, in the world of the single plate, I just know where the food gets stuck between my teeth and I use a pencil. I click the lead out a couple of notches and push it through.'

I could feel my face going red, though the colour wouldn't show out here. Kate laughed, which was better than Kate not laughing.

'You were obviously brought up right,' she said. 'I think Choice really rated that.' She sat back in her chair and crossed her legs at the ankles and looked out at nothing in particular. 'It's different being a kid now,' she said. 'Different to the way it was for us. More pressures, more things to do, more to keep up with. They live in a different world. But maybe you know all that. They buy your music, don't they? Teenage people. Among others. I'm old enough to remember when TV ran out of shows at night and went to a test pattern. The first time I told the kids about that they wouldn't believe me. They wouldn't believe that TV ever stopped.'

I realised I should be going – that Kate was easy company, good company, but the last of my beer was as warm as the evening and it was better to leave before the conversation ran out and left us stranded, two awkward people on a back verandah in the dark.

'I see the light in the granny flat some nights,' she said. 'I thought maybe you had someone staying there, but Annaliese tells me it's your studio.'

'Yeah, it said studio in the ad,' I told her. 'I got slightly the wrong idea. But a studio with a kitchenette and a bathroom – that's not a bad thing. I'm working on a record with a Norwegian band. I might have said that before. I'm producing. We just laid down some tracks in Norway, so now I'm . . . doing what producers do.'

'You say that as if it's selling shoes.'

'It's my version of selling shoes. I mean, it's great, but it's what I do.' That wasn't quite correct. 'It's what I'm trying to do. The chance came along, so I took it. I met the two main guys in the band, Gunnar and Øivind, at a festival a couple of years ago. Roskilde, I think. In Denmark. There was Tuborg involved, so it was probably Denmark. We got on well, and I watched their set and liked what I heard. And Gunnar was starting to write some really strong material with English lyrics. I think every band in Norway feels a need to break out of Norway. It's not unlike here.'

That's what I remembered of Roskilde. Our set – the Butterfish set – on the main stage in the falling light of the late summer evening was lost somewhere. Too many festivals, too many nights of Derek Frick morphing from tour-bus weasel into rock god, strutting and posturing, calling up all the love in the town. It didn't so much matter which festival, or which town – it was the same show, the same long shapeless memory.

The Splades signed with management in London. A deal came along. Not the kind of deal that would have them browsing the castles-r-us websites, but healthy numbers nonetheless. They tracked me down just as the future fell out of my diary, and they sent a charming funny email that lured me without a sign of struggle to Svolvær, and my producing debut. 'In Svolvær there will be peace and beer, and more dried cod than you have ever dreamed.'

'Annaliese is quite a singer, you know,' Kate said, but I'd lost track of what was connecting the threads of the conversation. Maybe it was a new thought entirely. 'We've got her singing on DVD. Let me show you.'

'Would she be okay with that?'

'Thousands of people saw her. Why wouldn't she be okay?' She was already moving.

I followed her inside, and she sorted through the pile of DVDs under the TV. She pulled one out of its box and pushed it into the player. There was a VCR wired in there as well, and a machine I didn't recognise. I wondered if Mark had gone to work on it all. He had probably charged her a fee.

'It's supposed to operate from one remote,' she said. 'This DVD is just Annaliese's segment of the show. If I can get it to . . .'

The screen burst into life, but on an analogue TV channel. Kate worked the volume down with her thumb, made an assortment of mistakes with the remote, swore under her breath. Then footage of a stage staggered onto the screen. Annaliese was standing alone in the back of a red convertible, with dancers around her. She was singing DJ Sammy's version of Boys of Summer, with the backing track ticking along at the requisite high BPM, and her only mistake was that she had too much voice to offer it. The original – the new original, anyway – was a dance track, and the voice deliberately pulled back to sound light on, but Annaliese was going for it, and she could really sing.

'She's great,' I was saying, honestly, when her door swung open.

'That's supposed to stay in my room,' she said to Kate angrily, ignoring me completely.

'But you were really good.' I was trying to defuse the situation, but also meaning it. I was feeling tired, feeling the beer in my head, wanting to be back at my own house.

'You're just trying to cover my mother's fat arse.' Still looking at Kate. Spleen was set to be vented here, and I could be collateral damage if I wanted to be.

'Did you really need to say fat?' These were Kate's first words, and I wasn't sure they would help.

'Okay, everyone,' I said, finding a peacemaker tone from somewhere. 'Great singing, great arse.'

'It was just an expression,' Annaliese said. 'And I'd like the DVD now.'

🎧

THE VERANDAH LIGHT CLICKED off when I was halfway to the road from their front door. The darkness felt almost total, and I had to stop. Then I saw there were stars, plenty of them. No moon though. I looked up, half-expecting to see the constellations mapped out, the clear lines of an archer, a plough, across the sky. But I couldn't name one thing up there.

Cities are awash with light. Light surges through them, with a pulse that's almost arterial. But there are no stars. Cities coast along without respite. The big ones anyway, blanking out starlight with the light blasting from Seven Elevens, traffic, office buildings.

I could just make out the way ahead, the bare earth between the patches of pale dry grass. I found my way to the road, and turned right. In the distance there were streetlights, the houses of unseen neighbours, the gap in the hedge that would lead me to my bed.

I had made a start on a new song when the band broke up. I had given it the working title 'The Light that Guides

You Home'. I tried bits of it out with Derek, enough that I could sometimes hear him humming or singing a line or two to himself as he gazed out the tour bus window. It wasn't coming together though. It wasn't right. I was blaming that on Derek, and I knew that wasn't right either. But he didn't get it. Derek could be a blunt instrument more often than he realised, and it wasn't always smart to set him to work on the finer details.

'An over-ripe overblown ballad' Rolling Stone had called Still Water, and given it two stars on its way to becoming our first US number one. It was our big break, the song that put us on planes and talk shows and stopped us seeing Brisbane for about two years. I can hardly remember finishing a conversation all that time.

It's where Derek would have taken the new song too. Rolling Stone wasn't entirely wrong about Still Water – it just misjudged the market's bottomless appetite for over-ripe overblown ballads. And I didn't want that for The Light that Guides You Home. Night after night Derek would sing Still Water, and each night I'd hate him for it just a little more. By the end, it was as over-blown as Elvis when he faced the final fried peanut butter sandwich, and Derek, as far as I was concerned, was the man who overblew it, who turned it into a big pompous bastard of a song that only a stadium could love.

I could do an acoustic version of that song right now – just me and an upright piano – and show the bits people never heard. Strip it back and make it small, make it lean and underdone, and show people the song it might have been. But we added Derek, and charisma, and sold twelve million albums instead. That was The True Story of Butterfish. We followed it up with Supernature, which

54

sold eight million, then came Written in Sand, Written in Sea. One hundred and forty-seven thousand copies sold, last time someone put the unit count into words and I didn't have my hands over my ears. 'Rarely can an album be called pretentious and directionless at the same time,' Rolling Stone said. 'Where are the effortless hooks from Frick and Holland that we became used to on their first two albums? Could be there's some turbulence in the still water these days.'

I also saw reviews that said 'File this somewhere between esoteric and bad' and 'It's either confused or confusing, neither of which is exactly a good thing'. So I stopped looking. Our US publicist told us she'd bundle them up at the end of the tour and send us each a copy. I hadn't seen mine and I didn't go chasing it.

We were in Frankfurt, drinking tall glasses of Schoefferhofer beer on a barge on the Main on a bright spring evening when we got the call to say our US label was dumping us.

'Fuckers. They were never behind us,' Derek said, holding his phone like a stone that he might throw into the river.

He had a jacket on, since there was a cool breeze coming up the river, and his collar was turned up as if he was in a video. He needed a shave, and some sleep. His eyes were puffy. He had spent days looking as if he'd just woken up. I thought he had taken some pills before we'd taped an interview for MTV Europe earlier in the day, and he was on his way down by the evening. He had been like a sleepwalker with his finger in a power point on the show – jangly energy, scratchy thought processes and somnolence, all in the one body.

The barge was called the Bootshaus Dreyer, and the massive ironwork of the Eisener Steg rose up behind Derek's head, carrying pedestrians across the Main.

The US tour had not ended well and, from my perspective anyway, there had been a feeling that the dumping was coming. This was our difficult third album and we had outsmarted ourselves. We had never been paid more, never had so much at stake. It was a long way from shopping demos around and hoping someone somewhere might take an interest.

Third time around, we locked ourselves away in Malibu for weeks, months, racking up huge studio bills, hiring and firing session musos. Derek behaved like Nero. Maybe I did too. I had turned up with some songs that were mostly done and a few half there, but Derek – given to grandiose metaphor at the best of times – arrived with a pile of ideas straight from an ugly seventies acid trip. I wouldn't have been surprised if he had turned up one morning with a puffy shirt and a sword, and a Celtic princess he'd befriended the night before. But there were great ideas in there too, and glimpses of a vision that might be too epic to contain.

After about six weeks of nothing getting back to New York but bad stories, we had a surprise visit from a few of the senior people at the music company. They turned up with boxloads of Krispy Kreme doughnuts, and played it as though they just happened to be in the neighbourhood and thought they might as well drop in.

'Mind if we listen to some of what you've been doing?' one of them said after his second decaf skinny latte, as if it was an afterthought.

We played a few tracks and they listened studiously,

and without moving. When they love you, you get some middle-aged-guy-type music-appreciation movements – the nodding head, the tapping foot, sometimes more – but they weren't giving us any of that.

'We haven't heard the single yet?' It was somewhere between a statement and a question, and it came from the one of the three I had met before. His name was Karl. He was a vice president of something.

'We're not about singles,' Derek said.

And Karl said, 'I know that. But is there a big song? You owe a lot to one big song, remember. Still Water, Iris, Drops of Jupiter – those songs make bands. They sell albums, they book out arenas, commercial radio plays them until they've put your grandchildren through college. We're budgeting for six million units with this album, but a big song could take it past twelve.'

'No pressure though,' Paul, our drummer, said, and Karl said, 'That's right,' and smiled. How many times had he, or someone like him, had the same conversation with the Goo Goo Dolls in the years after Iris had worked its big-song magic for them? He dusted doughnut sugar from his hand and asked where the bathroom was.

'I thought they were all big songs,' Derek said quietly and only to me, once they had left.

The last strand of that conversation unwound that evening in Frankfurt, almost a year later, when Derek took the call from our New York manager saying that he had had a meeting with Karl, and they were cutting us loose.

We ordered another round of beers in tall half-litre glasses, and not a lot was said. The beer was cloudy and slightly sweet, and I could taste bananas and citrus and cloves. Around us people ate fat sausages and schnitzels. We were under an umbrella – an orange umbrella emblazoned with the Schoefferhofer name in a Germanic script, with three ancient-looking gold medals above it – but the sun had gone and the wind rushed in as a huge barge loaded with rusty scrap metal pushed by. Three of us – Derek, Darren and I – had been part of Butterfish since before the first US deal. Paul was from Melbourne and had joined after the first album. Then we added Ben – from Cambridge, Massachusetts – just in time for the This is Spinal Tap remake that was Written in Sand, Written in Sea. The five of us sat awkwardly around a small wooden table for four, each of us trying not to take up an entire side and look like the alpha male. Each of us alone with his own complex arrangement of thoughts about what was going on, what might happen next. For Ben, it may have been as simple as wanting to get the hell out and hoping that the cheque would clear.

We walked along the riverbank where people had been lazing in the evening sun but were now wrapping up against the chill that had blown in, and we bought kebabs from a small white boat called the Istanbul. The others drank late that night and, no doubt, skirted around a morose deconstruction of our grand and soon to be public failure. I couldn't face it, and I went to my room. It felt as if several years of tiredness had caught me in a rush and tackled me hard.

I was up early the next morning, and I saw there was a market on the iron bridge. I almost bought a three-euro belt from a guy with a stall a metre wide that sold only belts, and all for three euros each. I remembered that I had kept the same crappy belt for years, saving money in case my career fell over and, in the moment of reaching for my wallet and then not buying the new belt, I realised that that was what had happened the evening before. My career had fallen over, without a sound, and I had met it with a beer-fuzzed brain and some ambivalence. Anger, relief, a sense of shame. A sense that some of the noise in my head might be about to go.

There was to be no fourth album, and the band broke up before I finished the song that may one day be known as The Light that Guides You Home. It had a chorus and one long verse, so it felt only halfway to being a song, and its bridge was problematic. Those were its shortcomings in structural terms. I also didn't really know what it was about, where it was heading. It was entirely true to life, in that sense at least. I walked away from the iron bridge market with the money to buy all the belts in Frankfurt, but I didn't feel rich, or even safe, and I had no clear idea about how to live a rich person's life, or any other. I had seen affluent lives and they didn't feel like me. For a while, nothing did.

We tore ourselves apart with Written in Sand, Written in Sea. We even argued about the comma in the title. Derek actually called it elegant. I was the one who ended up shouting, 'No one buys albums with commas in the title.' I had no evidence for that, of course. Not until we released the album anyway. 'Tore apart' is unjustly dramatic. We snapped like perished elastic, tamely and definitively. We wore out. Our best new ideas, our friendships, everything – we wore it all out.

So, it was over now. Derek was famously out of control and the others were, respectively, in Sydney, on tour with a side-project band, and last heard of back in his old bedroom at his parents' house in Cambridge, Massachu-setts. Where, presumably, he woke up every morning, took a look at the wallpaper he knew best and won-dered for at least a second or two if his whole Butterfish experience might have been no more than a bad dream with an Australian accent.

Since all the songs were Frick/Holland, I was still riding high on my share of the royalties. Still Water alone had clocked up US radio airplays in the hundreds of thousands, and had featured in two movies, a TV series and advertisements in Australia, New Zealand, Canada, Ireland, South Africa and Belgium, mostly promot-ing still water (no imagination required there). It was a steady earner as an iTunes download, and its chorus was a ringtone for which people around the world regularly handed over money. My grandchildren would thank me, if I ended up being smart with it.

I tripped on my own front steps in the dark, and won-dered why I hadn't thought to leave a light on. I found the door handle by feel, and the keyhole beneath it. The issue of grandchildren seemed very theoretical, like particle physics, or those equations that cross blackboards with a spray of sigmas in their wakes. I had no future planned, yet. I had a bunch of Norwegians to coax through the white-knuckle ride of their first major international album, and I thought that would do for now.

☊

ON FRIDAY I PLAYED a fierce half-hour of Space Invaders and then worked on a Splades song that I had been ignoring. I added bits, and then subtracted twice as much. D-verb, a Hammond-organ kind of keyboards sound. I had pulled off enough of the bells and whistles by late morning that I found myself recording an acoustic guitar track for its rawness rather than any other contribution it might make. I imagined a bar in a backwoods town, the drummer working the snare with brushes, and a guitar that had been carried across the country without much care. I recorded it to pick up every squeak of the fingering, and then wondered what Reason or Sample Tank might have for me when I went looking for the drums. I wanted leathery-faced old-guy brushwork that came with a battered hat and no teeth, and a sense of unshakeable rhythm that got built into the hands in the thirties.

No, wrong sound. Clever but wrong. My mind was on my father's old blues records – very old blues records – and that wasn't the way to take this. There was an element of it in the song, but just an element, and it was lurking in the background and meant to stay there. I threw most of Gunnar and Øivind's work back in, but tried to be selective about it. They had a sound, and I should go with that.

'What do you want? What do you want?' How many times had I asked them that in Svolvær? Plenty. We needed an album they could live with until the last interview in the last country. We needed a couple of potential hits to keep the music-company people in London happy, but we needed to avoid quirkiness, since there's no maths quite as certain as quirky plus Scandinavian equals one-hit wonder. We needed to keep their sound intact but bring it across towards the international mainstream.

I was enjoying the puzzle that presented me, and not minding at all being the grizzled veteran of the business, the one who had been through the mill and had all his excitement worked out of him, only to see it replaced by anecdotes he no longer had the grace to tell. And I didn't let Gunnar and Øivind know it, but they would eventually look on this as the best time – the last time they made a record almost for its own sake, full of promise and without the weight of expectations. Expectations existed, of course, but they had been calibrated in London and kept out of the heads of the Splades for now.

I brought up Øivind's guitar part, which played all over my half-baked work of the morning.

Then movement caught my eye next door, through the bushes. I realised it was mid-afternoon and school was over for the week. I heard the sound of a body entering the pool in a clean dive, and some strokes being swum. Annaliese got out at the end near me, topless. She picked up a towel and patted herself dry. She was almost facing me, but she seemed to be looking off into the trees behind my studio, though not at anything in particular. She was wearing only a black bikini bottom, and standing in the one place where she would be almost completely visible. Then she spread the towel out across a banana lounge – I could just see the end of it – and she disappeared from view. All but her feet and calves, as she lay face down in the baking sun. The rest of her was gone.

The green lines marking the volume of Øivind's guitar had tipped up into orange and then fallen away. The track had ended, and the only sound came from the airconditioning unit in the wall behind me. I told myself

I couldn't have seen what I had just seen, couldn't have watched.

I wondered if it would be best to re-record the bass, once everything else was right.

☊

'IT'S A BIG YARD,' Mark said as he looked it over. We both knew it was a big yard, but now it had to be put into words, with an appropriate sense of the burden it was about to place on him.

Despite the heat, he was wearing black shorts and a black T-shirt again, though the design had mostly flaked off this shirt, which hung like a sack. It might have once said Slayer or Stryker or something else that was almost certainly heavy metal, in a gothic font and inappropriately umlauted. He was leaning like an old hand on the mower he had clattered along the street from his house. He was wearing a black cap on which someone had had the word 'dude' embroidered, in black. The sun glinted from his ear nail.

'Could be fifty bucks, I reckon,' he said, with the gravitas of the large-animal vet who's telling you the whole herd has to go. It's hard news, but he knows you're man enough to take it on the chin. 'Plus ten for providing the mower and the petrol. So, sixty.'

I nodded, and tried to appear as though I was giving it the right amount of thought. I looked around, appraising the furthest mowable parts of the block.

'And the price stays fixed regardless of fluctuations in the price of fuel, and you rake the grass once you've mowed it?' I nearly mentioned the ten-day rolling-average oil price out of Singapore, but I would have laughed then. I already had to look away from the dude cap as it was.

'All part of the service,' he said, still cheerless.

He reached out a pale sweaty hand for me to shake, and the deal was done. I went back inside, and heard the mower squeak and rattle its way to a corner of the block near the road. With a couple of pulls of the cord, he had it started.

I was taking a day off, determined to take a full day off. I'd been squinting at the screen and hunched over like a monk for too many hours of the preceding few days, and I knew I wasn't hearing anything the way I needed to.

So, I had read three newspapers in their entirety, slept through lunch and was starting on a slow-simmering curry while drinking the day's first ice-cold Stella. The curry was a lamb rogan josh, with bay leaves and a stick of cinnamon and whole cardamom pods and cloves, and it worked out best with two hours or more on a low heat.

Mark pushed his way up and down one side of the house. I gave the spices a couple of minutes in ghee before adding the onion, then the garlic and ginger.

'I'll do yours if you'll make that curry,' Derek had said to me more than once when we'd been handed our updated interview schedules on the Supernature tour. And I'd hang out in my suite's kitchenette, giving the pot an occasional stir while he served up identical anecdotes in interview after interview. Then someone labelled me enigmatic, and we got to do that a lot less.

I was becoming a candidate for the 'so how does it feel to be the quiet-but-fucked-up guy in the band?' interview, and that's best dealt with by cooking quicker meals and pulling your weight.

Mark methodically worked his way around without a break until all the grass was mown. I went out onto the back verandah to find him leaning on the rake under the shade of a tree near the studio.

I offered him a drink, and he said, 'A beer'd be good.' He was bright red in the face and his shirt was drenched with sweat and flecked with grass clippings. The dude cap was pushed back and wavy strands of hair were stuck across his forehead.

'I'm not having that "special occasion" debate with you,' I told him. 'I was thinking of your hydration. Water, you know.'

'I'm aware of it. Water, yeah.' He put on some kind of smile then. 'Water'd be good.'

I went inside, saw my own beer on the counter and felt like he'd brought out the mean old man in me. But, no, I couldn't go giving out beers to fourteen-year-olds to avoid feeling old. I put the stubbie in the fridge and took out a jug of cold water.

Annaliese was walking around the side of the house as I opened the screen door. She saw me and stopped.

'Hey, Curtis,' she said. She was wearing oversized round sunglasses of the style favoured by people like Paris Hilton and Mischa Barton. They were almost half the size of her face. 'Mark has to go home.' She turned to look at him. 'Dad's on the phone.'

'Really?' he said without much interest. 'Do I have to?'

65

'Apparently.'

He gave the ground a scratch with the rake, but didn't move.

'Some school report,' she said. 'You're being dysfunctional again.'

'Oh, that,' he said, as if it was old news. It probably was. He looked up at me. 'I'll come back and do the raking. If that's okay. This might take a while.'

He leaned the rake against the tree, pulled off the dude cap and pushed his wet mat of hair away from his face. He smiled, as if set to be amused by the interrogation about to come his way, and the deadening monosyllabic replies I was sure he was going to offer.

'Right, then,' he said, and he walked off across the dry mown grass, in no particular hurry.

Annaliese made no move to follow him. She was dressed in a short skirt and a singlet top, and they didn't quite manage to meet in the middle. I stood there with the jug of cold water and the glass.

'How about a tour of the studio?' she said.

'The studio? Sure.' I didn't know what I had expected her to say, but that wasn't it.

I left the jug and glass on the verandah table and walked down the steps. A tour of the studio. She was about to be underwhelmed. I noticed the closed curtains and realised the key was back in the house. I was practically standing at the door by then.

'Pretend you didn't see this,' I told her, and I reached under the steel beam that ran beneath the front of the studio and found the spare key in its magnetised holder.

'Who are you?' she said, and laughed. 'Maxwell

66

Smart? You'll show me the studio, but then you'll have to kill me?'

The studio air felt trapped and stale and warm when I opened the door, so I turned the airconditioning on as I stepped inside. Annaliese pushed the door shut behind her and stood next to me, her sunglasses in her hand.

'It's um . . .'

'It's early days,' I told her. 'Still halfway between a granny flat and a big studio, massive mixing desk, the remnants of lines of coke on every horizontal surface.' She either played it cool or thought I was serious, or thought the line was too stupid to acknowledge. Whichever way she took it, she said nothing. 'Or in my case, the rings of forgotten coffee cups on every horizontal surface.' With that I looked like either a wimp or someone with something to hide. Almost certainly the former.

Annaliese took in the array of mute machines and powerboards, and the musty odour that had been locked up here when I first arrived. In her mind, this room had been different. It looked like a bachelor loungeroom prior to its Queer Eye for the Straight Guy makeover. And I was playing the role of the slob with the grey ponytail and the food-spattered shirt who called it his little slice of a shambolic heaven. Then in would come Carson and the gang, and I'd be given a red raw screaming body wax and mocked and prodded into something fit to leave the house, maybe even bring a tear to the eye of my long-long-suffering girlfriend.

'Right,' Annaliese said. She had expected a place where magic happened, and there was none on offer. 'What's this?'

67

She had managed to pick the one frivolous purchase in the room.

'Space Invaders,' I told her. Or, to be more precise, an original circa 1978 Space Invaders console, refurbished and in full working order, sitting there low and sleek and black with its red knob and glass top. The perfect antidote for overthinking or boredom, or the times when every sound seemed like a big mistake.

'What? Who are Space Invaders and what space are they invading?'

'Don't do this.'

'Ha,' she said, and smirked, looking down at the smudgy surface and, yes, coffee rings. 'I was just kidding. Maybe. It's a toy from the twentieth century, right?'

If I had come back to Brisbane to stop being a rockstar, Annaliese was determined to get me there as quickly as possible. I wanted to be much cooler than the ageing flabby man I felt I was at that moment, the gormless stack of a creature showing the young girl his old grubby toy.

'I think I'm missing all those people I used to pay to give me self-esteem.'

'I'm sure it's a good toy, Curtis,' she said, without a hint of esteem-support in her tone. 'Hey, in the language of your time, I dig you, man. I dig you like a fossil.'

'That's so not my time.' Fossil. Excellent. Dig you, man. Also excellent.

'Fifties, eighties, whatever – it's all history.'

'You can't say that. There's a generation difference. You can't just dismiss it as being all the same.' But she could, and she had. 'The fifties is my father, and he was this old high-panted guy who didn't think there had been any real music since the war. By which he would have meant World War Two.'

'Every guy over thirty looks high-panted to me.' Dismissed again. 'So, can I hear something?' She was looking towards the Mac and the keyboard.

'Yeah, good idea. It'd be nice to have a chance to show you this isn't just the junk room.'

'Well, yeah. I guess you didn't know that you'd be having a visitor.'

Behind her and through the window, I could see Kate step into the gap between the bushes at the back of their house. She had a pool scoop in her hands and was lifting out leaves. Annaliese followed my eyes, and turned to see her mother.

'Okay,' I said, filling a space in the conversation before it seemed like a space.

I wasn't sure if I saw her smiling before she looked down at the keyboard and said, 'So show me. Show me how it all works.'

I thought of her, in that same gap between the bushes the day before. And now here in her midriff top and her short skirt. I wanted to open the window and call out to Kate, let her know Annaliese was here for the studio tour. I was sweating. The airconditioning was blowing cold air at my head, but the room was still full of trapped heat.

I woke up the Mac and the track I'd been working on was sitting there, laid out on the screen.

'Wow,' Annaliese said, as if my job had turned real in that instant.

I opened a new file, and set up master, midi and two audio tracks. I fed the keyboards in through the M box and assumed that a few bars of something I could work with would just find their way to my fingers. Annaliese was beside me, close by my right shoulder. Her eyes were on my hands, which were sitting neutrally on the keys. Her own hands were held as if they were ready to follow any move I made.

'Actually, why don't you?' I pushed the chair back from the keyboard. 'Why don't you play something and then I'll do some work on it?' I stood up.

'What?' The self-assured Annaliese of the fossil remark was momentarily absent and she seemed, for just a second, fragile. 'All right. All right, I will. I'll give it a try.' She sat, manoeuvred herself in the chair, touched the keyboard with the tips of the fingers of her right hand. 'Anything?'

'Anything. Just let me get it started.' I reached for the mouse. 'As soon as I set you up with a click track, you're right to go. This'll give you a rhythm to work with. If you put the headphones on, you should hear it coming through.'

'So it's like a metronome,' she said, correctly.

'Yeah. A metronome's kind of like a click track for old people. Mozart, people like that.'

'Bastard,' she said, and laughed. 'I just happen to be classically trained.'

'So, I should expect a lot then.' I set the rate to a hundred beats per minute. 'Something modern might be nice, if you've got it. Something from your own non-high-panted time. Unless classical's all you do.'

'Non-high-panted. Right. So, tragically, Asia's Heat of the Moment is out . . .' she said, pretending to give her song selection serious thought.

'That was one second of weakness.' And yet, somehow, another small victory for Annaliese over the fossil. 'Now, put the cans on and play me something.'

I got the click track started, she nodded her head a few times to settle into the rhythm, and she played. The song she picked was Missy Higgins's Scar, or something improvised from it, and my keyboard setting wasn't right for that, but I could change the sound once we had it down.

She played maybe ten bars and said, 'How much?' She was taking it somewhere new by then. I'd been right to think that she could play.

'That'll be fine. Let's work with it.' I pulled another chair over and she moved along. 'I should have set it to "grand" before you started, but we can fancy it up a bit.'

She watched everything, every move as I lushed it up, went for D-verb, pushed it up to one hundred percent wet and clicked on 'large plate'. I went into Reason and tested some drum loops, and then had to admit we should have gone there first. I was doing it all out of order.

'Okay, I'm going to try some fake bass now. It's not my best thing, so bear with me.'

I listened to her piece twice more and thought I had enough of it in my head. I played it again and recorded a painting-by-numbers bass line using the keyboard. There was nothing clever about it, but it would do to make the point.

Annaliese took the mouse from my hand, and played my bass track back. 'Let's see,' she said, bringing up the screen box that looked like a mixing desk. She twiddled

71

knobs, pulled and pushed, compressing it mercilessly. She listened and said, 'Oh crap,' and pulled it back the other way. 'Show me how to make it real. Then let's add some horns.'

Kate was gone from the pool by then, I noticed as I looked past Annaliese and out the window. I heard a rake outside, Mark scratching up the cut dry stalks of grass beside my house. And I remembered I had a curry inside, simmering.

I COULDN'T DENY ANNALIESE was on my mind as I drove across town to meet Patrick in the Valley that night. I wondered if any sixteen-year-old boy in the city understood her at all. I could see them at parties, sneaking in rum, trying to get her drunk. But I also pictured them in eighties clothes and I *remembered* the parties instead of imagining them, and the sixteen-year-old boy who looked like me – dressed like me, was me – threw up the rum and felt the Coke fizz through his nose as it washed back out and the girls didn't seem greatly attracted to that.

I couldn't graft Annaliese onto a memory of a party from the eighties and see how she would fare. She was right. It was all history. My version of sixteen seemed truly old for the first time.

I parked miles away, and Patrick was already at the Troubador when I arrived.

'You're crap without a publicist, aren't you?' he said.

'I'm not *that* late.'

'You can buy me a beer.' He was wearing a paisley shirt that, in daylight, might or might not have been salmon in colour. The Beck's on the coaster in front of him was almost empty. 'Another one of these,' he said, holding it up, 'to thank me for fighting off the hordes who wanted this discreet dimly lit corner table.'

It was early for the Troubador. There were not yet hordes present, not that it took much of a horde to fill the place. The entire venue was as wide as a lounge-room and about three times as long, and decorated in the mustards, chocolates and burnt oranges of the seventies, with sagging vintage furniture and a large print of junks in Hong Kong harbour at sunset. It was all history, as Annaliese had said, and all history sat in op shops across the city ready to be plundered with whatever sense of irony could be mustered. Patrick had moved into a house that had looked just like this when I was still at school, but there had been nothing chic about it then. I was sixteen, he was twenty. That was where I came temporarily into possession of quite a volume of rum and Coke, before I lost it over the verandah railing and was sent to bed. He told me the next day it wouldn't have counted as a house-warming party if no one had done that.

It was my first and last experience with rum. I couldn't really remember if there had been girls there that night or not.

I waited my turn at the bar and shouted out my order for two Beck's as soon as I got the look from the guy serving.

'Hey. Curtis Holland.' Next to me stood a teen-ager in a pork-pie hat and his first straggly attempt at a goatee. He was the height of my shoulder and gripping his beer as if it was a handweight. He was the kind of person who, I was sure, blogged regularly about what a talentless arsehole I was. Or maybe I had disappeared sufficiently from view that there wasn't as much of that now. Surely those people are always cruising for new targets. Surely the target isn't really what it's about. He reached across and clinked his beer against both of mine. 'Man. Curtis Holland.'

I nodded, and reached over and clinked both my beers against his.

'So, what have you been doing?' he said. 'Could I get you to sign something? Anything?' He was patting down his pockets for pens. He saw one behind the bar, next to some spiked receipts, and he leaned over and picked it up. 'A coaster? How about a coaster?'

'Are you bullshitting me, or . . .?'

No, he was playing it straight. 'What?' He was too drunk to carry it off if it was an act, too drunk to whip the coaster scornfully out from under the pen or to walk away shaking his head and saying 'As if . . .' and leaving me signing for no one. Curtis Holland thought I actually wanted his autograph. Hilarious. 'No, seriously. It's for Josh. That's me.' He slid the coaster along the bar, with the pen on top. 'J O S H.'

I wrote: 'Josh, If you drink too many of these, they'll come out your nose.' And I signed it, though the pen hit a soft damp spot near the edge of the coaster so the D in Holland was nowhere to be seen.

'Wow, excellent,' he said, as he struggled to read what I'd written in the dim bar light. He put the coaster in his shirt pocket and clinked his beer against both of mine again. It seemed as good a sign as any that the interaction was done.

When I turned around, I could see that Patrick had watched the whole thing. He looked away, towards the empty stage at the far end of the room, and drank the last mouthful of his first beer. I moved away from the bar, head down and with a beer in each hand. Two people slid by me to claim my spot and order drinks.

In my second week back, I had been buying groceries and had slowed down to test the ripeness of the avocadoes when someone called out my name. 'Hey, Curtis Holland.' Just like the guy at the bar. Her name was Dana and she was a stripper, tattooed and lithe, but with firm biceps from pole dancing. She showed me the biceps, made me feel them. She said she had finished work around three that morning but a friend had dropped over and they had all had a few bourbons, otherwise she wouldn't have come up to me. Once she'd mentioned it, I could smell it on her breath.

She was a fan, she said, but her friend Loretta, another stripper and one of the drinking buddies awaiting her return with food, was an even bigger fan. She asked me to sign something, anything. She had a pen in her bag, but no paper. I offered to sign my shopping list, since I could keep the last few items in my head.

I checked the piece of paper for somewhere to write and noticed the word Cointreau on the list. It was part of a recipe. I circled it and wrote: 'Loretta, Trust me, this is not an everyday purchase.'

'Oh my god,' Dana said, completely sincerely, when I gave it to her. 'This is such a regular shopping list.'

I handed Patrick his beer and sat down. A yowl of feedback came from the speakers as the band started to set up. A girl with a guitar and long blonde hair was leaning over, adjusting her amp.

'You know what I found when I was clearing out Dad's wardrobe?' Patrick said. It was clearly rhetorical. 'I found two pairs of identical shoes. New shoes. Not new, but never worn. Still in their boxes.' He took a mouthful of his beer and leaned closer towards me. 'You know what I think it means? I think it means there was some time, from the look of it in the eighties, when he thought he'd found the perfect shoe, so he took a guess at his life expectancy and bought up big.' There was an intensity to his expression that I hadn't anticipated tonight. He had given the shoes some thought, and now was his time to share it. 'He overestimated it by two pairs. But most of us would, I guess.'

'Maybe the pairs he got to wear just lasted a really long time.' A better brother might have answered differently, might have kept the metaphor of the unworn shoes intact. 'Or maybe they were on sale because they were so out of date.'

He frowned. He looked as if he was going to say something. On stage, the bass drum gave a couple of practice thumps.

'You have the same size feet as him,' he said, 'which I don't, but I don't think you'd wear them.'

'No.' I wouldn't wear them. I knew I wouldn't. They couldn't, for either of us, ever play the simple role of shoes, whatever they looked like. And they wouldn't look right, not my father's shoes. They had been bought to go with high pants and cardigans and a different time.

76

'I also found his Caloundra Powerboat Club membership card.' He watched for a response, as if there was a secret I was holding and that I might spill. There wasn't though. 'Did you know he had that? He never lived in Caloundra. I never saw him on a boat.'

'No. He never even talked about boats.'

The idea was wrong for our father, nothing like him. He had never baited a hook or even tied a complicated knot. He had never dragged us along to the Boat Show the way some other people's fathers did. In fact, the one time I went it was with a friend from school and his father, and they both got worked up over big fat Evinrude outboards and went home to make a case for buying a half-cabin cruiser. My own father didn't ask a question about the evening, other than to check that I'd had fun. I hadn't, but said I had.

'I wonder if he had a lady friend who he'd take there for the Sunday roast.' Patrick's imagination had gone to work on this artifact as well. 'I bet they do a good Sunday roast.'

'Don't even get me started on the lady friends.'

He laughed. 'We should go sometime.'

I laughed then, but my timing was out.

'No, really,' he said. 'We should go. I meant that.'

'Sure.'

'No, don't bullshit me like that. Don't say "sure" and not mean it.' He was irritated with me now, and it seemed to have come out of nowhere. I didn't think I'd disagreed. 'I'm trying to work Dad out.' He said this more slowly, weightily. 'It matters to me to work Dad out.'

I nodded, first to pay his measured tone its due, and then because I understood what he meant. There were gaps, things neither of us knew. I had looked away from them – maybe even run away from them, however inadvertently – and relied on sideways glances at the bits of our father that I did know. It was hard to bear not knowing him completely, hard to bear that along with everything else.

There was another yowl of feedback. A girl's voice, close to the microphone, said, 'Ah, shit.' I didn't look up.

'You just assume things,' Patrick said. 'You think things stayed the way they were when you were twelve or something. I can't believe you don't want to know more. You weren't here for years. You weren't here for the crazy bits.'

'One two three four . . .' With a four-count, the band went into action, in an instant blowing us all back in our seats with noise. They were an all-girl thrashy punk outfit, punk in a genuine way and not the new punk that was more about eyeliner. Everything was turned up to ten, if not eleven.

Patrick leaned back from the table. He shrugged. We couldn't talk now. He drank his beer.

What crazy bits? What had I missed? More than shoes. I could picture the shoes – tan, conservative, Cary Grant-style shoes, or at least the type of shoes I imagined Cary Grant wearing in all those movies from the middle of the century when he had played different kinds of solid citizens. It didn't matter so much that there were two more pairs, unworn. I didn't assume and I didn't think anything had stayed the way it was since I was twelve.

I thought of my mother then, and the next to nothing I knew about her and the memories I had faked from

78

what I'd been given. They weren't assumptions either. They were the best I could do.

Patrick watched the band, or in fact gazed through the band to nowhere in particular, and took another mouthful of beer in an absent-minded way. He had gold cufflinks on, and his salmon paisley shirt had its top few buttons undone, exposing a triangle of his tanned, muscular, hairless chest. Meanwhile I pudged along next to him, showing as little as possible, missing the crazy bits, other bits, a lot. More than I could define.

We were a family of two, Patrick and me, trying to work out if we were a family at all. This was a series of summit meetings, conducted undercover and un-declared, as we looked for a way forward. Conversations that dwelt on memories only the two of us now shared, and in which the meanest shots needed to and would be taken. I couldn't be certain where we would be at the end of it, where in the world I would be.

In the seconds between the third and fourth songs, he leaned over towards me and said, 'I don't know what you assume. I'm sorry about that.' That's what I thought I heard under the two-sentence intro before the new song came crashing down.

Did he like this music? I thought he was more a 180-beats per minute kind of guy now. Maybe we were here for me. I realised that we hadn't talked about music for years, not properly. We had talked around things, not about them, with the occasional sniping assault when the pressure built up. 'What are you listening to?' It had tended to be the first question he would ask me when he visited, back when I was sixteen or seventeen and he was dropping in to eat a real meal or use the tumble dryer.

The band finished their set. I wondered if I was supposed to buy another round of beers. Patrick straightened in his seat and moved his near-empty Beck's stubbie around in the ring of condensation on the table.

'Did you know he was signed up to internet dating sites?' he said, watching his hands peel the corner of the label away from the bottle. 'We might have been just a few emails away from a Russian step-mother, Chubs.' He laughed, and the label started to tear.

I laughed too, at the implausibility of it, and with relief that it hadn't happened. 'I don't think internet dating necessarily means a Russian bride. I think people do end up with people in their own town as well. I was under the impression the Russian bride thing worked a bit differently.'

'Just imagine it. There'd be three of us here now. You, me . . .' He pointed to the space beside me where a third chair might go. 'Svetlana. Younger than both of us, big hair like a blonde helmet, buxom as buggery, a stash of cheap cigarettes in her bag, full of complaints. And people say I'm high-maintenance.'

'Is that last bit rhetorical or . . .'

'Rhetorical. Not even a question. It was Svetlana I was talking about.'

I wondered if there had been a Svetlana – clichéd or otherwise – or if this was merely the name Patrick had given her during months of contemplation about his discovery, about the strange shape our family might have taken, but didn't. No, there may have been Catherines and Elizabeths and Yvonnes – there might well have been emails that could make us both blush as my father fumbled his cack-handed version of romance over the internet – but I couldn't see a Svetlana at the end of it. I wouldn't let myself, couldn't see the two of us sitting here adding a baffled young Russian to the mix.

'I think he may have been working on an opera,' Patrick said. 'I've found some notes.'

'Notes for an opera. I'd like to see them.'

'Sure. They're just notes though.' Someone had turned up the recorded music and it was harder to hear him. 'But sure.'

He pointed to my beer, and his, indicating their near-emptiness, and he pointed to the bar. This was his signal that he was buying. I nodded.

Notes for an opera. Was this the same extrapolation as a Russian bride from a few emails, or were there really notes for an opera? Patrick stood at the bar, and quickly got attention from a bartender who had lightning bolts shaved into the close-cropped hair over his temples. The guy with the pork-pie hat and my autograph in his shirt pocket was at the bar again too, but with his back to Patrick and a twenty-dollar note in his hand. He didn't seem to be a high priority for the staff. I tried to remember his name, but couldn't.

Patrick steered his way back through the crowd with two beers and took his seat before sliding my stubbie to me across the table. The music volume dropped by half, then came up a little. We might get to talk more after all.

'Do you know how many times people ask me why your band broke up?' he said. 'How many times clients, when they work out or find out who my brother is, say "Why don't we get Still Water?" or some other Butterfish song to sell their fucking car parts? Or kit homes, or cheese?'

'Let's go for the cheese,' I told him. 'As long as they pay us in cheese.'

BY THE END OF my second beer, and Patrick's third, another band was setting up. I knew I didn't have the staying power. I offered him a lift home, and he accepted.

The crowds in the mall spilled over onto Ann Street and cabs tried to nudge their way through without much luck. There were long lines outside the Press Club and the Sun Bar, shaven-headed bouncers in black making skinny girls wait and turning away men with the wrong look. They had once, famously, rejected Powderfinger when the band was well on its way to being the biggest in the country. Or maybe that was apocryphal. Those stories often were.

On the other side of the street, I pushed through the crowd, head down, past a busy kebab shop and pizzas being sold by the slice, past Ultrasuite and Mayocchi, with their window mannequins lean and wan and lightless, catching the style of the time but by-passed at this late hour. The traffic was snarled and people were crossing the road wherever they wanted, stopping to talk through open windows. Someone from a dark Monaro shouted an order for four slices of supreme.

Within two blocks, the crowds were gone. We turned down a side street.

'I'm now officially halfway home,' Patrick said. 'Thanks for the lift.'

'It'll do you good,' I told him. 'It can't be all about the abs, you know.' The abs that didn't rate in my part of town, but Kate's remark would stay my secret for now. There were cars parked in every available spot, warehouse apartments on both sides of the road. I could see a lit cigarette on a balcony three floors up and make out the sounds of conversation against the receding Valley hum. 'I'm going to have to come round to your flat some time. I've been back for weeks and I've never been there. And I haven't seen Blaine for ages. I guess I assumed he'd be coming along tonight. Maybe the Troubador's not his kind of venue?' Blaine's nights out definitely operated at 180 beats per minute.

'Yes, well,' Patrick said. 'Where *did* you park?' He stuck his hands in his pockets and looked at the ground. 'You probably won't be seeing Blaine.'

'So . . .'

'So, it's no more. His choice, not mine. A couple of months ago. Actually three months ago. I've stopped counting. Good sign.' It wasn't coming out sounding good. 'He said he wasn't ready for two dogs and a white picket fence.'

'When did you ever . . .'

'Exactly.' He waved a hand around for emphasis. 'Exactly. I said to him at the time, "Do I look like someone who copes well with dog hair?"' Even now, recounted three months later in a Valley side street, it came out sounding histrionic, like something that should come with a sitcom laugh track. It was a good line though. I was glad he hadn't let Blaine dictate the terms. 'And I told him I was perfectly happy anyway with a New Farm apartment with practically nothing in the fridge

83

but vodka and strawberries. He said it was just a meta-phor and he couldn't imagine either of us with dogs, but that wasn't really the point. So I told him to stop being such a coward, hiding behind metaphors . . . and I don't have to tell you where it headed from there.'

'Is this where I tell you I never really liked him, and that I always thought he was a slimy narcissist and you deserved better, and then you get back together, etcetera etcetera?'

'Oh god,' he said, and laughed. 'He had so little to be narcissistic about. And yet he managed, against such odds. He won't be back. I'm free. Sad, but free.'

'And you have much more to be narcissistic about than he does.'

'I've always thought that,' he said, conspiratorially, as though it couldn't be owned up to until now.

I unlocked the car and its lights flashed at us. Did he have friends around to see him through the break-up? I wasn't sure. They had been together three years, or four, which meant I didn't know Blaine well. Before our father's funeral, I might have met him only half-a-dozen times.

'I'm about to leave town on another shoot,' Patrick said as he got into the car. 'But you should come over when I get back. I can cook some things now. The fridge is still *mainly* vodka and strawberries, but not entirely.'

He was an expert buyer of food, but I hadn't known him to cook much. He would know not just where to get haloumi and quince paste, but where to get the best haloumi and the best quince paste. He once told me that, when it came to making food rather than merely acquiring it, he maxed out at canapés, and meals would have to wait until later in life. That time had come while I had been on the road. And he might have lost Blaine along the way, but I realised that, over the years, he had been finding himself bit by bit. He was not the wayward student in the house with milk-crate furniture and too much rum. He was a long way from that. Vodka and strawberries, and beyond. And I'd racked up an awful lot of frequent-flyer points, but wasn't sure I'd come as far.

'I cooked a hell of a curry tonight,' I told him. 'I should make it for you some time. It's from scratch, leaves and seeds and a lot of simmering, no jars.'

'Ah, those boys in that band. How do they eat now that it's all over?' He fiddled with the radio, clicked between stations. 'I can show you the opera notes,' he said. 'When you come round. I think they're opera notes. You can take them away if you want. Have a proper look at them.'

I turned right onto James Street, heading for the river.

Patrick organised our father's funeral. He kept calling to run details by me while I waited for my flight back to Australia, but I couldn't cope with the speed of it. I couldn't talk to him about flowers and hymns and who should say what. I told him he was always better with those things, and he should choose whatever he wanted and I'd be happy to pay. We had a fight at O'Hare about that. I was at O'Hare, in the American Airlines Admirals Club next to a huge bowl of pretzels, Patrick was at a funeral home somewhere in the suburbs of Brisbane.

I didn't stay long, so the funeral is stuck in my memory now like some strange thing, not like a funeral. Three days of warm steamy autumn before flying back to the US, to a spring that had yet to arrive. The service was in a brick building I'd never seen before. It was hexagonal or octagonal, and I noticed its roof line sweeping up to a white cross as we drove up. There wasn't a cloud in the sky. It sat in a garden of well-mown grass and rose beds and poincianas, like a reception venue or a corner of New Farm Park.

I came back from an absent moment during the service to find Jess holding my hand. We got married shortly after. We broke up not that long after that.

♁

'OUR PLACE IS SO hot it's totally disgusting,' Annaliese said when I opened the studio door. 'Can I please pleeeze sit in your airconditioning for a while?' She groaned, and hung out her tongue like an overheated dog.

It was Monday afternoon and she was in her school uniform. Her tie was half undone. She was already inside before I could say anything.

'Ah, much better, much better.' She threw her hat like a frisbee onto the Space Invaders console and stood with her face in front of the airconditioning unit.

I'd had the headphones on when she tapped on the glass, and at first I thought it was an artifact on the recording. I was working, but that seemed inconsequential.

Annaliese groaned again. 'Why can't we have airconditioning at home? Why can't we kill the planet just a little bit, the way you do?' She turned to let the air blow on her back. Her cheeks were radiating heat. 'My mother likes trees. That's why we live out here.'

'And you don't like trees?'

'I have no position on trees. I'm fine with trees, but they could share the planet with some airconditioning.' I offered her a drink, water or tea, and she said, 'Water or tea? You rock, man. I thought you were supposed to be doing lines of coke off the top of your dinosaur Play Station by now.'

'Rude, even when overheating and begging for the mercy of my airconditioning . . .'

'Water. Please.' She rolled her eyes, as if I'd just told a five-year-old to show some manners.

I went over to the kitchenette, which was almost as empty as it had been when I moved in. When the granny flat properly morphed into a studio there might one day be a lot more to it – to the kitchenette and the rest – though maybe not coke on the Space Invaders machine, the playstationosaurus. The bar fridge held only two carafes of cold water and a carton of milk which, I noticed, was two days past its best. I poured her a glass of water, and brought the carafe over as well.

I noticed that it said 'A WINTER' in black marker pen along the band inside her upturned hat.

'So you're Winter and your mother's Winter as well? She kept your father's name after their marriage broke up?'

Annaliese held the glass but didn't drink. 'No, actually. I decided to be Winter.'

'Decided? You can just do that?'

She shrugged. 'I did. They had to sign off on it to make it official. I got this talk about being eighteen, waiting till then. But that sucked, obviously.' Another shrug. 'Marky's still a Fletcher for now. But don't think he's totally on Dad's side or anything. Dad bought this car . . .' Her tone swung up on 'car'. There was a story to be told. 'It's a yellow sports car, canary yellow. He drives it to work some mornings, even though he could walk. It's about ten minutes away. Admiralty Towers to Waterfront Place, lawyer central. How lazy is that? Anyway, he drove it to work when he bought it, and he took all his staff down to the car park and made them stare at it. Most of them had never even seen the car park before. These people catch the train in twenty stops from Thornlands or wherever, and bring their own lunch in a box, and here he is making them ogle his new toy.'

Twenty stops from Thornlands, or wherever – where had it come from, this fierce and detailed deconstruction of the callous lord among his serfs?

'I'm so glad you don't have a dick-swinging car.' She stopped to drink some of the water, finally. 'So Mark had to write this story for school. The topic was "revenge", or something, and in it this guy is so angry with his dickhead boss for dragging them down to the basement and making them walk laps of his new car that, when the boss tells him to go off and get it detailed, he pays four guys to smoke in it and then gives one of them twenty bucks extra to shit on the passenger seat.' She laughed. 'The boss had always been an arsehole and the car thing was just the last straw. They called Mum in to school to talk about that one, since they knew Dad had the same car. The teacher said it was good writing, actually, but that the guy wouldn't have done it since the boss would have got him back.'

'So that's the only reason no one's dumped in your dad's car? Consequences?'

'Probably.' She sat on the edge of the one desk that wasn't cluttered with equipment. Her cheeks were less red now. She pulled her tie off and dropped it into her hat. 'If you were up for it, I'd get you the keys.'

She told me more about her father, whose name was Campbell Fletcher. It almost went without saying that he was a partner in a big law firm. When friends came over – which didn't happen often – they were always people he wanted something from and his best conversation topic was how to minimise tax. He could only cook bachelor food – I assumed the expression had come from Kate – and called in caterers for his rare dinner parties, even when there were only six people. He and Mark butted heads regularly. He had a vein that popped out on his scalp at times like that. He had had a series of relationships with younger women, a number of whom may have been junior solicitors. Kate, Annaliese and Mark had taken to referring to them as his PTGs, or pony-tailed girlfriends.

'Mum started that,' she said. 'That was years ago, with her friends. I probably wasn't supposed to hear. I used to think it was because he played squash with them a lot. That's why they had the ponytails. Not that they all do, of course. It's how he'd introduce them to us, the squash. "This is Caitlin. We play squash together sometimes." Which of course ended up with Mark using it as a verb and not a noun. "Dad, are you squashing Caitlin?" He couldn't even fit us in his yellow car. It's a fucking sports car. It really only has two seats.'

89

Enough room in the back for two racquets and a small black ball, but not for your adolescent offspring who would not forgive you for much, and who would dog your every move with their harsh reading of your motives. I couldn't guess what Campbell Fletcher was really like, or entirely like, but he wasn't shaping up well in Annaliese's portrait.

'We're at his place tomorrow night,' she said. 'That's a regular thing, Tuesdays and every second weekend. Hannah's usually there, but she doesn't live there. She's the current PTG. She's nice. She cooks. That's good.' She sighed, and looked out the window. The airconditioning blew through her hair and its school-coloured ribbons, maroon and white. 'Sorry,' she said, turning back my way. 'You're working, aren't you? I didn't mean to distract you.'

I could see the green and orange sonic hills and valleys on the screen to her left, twenty seconds of sound drawn out for editing and realigning. I had been going well, but I needed a break. I needed to clear my head and come back later with fresh ears and a few new ideas.

'I can remember my father and his attempts with women.' It was the start of an answer, or at least a thought put in my head by the mention of Hannah and her status as the current PTG. 'My mother died when I was young. There's nothing worse than listening to your father work his cheesy lines.'

'Oh god,' Annaliese said. 'Nothing worse.'

My father's lines were straight out of history, lines that fitted with his Cary Grant shoes and old black-and-white movies. He had the moves to go with them too, but he never quite delivered them. He would circle halfway around the table to pull out a chair for them, and then slink back as if he'd done the wrong thing. He worked through gestures like that that we never saw at other times, and each one looked like a rehearsal the director had called a halt to halfway through. They weren't natural, they weren't ever quite right. And the women were rarely at ease, facing us, the two boys who, if the cards fell a certain way, would be sons of a kind to them. More than that, though, on their first visit to our house they had to face down the ghost of our long-gone mother in the faded photos that stayed forever all over the loungeroom.

'Do you want to hear what I've been working on?'

'Yeah. Sure.' She slid off the desk and turned to face the screen. 'This is those Norwegian guys, right?'

I unplugged the headphones and sent the song through the big speakers. It sounded better now, after a gap and with my head in a less critical place.

'Wow,' she said when we were through the chorus for the first time. 'This is good.'

I had a new idea for the piano part, and I stopped the song and played it before it slipped my mind. I opened a new track and recorded a few bars, which was all I had. I could do more with it later. I played it back. There was something there. Annaliese said 'Wow' again. I hoped it didn't look like some kind of showy trick.

I told her the piano parts were sometimes the easiest bits for me, since I knew piano better than anything. That was partly true, but it often wasn't easy to find some new melody that worked, that took a song forward and helped it find its place. I told her I'd grown up wanting to be Billy Joel but, importantly, the Billy

Joel of the seventies. Specifically the early seventies. He had become a big star towards the end of the decade with The Stranger and The Piano Man, but I had really wanted to be the Billy Joel of Cold Spring Harbour.

'I've had fights before about that album,' I told her. 'So don't pick one now based on your smug post-millenium perspective of Billy Joel.'

She laughed, and I played her She's Got a Way. Cold Spring Harbour was an album less played and less remembered than it should have been. It was a cluster of small songs, melancholy and warm and often optimistic, and most able to be perfectly rendered with just piano, vocals and, importantly, no fuss at all. I played and sang, and the song was as true as ever, and still a map that showed where melody came from, and no less a song to aspire to than it had been when I was ten or twelve, in the early eighties. I was hopelessly nostalgic about it, and had no inclination to be otherwise. It had been *my* map. It had been part of turning me to music.

By the third time through the chorus, I caught her humming a harmony – not the melody, but a harmony that had just cropped up in her head – and I made her sing it. Then I made her sing the song while I played, feeding her the words line by line and playing through.

'Yeah, you've got it, easily.' It was in my mind, but I found myself saying it. 'You've really got a voice there.'

She half-shrugged, and looked awkward. 'It's just singing. Everyone can sing, can't they?' She knew I was right though. 'My father wants me to do law. Business or law. But he would, wouldn't he?'

'And what do you want to do?'

'I don't know.'

'I think I still want to be the Billy Joel of the early seventies, but you can't tell anyone that. The dagginess coefficient is just too high for anyone who doesn't know specifically what I'm talking about. I want to get a grand piano in here. I think there's room.' I knew where it would go. There was a corner in which unsorted junk sat on an area of two-tone brown carpet where the previous resident's lounge suite had spared patches of it from the light. 'My father was a piano teacher, so there were always people coming round to our house taking lessons. The piano was our only expensive piece of furniture.' Another memory had surfaced. I didn't know why. He had once thought of selling the piano to pay school fees. 'Sorry, that sounded like one of those fake-humble statements rich people make, or politicians.'

'Ah, yes,' she said. 'Back in the days when life was simple and before fame came along and complicated everything. Would you do it any differently, if you had the chance?'

Definitely yes, definitely no. 'That's the kind of chance no one ever gets. I don't have any regrets about doing it though.'

'You have plenty of regrets.' She was sure of it. She poured water from the carafe into her glass. 'I've read that article – it was in some magazine in America, and the title of the article was Curtis Holland Regrets. I saw it online.'

'Will you please stop googling me? It puts me at a distinct disadvantage. I wasn't always myself in those interviews.'

'I think you were completely yourself. Maybe not everyone else was.' She was back sitting on the edge of the desk again, one leg crossed over the other at the ankles, short white socks showing just above the tops of her black school shoes.

'Okay, but the main thing is that you stop googling me. I don't want to shock you, but it's not entirely reliable. I'm the definitive source. Come to me. And, anyway, who's lived and regrets nothing? What kind of psychopath, really? I'm sick of this "I've got no regrets" thing that people keep coming out with.' I was sure it only *sounded* as though I'd just contradicted myself. I knew what I meant. 'Why do we have the word regret if we all decide not to have any? There are things I regret. I could write you a list. I was on tour when my father died. I regret that. I can't change it and I couldn't change it at the time, but I can still regret it.'

I was on tour when it ended with Jess. I was on tour looking out through the tinted windows as my life passed in a whir, in a blur. The US Midwest, pale flat roads six or eight lanes wide sliding through cornfields and forests and over rivers with names I would never know, white barns and siloes, endless lines of Buicks and Plymouths and Dodges humming along at the speed limit. Down in those cars, the lives looked more real. I felt minuscule there, in the face of all that traffic. And lost, in a way.

'So, what about the band?' Annaliese said. 'What about Butterfish?' She was on her way out the door by then, hydrated and cooled down. I had my one new idea to get back to, though I had lost the spirit for it temporarily.

I walked with her around the side of the house. The afternoon was still hot, and the heat felt like it was there to stay. The air was thick and static, but the sky was cloudless and again there would be no storm coming through.

'It's really Derek you're asking about, I guess. Derek and the end of the band. And that's the question I've been pretty good at not answering.' It was always Derek who people asked about, and there was always more that I could have said about him than the others. I regretted yanking Ben away from a relatively normal life and dumping him into the band's mad final year, but that regret was a simple matter, and he had survived it and made some money. I had said almost nothing about Derek after the band had broken up, since it was hard to talk about him without shitting on him, wilfully and at length. 'Derek needed a break from it as much as me, I think, really. There was a certain amount of unravelling on that last tour. Derek was James Dean and John Belushi, but still alive. And if you don't know who those people are, you should google them. But continue to be sceptical about what it gives you. There are lots of innocent non-facts out there, not to mention stories made up to sell magazines.'

So, even then I was guarded, cagey in the way I put it. However much I told myself this was a straight honest conversation with a person who was literally the girl next door, I could also see the words travelling home in Annaliese's head and scrolling out across the internet, on a blog first and then worse. If I maligned Derek, it would be no secret and it would come back my way. It would hunt me down, all the way west out of town, along Gap Creek Road to my hidden dry block of land, and I would have to answer for it.

'Maybe I meant the whole thing,' she said. She half turned towards me, and the sun caught the side of her face. 'The whole Butterfish thing.'

'That's a more interesting question.' A better question, a smarter question. 'People don't ask that one. And I don't think I regret the whole thing. No. It's too much of my life.' I couldn't separate myself from it. I couldn't picture my life without those years. 'There was a reason for doing it, for trying it in the first place. And when it was good it could be great.'

As I watched her walk along the road towards her house, sticking to the shade wherever there was any, I knew she wouldn't be blogging about me, or the band. She wouldn't even tell her friends, and I had a new regret about my instincts and the way they had leapt up to protect me when, surely, I hadn't needed protecting at all.

♀

JESS SENT ME AN email from a Louisville internet café after a fight that I couldn't distinguish from any other, and then she went to the airport and flew out. By the time I picked it up, her phone was switched to voice mail and she was boarding, or perhaps even in the air. We had been together on and off since I was twenty or so, and been married less than a year.

I saw the email backstage after a soundcheck. I printed it and put it in my pocket and walked outside with it. I sat under a tree at the edge of the car park, reading it, not reading it. She had left me. She kept it brief and clear, and said we had grown apart and knew each other less now than we had years ago. 'I know this is the right thing FOR BOTH OF US,' she said. Actually, she said it was the '5ight thing', with the keying error going uncorrected. I had left her with a migraine in our hotel room, and now she was gone, with this email equivalent of a scrawled note the last piece I had of her as she left town.

I saw the others coming out of the venue, their hands in their jacket pockets as the wind blustered around them and rain started to spit from the cold steely sky. They were heading for the bus and assuming I was on it already. I folded the email and put it back in my pocket, and I told them later that Jess's migraine wasn't letting up so she would be staying in the room that night. Halfway through our set, I realised in one ugly moment that that wasn't right, that she was in fact gone, that I had lulled myself into keeping the migraine story at the front of my mind, and that the truth was a sad, demoralising secret that I would have to own up to the following morning as we got ready to drive on to the next city.

I told them over breakfast, and they said almost nothing. 'She's gone home,' is how I put it. 'This really wasn't working out for her, all the travelling.' I was telling a stupid story, and we all knew it. 'It's probably for the best. We can take a look at it all after the tour.' And there the fiction tailed off into nothing, and the others let it sit that way.

'Fresh flapjacks,' Derek said. 'They're just coming out from the kitchen. Let me go get you some.' They were, he knew, my favourite part of the American hotel breakfast. Comfort food.

When I last spoke to Jess, months after that, it was amicable enough but she came across like a stranger with whom I shared a history by chance – someone who had, freakishly, been in the same places and at the same times, but lived a rather different life there to the one I thought we had both been living. She was in Sydney working as a physio, living in a mortgage-free house paid for by songwriting royalties. And fair enough, since she was tossed around on that ride as much as the rest of us.

Derek knew best that it was over. I was in the habit of under-rating his instincts with people, but he knew me and he knew Jess. For several days he set aside any differences we had, and replaced them with stilted conversations on the bus about how I was going. I could be staring at a novel and all of a sudden he would slip into the opposite side of the caravan seat with a new cup of coffee for me. He would have made us both cappuccinos – forgetting that I'd never drunk cappuccinos – and dusted the foam with chocolate.

He wasn't James Dean, or John Belushi. He was riven by self-doubt and the fear that he might be only a try-hard, promoted to fame by a world that no longer had the attention span to judge a person properly.

Some of the very worst contestants on American Idol had become *famously* bad and worked the same talk show circuit we did, singing flat and proud and backing it up with the dance moves of a Ken doll. At a chance green-room meeting at a TV studio, one of them said he was practically our biggest fan anywhere and pressed a copy of his CD into Derek's hands. Derek stared at it as if the badness might seep through his skin and do him harm.

'Get that kryptonite off this bus,' he shouted from his bunk the next day when the rest of us decided to give it a play. He made the driver stop and he flung the CD like a frisbee into a Pennsylvania field, and threw the case after it. 'Jesus Christ,' he said. 'It's fucking karaoke. People can get famous with karaoke now.'

Derek had launched himself at fame looking for vindication. Twenty million album sales were supposed to tell him he had some kind of talent, but people bought indiscriminately, impulsively, and sometimes they bought karaoke. There was a real risk that, if he questioned it too closely, fame might not be able to tell him he was okay.

With the third album now behind us and the band wound up, Derek seemed to need to put his fame to the test just about every day. He was living the life, the 'live fast, die young' version of life that keeps magazines hovering, waiting for the best fresh pictures of the wreckage. But most people like that survive, I suppose. They give their organs a pounding, but they end up growing old despite themselves. They end up white-haired and living in a big house at the edge of things with a movie not-quite-starlet who is on the brink of middle age and trying to hold it at bay with some breast work, and who might have been killed in the opening sequences of a few schlocky horror films and who spends her days trying out unsuccessfully for infomercials and her evenings mixing his scotch and whatever, and listening to his grand embellished stories of an erstwhile better life.

Derek at sixty, high in the Hollywood Hills, might then be well placed to offer something on regret. At thirty-five, close to thirty-six, he was definitely one of the 'no regrets' crowd and, of them all, he was of course the one who shat me most. I didn't know if every famous 'bad boy' was just selfish at heart, but it's where I put Derek. He would try anything, trample anyone, in the hope that not one possible life experience would pass him by. He never looked sideways, never saw collateral damage. If I delivered some diatribe on regret to a poor unsuspecting American journalist, it was no doubt because Derek had done something that day to rile me more than usual. It was a coded message to him as he scrutinised the press coverage, and one that he would never heed.

Together, we had moved to bump Patrick from the band and, whatever he said at the time about his ad agency job offer, it had ended up looking as if it was all my work. Another regret of mine.

It was our father who had thought, perhaps even decided, that we should each learn an instrument. My first choice was guitar, but I was happy to settle for piano instead. Patrick picked saxophone, but ended up with a second-hand clarinet because saxophones cost a lot more. He had a fight with our father in which our father said he doubted that he had the application to justify the investment.

Patrick stuck with the clarinet, and became good enough that he could play a version of the sax solo from Gerry Rafferty's Baker Street on it, and resent every woody, reedy note. Around then I heard Cold Spring Harbour for the first time, and I saw how a person might write a song. I saw the music and the words and how you could make something of them, just you and a span of black and white keys. And I worked at a melody in my head until I had to make written notes, and then had to sneak in some time at the piano in the loungeroom when Patrick and my father were out of the house, and I wrote my first song. I was twelve.

Back in the studio, I played my few new bars of piano again and fleshed it out a little. How far could I take it down this track? What else did it need? I knew it might be the worst idea I could have, but I called next door. Annaliese answered the phone.

'There's an experiment I'd like to try,' I told her. 'Just an experiment.'

'Yes . . .' Her voice was all mock wariness, like the voice the sensible person uses in a sitcom when the hapless fool is about to pitch a hare-brained scheme.

'I'd like to try some backing vocals with the track I played you earlier, the track from the Norwegian guys. But I think it needs a female voice. I want to give it a go, but there's no guarantee it'll work. So I can either junk the idea, or face the logistical nightmare of getting someone in somewhere to do it, or you could drop over sometime and in about five minutes we could work out whether or not the idea has any prospects.' There was silence. I heard Kate's voice shout something out in the background. 'We could maybe record it and see how it sounds.'

'So,' Annaliese said, sounding disappointed, if anything. 'Are you bullshitting me and, if so, why?'

'No. No, not at all. I'd really like to try it. If you're fine with it, and your mother's fine with it, and . . .'

'My mother? Jesus. She's fine with it. As fine as she needs to be. I'll tell her.'

'It's just an experiment.'

'Sure. I thought it might have been some joke of Mark's. But if you really think I can do it.'

'Yeah, I do. Your voice'll be right, I think.'

'Wow.' She put her hand over the mouthpiece for a few seconds and then came back. 'All right then. I'll get my people to talk to your people. But, yeah, for sure. I'm in. Thanks. And I think Mum wants to talk to you about something now anyway.'

There were some more muffled noises as the phone was handed over.

'Annaliese's people here,' Kate's voice said. 'I've actually got a food question, but first . . .'

In the distance, Annaliese's voice shouted, 'Oh my god,' very theatrically, and she let out a big squeal. Mark bellowed, 'Shut the door,' as though for the thousandth time.

'First, you're recording something with Annaliese?'

'Yeah, I'd like to. If that's okay with you. I want to try adding female backing vocals to one of the tracks I'm working on.'

'Okay,' she said slowly, processing the truth of it. 'Okay, that's what she told me. Well, I can't see why not. Just, if it doesn't work . . .' Her voice was quieter now, her hand perhaps cupped around the phone.

'If it doesn't work, it won't be about her, and I'll make sure she knows it.'

'All right. All right then. Well, the two of you have fun.' She laughed. 'I'm glad I played that DVD. It was worth the lecture I got in the end. Now, something much more mundane. Salmon. What can you do with fresh salmon? Something simple. Make that foolproof. I've got a friend who bought some in bulk and she's given me some of it. I'll need to go back to her with a story of the great, or at least passable, meal that I made from it.'

'Is it steaks or cutlets?'

'It's salmon. That's all I can tell you. Pieces of salmon. Kind of rectangular.'

♁

SO, THE NEXT DAY at lunchtime, I cooked salmon with Kate Winter. It was her day off, a mid-week reward for rostering herself on with the casuals on the preceding Saturday. The store was part of a chain and that was policy for managers, but she said it gave her 'me time' during the week, and this Wednesday's me time was to be her learn-to-cook-salmon lesson.

I showed her how to crush garlic the way I had seen Nigella Lawson do it on TV, and we tossed it into the plastic bag with the salmon, along with some mirin and soy sauce.

'And that's pretty much it,' I told her. 'You let it marinate for a while, maybe an hour, and the only other things you have to do before frying it are chop the oyster mushrooms and put the rice on.'

'It can't be that easy,' she said. 'Anyway, there was all that chopping of the garlic. I never seem to get that right, and it takes ages.' She looked down at the chopping board and the knife. It still had flecks of garlic on it. 'Chefs on TV chop like machines.'

'That's because they have sharp knives and they chop a lot. They also have arthritis in their hands by the time they're twenty-five. You need a real knife. I think this one's just bending the garlic.' I picked it up and tapped its edge against the palm of my hand. It didn't come close to breaking the skin. 'The reason you have issues with chopping is that, in some circus somewhere, there's a sad clown with a tear painted on his cheek because you stole his comedy knife.'

'Well, that's a relief. I thought I was just a crap cook. I think I'm the bad carpenter who, by coincidence, also has bad tools.' She was leaning against the bench with her arms folded, turning her head to look at me and her enemy the knife through a spray of uncontrolled blonde hair. 'Marinating,' she said. 'That takes time. So I should open some wine. I have some expertise there.' She pushed herself away from the bench and went to the fridge.

'I'm not sure you're really connecting with the cooking task.'

'How would a sauv blanc be? That's what I've got cold.' She lifted the bottle from a shelf in the fridge door and showed it to me.

'There's no way you're getting out of doing the oyster mushrooms.'

She cracked open the bottle cap and went looking for clean glasses. I sliced one mushroom to demonstrate, then handed her the knife. She chased her first mushroom across the board with the knife edge, then trapped it and cut it.

'I know,' she said. 'I know it should be thinner.' Her hands were neat and compact, and made the knife appear large. She had a ring on the fourth finger of her right hand. It looked like it was made of jade.

'It's fine. There's no rule.' I had the hands of a giant, big ungainly hands in comparison.

She sliced another mushroom, still hesitantly, as if

it was working against her and would make her do a bad job.

'Annaliese misses her dog, you know,' she said, without looking up. 'Oscar. You never met Oscar. She went round to your place looking for him. There was a ceremony. We had a wake.' The photo was still on the fridge, Annaliese with a bug-eyed baby Oscar cupped in her hands. It was fixed squarely in the middle of the freezer door, at eye level. 'I think you're some kind of replacement.' She half-smiled and stopped chopping. 'It's really nice of you to get her to record something.'

'I wouldn't do it just to be nice. I mean, I am nice – of course I'm nice, I'm a hell of a guy – but I like her voice. And I need to hear the idea I've had. I don't know if that makes me a great replacement for a dog . . .'

'I was never a big fan of the dog.' It came out sounding more weighty than it was probably supposed to, and her cheeks started to go red. She blew stray hair from her face, put down the knife and picked up her wine. 'How much is Mark charging you for the lawn mowing? I bet he's overcharging you.'

'Am I supposed to tell you how much he's charging me?'

'Now I know he's overcharging you.'

'Well, part of it's to cover the fuel and the equipment.'

'And do you think any of that's coming back to me, the owner of the mower and purchaser of the fuel? Oh, that boy . . .' She shook her head, and laughed. She lifted her wine glass up to drink, but then stopped. The ring she was wearing tapped against it. 'Back at our old place, he used to charge the kids next door to use the trampoline. That's a pretty embarrassing thing to hear about over the fence.' She took a sip of the wine, put the glass down.

'I'm not a big trampoliner myself, so . . .' I had no idea what I should be paying Mark to mow my lawn, no idea of the price of a lot of things. I had never had a lawn before.

'Neither am I. They come with all kinds of safety gear now, and where's the fun in that? What's trampolining without those moments of horror when you're way up in the air looking straight down at the springs?' She sorted through the punnet of mushrooms, separating some that were clumped together. 'You're surprisingly down to earth, you know.'

With that, my job was back in play. I had wanted to be a neighbour with some ideas about salmon. I was okay with being a dog replacement. 'I've never been much for applause,' I told her, and left it at that.

She gave me a look, as if there would be more, must be more. The end of my sentence drifted out like an ellipsis, and the ellipsis would take all but the most casual listener straight to Derek, who was much for applause, for the grand-scale loveless love of a big crowd out in front of him in the dark. He would make them clap overhead, sing choruses. He would shout 'Hello Cleveland' and they would roar. Hello Louisville, goodbye Jess, goodbye.

Kate picked up the knife again and straightened a mushroom out on the board. 'Is it true that you and Derek don't get on?'

'It's not quite that simple. But nothing ever is, really, is it?'

She pressed the knife down on the mushroom, but the dull blade squished rather than cut it. She had another go, and the mushroom skidded away from her.

'Fuck it,' she said. 'No, I guess it's not.'

'The problem's with the knife.'

'The clown knife, yes. So I should cook with a big red nose on, and crazy oversized boots?' She tried again, this time with more of a slicing action, and more success. 'Has the salmon marinated enough yet?'

☊

THE EMAIL FROM DEREK arrived the following morning. It said:

> Fat Boy,
> Do you ever turn your phone on? My father has to go in for a brain op next week, so I'll be home on Tuesday. My mother will drive me insane if I stay with her and the secret'll be out if I book into a hotel, so I was thinking your place – how about it? Room for a guest? It should only be for a few days. I think they only need to make a small hole. I'll be on QF 176, so maybe you could let Andrea at the Chairman's Lounge know I'm coming?
> D

My phone – the mobile for which Derek had the number – was in a drawer. It had been there, turned off, for about two weeks.

So, they were about to put a small hole in Derek's father's head, but a big enough hole that Derek would let the hedonism slip for a few days and fly back here, to a room he assumed I was keeping for guests. It was typical Derek – sketchy details, a favour, a snarky remark in the opening line. Thanks very much. But the code behind it said to me that his father might be quite ill, and we both knew I was his best choice. So I would say yes, I would take him in, and I would ask a decent minimum number of questions about what was going on. That was where our history put us.

I wanted to tell him to stop being a fool, to stay for far more than a few days. I wanted to tell him that you don't get forever with these people. I wanted to poke a small hole in his own skull and shove in a few lessons about the obvious. But we both knew I wouldn't. Not yet, not today, not sober and months after our last proper conversation.

D,

You should get over your big ideas about yourself and celebrity arrivals. I'll pick you up. No Chairman's Lounge to hide you, no orange plastic crash barriers to keep the crowds at bay. Just me and my average car, doing it the way the little people do. You'll be surprised how well it'll work. I'll even turn my phone on so you can let me know when you're on the way through. And, yes, stay at my place. The last thing your dad needs is you being spotted in hotel foyers, and questions being asked about why you're here. Though be aware that my new life doesn't exactly run Derek-style, so if you bring any substances into the country and befriend a sniffer dog in customs,

108

your best call from the watch house would be to a solicitor from the Yellow Pages, since it won't be my problem. Stay clean and mi casa es su casa, for as long as it needs to be. I'm sorry to hear that about your father. I hope all works out okay there.

C

That would do for now. I wasn't at all ready for Derek to come crashing into my new neighbourhood, with the sarcasm and reopened wounds and badly managed anguish that would entail. But at the same time there was a better side to how it all felt. It might even have been nostalgia for the times, years before, when he had ended up on my floor in whatever house I was sharing, back when he seemed to the world like a grandiose pretender, but I knew he had what it took.

☊

ANNALIESE WAS DUE TO come over to record at five that afternoon. I heard nothing from Derek after my reply to his email, though the day had passed into night in California, where I assumed he was, and he was unlikely to be sitting at a keyboard. I wanted to keep him from my neighbours. I wanted to stop him spoiling them.

Once the mushrooms had been dealt with, the salmon with Kate had gone well. She was only a sharp knife away from recreating it with ease. The green zigzag of wasabi sauce on the top at the end was the clincher, the trick that turned it into a dinner party meal. I had left with half a bottle of sauv blanc in me, knowing I'd be next to useless for the afternoon. But I could afford to lose those few hours, and nothing about the day felt wasted. I would buy Kate a knife, I thought. It was an idea half-full of wine, perhaps – the two of us, shopping for a knife – but bits of our lunch-making conversation were still in my mind. She had left me feeling less inclined towards silence, and for years I'd craved it. I walked up my front steps with the idea of calling her, just to keep talking to someone, but she would have been back into her day already and I was supposed to be getting back into mine.

The next afternoon, with a clear head, I was in the studio at four-thirty. I was gazing out the window, across to the trees next door, when Annaliese stepped out again between the bushes at the end of their pool. Again she was topless. She arranged her towel on the banana lounge and I couldn't be sure if, for a moment, she had glanced my way before turning and diving into the water.

At exactly five, she came to the studio door and tapped on the glass.

I let her in and she said, 'Aircon. Beautiful.'

'It's hot out there.' It was redundant, but I said it anyway.

'I've just been for a swim,' she said. 'You could come over and swim any time it's hot. When you're not work-ing.' Her hair was still wet. 'It's very private.'

So, she had seen me. I hadn't stared, but I had looked and she had seen me. That's what she was saying, surely. It was the gap in the hedge – one drought-dead bush –

that stopped it being completely private, and the only view in came from right here. She sat on the edge of the desk under the airconditioning unit, and shivered as the cool air hit her. She ran her fingers through her hair. Her nipples pushed out against her T-shirt. She wasn't wearing a bra.

'So . . .' she said.

'Okay.' I kept my eyes at face level. 'Let me play you a few things. Take a seat.'

I went to the Mac, and she moved to the other chair and rolled over my way, clunking the plastic arm of her chair into mine.

'Sorry.' She turned so that the arms were parallel. 'So, play.' She was wearing a short skirt and she sat back and stretched her long brown legs out under the desk.

'This is Thomas Dybdahl.' I already had the CD in, and I clicked play. 'This guy is big in Norway, and the album's all in English. This is the kind of thing people might be expecting Gunnar and Øivind to do, if they weren't looking at doing something different. Something a bit poppier, but not disposable Europop, if you get what I mean. Thomas Dybdahl is sort of where they are now, or where they would be if they'd been recording in English.'

I played her the first track with Thomas Dybdahl's melancholy reedy voice singing over melodic lap-steel guitar and measured brush work on the drums, his own backing vocals swelling and lifting the sound of some lines in the chorus. It had a rawness, a lack of fussiness, that I liked. It felt like a bunch of people in a room making music.

111

Then we moved on to my iTunes library and tracks that were much more overtly produced, first the Cardigan's Love Fool as an example of what the music company might be expecting, something Nordic and quirky. Even though it held together musically, and stuck in your head because of a real melody, it would be a mistake to try to squeeze something like that out of the Splades.

'Now, for comparison, Alphaville's Forever Young.' I clicked on the track and it started to play. 'This is the trance mix. There's something a little unreal about the vocal sound, a little electronic.' That's what I wanted Annaliese to listen for. 'Whereas with the Cardigans it's straighter, other than the accent. The Alphaville sound is really crafted, but in practice one is probably just a few Pro-Tools tricks away from the other. I want to make the backing vocals sound more like Alphaville, but to get there we'll try it with you delivering it pretty straight and me putting the work in after that.'

'Okay.' She was getting down to business now. She had her arms folded and she was sitting up in the seat. 'Okay, I get that.'

'We'll also double you, maybe even more than double you.' I stopped Alphaville and clicked on 10CC's I'm Not in Love. 'Listen for the aaaahs behind the chorus. I heard once that there were 246 vocal tracks on this song.' It was Countdown, Molly Meldrum, I must have been about eight. And the show might have changed the country's music industry, but it was gone before Annaliese was born. This was dinosaur knowledge, musical palaeontology, however valid the point might be. 'Listen to how it expands the sound.'

'Good,' she said. 'Nice to know I don't have to do all that in one go.'

Finally I played her my best current version of the Splades' It's Not What You Think. I picked out the parts of the chorus where I wanted to try backing vocals, try out her voice, and I played the notes I was looking for on the keyboard.

She nodded, and said, 'Yeah, yeah, I get it,' and she sang along without any apparent effort, trying it out quietly but hitting every note just the way I needed her to.

'Now I'm going to get you to stand, so you can breathe properly, and get you to make it a bit bigger, and we might try recording a few.'

I had my vocal mike already set up, and I gave her the headphones. She walked around to the other side of the desk and put them on. She stood close to the mike, then further away, then she reached out and tapped it with her index finger. The sound popped in her ears.

'About this far away.' I measured the distance with my hand in front of my mouth.

She nodded.

The first time through she came in late, half a beat late. Then she heard her own voice and said 'Yuk,' and took the headphones off.

I told her it was like that for everyone. No one was used to hearing their voice that way. 'Just sing. Pretend no one's listening.'

By the third or fourth attempt, she was giving me something worth keeping. I got her to push it a bit more, hold the last note a bit longer, and with that she showed me the sound that had been in my head, the sound I had been wanting for the song for days. About six times

113

I asked her to give me exactly that again, and she did, exactly. I had what I needed.

'That's it?' she said when I told her her job was done. 'I thought it'd be more . . . I don't know.'

'It's all there. And it is just an experiment but, from my point of view, it's working.'

'Oh.' She looked proud of herself for a moment, as if she had been expecting that it would take some kind of magic that she didn't have.

She took the headphones off and hung them on the mike stand and went to get herself a glass of water from the kitchenette.

'Hey, you have a whole bathroom here.' Her voice echoed as she looked around inside it. I thought I'd talked to her about the bathroom, and then I realised that had been a conversation with Kate. 'Nice robe.' She swung the door open and came out again. 'It looks like it's stolen from a hotel.'

'Yeah. There's a reason for that.' It was a Derek story, Derek who would soon be on his way here. 'It's that bored rockstar thing when you've seen one hotel room too many and you can't stand it any more. The real problem is the TV went out the window in the seventies, Fleetwood Mac herded pigs around their floor in the seventies and anything you do now looks derivative and not quite up to the mark. It's all been done thirty years ago. Anyway, Derek, who may or may not have been high on something, in the early hours of one morning ransacked his entire room of everything that wasn't nailed down and recreated a hotel room on the bus. I think they stopped him on his way out with two chairs and the TV on a baggage trolley.'

114

'Wow.' She was impressed. I had only told this story a few times and it seemed there was no way to tell it without impressing people, though they hadn't been there in the morning to see Derek, dazed and confused and hovering behind the tour manager as he negotiated our way out of the building and back on the road.

'The robes stayed on the bus, and ended up on our account. Ninety US dollars each.'

'I never heard about that.'

'That was the idea. We got the hotel to wipe the security tapes, and no one got hurt, so . . .'

She took a mouthful of water. 'So, what do we do now?' She was standing in front of me by then, just on the other side of the desk. She put her hand down lightly on the top of the Mac, tapped it with her glossy finger-nails. 'You should have more than water in that fridge.'

'I should have Cristal in case Diddy drops over? I keep that in the house.'

She laughed into her glass.

'You session singers. You're always asking for more. If I provide fancy drinks you'll be hitting me up for sushi and a car park outside the door.'

'A car'd be a good start,' she said.

She was leaning forward against the desk, several centimetres of thigh showing between the desktop and her skirt. The airconditioning billowed against her T-shirt. She was at least months away from sitting for her learner's permit, I realised, as she stood there less than a metre in front of me, looking down at me with her dark eyes as if we were playing a game and she was winning.

'I think I might get your mother a knife. Do you think she'd be okay with that?'

115

She lowered her glass, took a half-step back from the desk. 'I don't know. I don't know what she thinks about knives.'

'I think every chef needs a good one. Now, to get back to your question about the next step, we play around with what we've just recorded.' There had been a tension in the air. She had put it there, I thought, and I had spoiled it. 'So if you want to see how that works, come back around here.'

She walked around the desk and took the seat next to me again. 'Why did you ask about my mother and knives?' she said, looking at the screen. She wasn't happy with me.

Because this doesn't work, can't work, when you stand in front of me without a bra on, turning on the charm. That would have been my honest answer, but I didn't give it. 'Her knife's blunt, and it's not a very good knife. Ask any chef what single thing they couldn't do without and they'd say their knife.'

I opened a mix window and moved her vocal tracks around between the speakers, biasing two towards the left and two to the right, and keeping two centred.

'Hey, that's good,' she said, listening to the arc of six versions of her spread out in front of us. 'It sounds good that way. Still too much like me though.'

'This is still raw material. But it's quality raw material.'

A few minutes work at the Mac and it was less raw. I had compressed her vocals, but also made them more ethereal, taken them away from nature and towards something more invented. It was one step away from done. I went into Audiosuite.

'Once you pick something here it sticks, so I've saved the version we've got but, since we might as well go all the way, I'm going for the flanger. This is a bit eighties, a bit Britpop. It's typically used for guitars but, anyway, I think it'll work.'

It did. It came up shimmery, metallic, just right.

'Hey,' she said after the first chorus. 'I get that.' She had moved closer and was leaning forward. I turned the right speaker around to face her. The song reached the second chorus. 'I can't believe that's me. And you, obviously.'

'I don't know if the Splades'll get it, but I think we have something.'

She swung her chair around and it clunked against mine. 'This,' she said, 'this is amazing.' Her knee was against my thigh. 'Oh my god.' Her eyes were looking right into mine. She put her hand on my arm. 'Thank you.'

Here she was, in my backyard studio, stirred up, caught realising that her voice could do far more than she knew. She was out of words then, half-smiling, half-looking at me quizzically, her head on an angle. She bit her lip, made a 'Hmm' noise.

'I said you'd be good.'

She straightened her head, lifted her hand. 'Yeah, you did.' She tapped the arm of my chair.

'Could I get you to try something more?'

I searched around through my folders and found The Light that Guides You Home. I told her it was only a verse and a chorus so far, and they were in need of a fresh start. She went back around to the mike and I asked her to harmonise with the chorus, pick any

117

harmony that worked for her and give it to me. She listened, hummed, sang. She sang with the verse and with the chorus, melody and harmonies, and I recorded it all, figuring I could edit out the bits I didn't need. I was about to tell her I had no idea where this piece of song might go, when she stopped me. Mark was at the door, black Korn T-shirt, baggy black shorts.

I waved him in. I noticed it was getting dark outside.

He smiled his bent ironic smile and he looked only at Annaliese. 'Mum thought you might want to do some homework before dinner.'

🎧

LATER THAT NIGHT I sent the two versions of It's Not What You Think to Gunnar and Øivind. I spent another half-hour listening to them first, and wondered if I had found the sound of the Splades or not. But it was time to let the boys in on what I'd been doing. I told them I'd taken a chance and added some female backing vocals. I said that Annaliese Winter was a fairly big name here, but not one they'd know.

Annaliese Winter, who had gone home to do homework before dinner.

I turned off the airconditioning in the studio and opened the sliding door, and the warm air came in with its smell of the sclerophyll forest and the dry baked ground and, somewhere that I couldn't see, small flowers blooming despite the drought.

Annaliese's chair was turned at the angle she had

left it when she went round to the mike to try out the chorus of The Light That Guides You Home. I straightened it up.

If she had been twenty-five and not taken away for homework, would I have handled the day differently? Probably. If she had been eighteen? That was just two years away. There was no answer for eighteen. And she wasn't eighteen.

I turned the light out, and locked the door. In the dark I nearly tripped on the stairs on the way up to the back verandah. I had stayed in the studio hours longer than I needed to, sometimes with music in my head, sometimes Annaliese.

🎧

THE NEXT MORNING THERE was an email from Norway waiting:

Hey Curtis,

We googled Annaliese Winter and didn't get too far. It's fine to use your girlfriend, man, since her voice is great. Maybe not the style for that track though. We think maybe this is more of a 'guy' track, so we have tried your backing vocals idea with a guy (Gunnar). We like the idea, and we think this way the track is 'The Splades'. Have a listen – we've posted it on yousendit. You probably already have the note telling you it's there. We expect you will want to flange it, because you have love for the flanger. Any more flanging and you will go blind. So would my grandmother say if she was still here.

119

There is also a new song, Lost in Time, which we are demoing now. Could be a single. Could be one for Annaliese Winter backing vocals. Even if you are only pretending she is famous anywhere in the world. We'll send it soon, when it's ready for your ears. Why did we not write it before you came to Svolvær? Good question. There is no good answer. But we have it now and we like it.

Øivind

In the give and take of producing, this was a good result. I picked up the track they had sent, and I played it. Gunnar could stretch himself to Annaliese's harmonies, though his voice was thin where hers had been husky and rich. This was the beginning of the new sound of The Splades, the sound that would take them to the UK and beyond. They had gone with my ideas, with everything, except Annaliese's vocals. I wasn't certain it was the 'guy track' they thought, but it was theirs, and Gunnar's vocals worked.

I couldn't see, though, how I'd get it across to Annaliese that this was any kind of good news. That quality work gets cut all the time because someone chooses a different direction. That she had ended up singing guide vocals for Gunnar's backing vocals and not something anyone but us would ever hear. I hoped I'd got her ready for it, but I wasn't sure I had. Maybe I had let the moment get the better of me.

I listened again to her singing the chorus of The Light that Guides You Home, and I wished it was a whole song. I wished I could give her that.

🎧

'GOD, SO MUCH FOR the hair being a disguise. Do you realise how many people look at you?' Kate said as we manoeuvred past strollers and loiterers and a man struggling under the weight of a boxed plasma-screen TV. She was on her lunch break at Indooroopilly and we were on our way to King of Knives.

'I try not to notice.' It was the first time I had been there for years. It was different to buying groceries at Kenmore at ten in the morning. This was hundreds of shops, a city's worth of people. To see people looking would mean eye contact, and the plan was – always was – to keep moving forward with speed and a sense of purpose and no eye contact. In the absence of Steve Irwin's teeth and trucker's cap, it was the best tactic I had. 'I hear them though. I try not to listen, but you hear your own name. They say it surprisingly loud. It's almost as if you aren't real.'

'What will they think, seeing the two of us together?' She was in her uniform – a burgundy skirt with a white top and two badges. One said 'Kate', the other 'Manager'. The manager badge hung at a slight angle, as if she'd put it on in a hurry, or been distracted.

'The harsh reality is they probably won't see you.' We passed a bookstore, a stand selling watches, a shop selling art supplies. There were escalators ahead, more people. 'It's a strange phenomenon. Publicists, girlfriends, anyone else – in the case of Butterfish even the guys in the band other than Derek and me – all invisible. So if we get stuck and you get snubbed or stepped on, it's not about you. If they wanted to talk to me, or wanted an autograph, you would be a speedbump. That's the official term for it.'

It was Jess's term. Jess, who had taken an elbow in the ribs, a knock to the head, a shove into the gutter, all entirely by accident. Jess, who had been introduced to some industry people by name ten times, and each time they had had no idea they had met her before. When 'favourite superhero power' turned up on one interviewer's emailed list of questions, it was Jess who told me not to put invisibility, since it was altogether too demeaning.

'I'll bear that in mind,' Kate said. 'I think I'd be happy to leave the autographs to you anyway.' We passed Kmart and a shop where a vacuum cleaner kept a ball bobbing in the air. 'King of Knives – what kind of a name is that? I'm surprised they even let them register it.'

'It was probably a few years ago. There was probably even a time when you could have King of Guns, but those days are long gone.'

'I think it used to be on the second floor, King of Guns. Just down from Queen of Semtex.' She stopped, and gave an appalled kind of laugh. 'I think I just made a terrorist joke. That's probably very bad.'

'We'll have to get you an orange jumpsuit and put you in a cage.'

'Orange is *so* not my colour.' She rolled her eyes, Annaliese-style, and laughed again. Or maybe the eye rolling had been Kate's style all along, and Annaliese had taken it on.

King of Knives, it turned out, was very business-like, very culinary. A middle-aged man with big glasses was running a knife through a sharpener and talking to a customer about the technicalities of the edge.

'Probably not the place for your Queen of Semtex material, I'd be guessing,' I said quietly to Kate as we stood at a glass cabinet.

'Don't,' she said, trying not to laugh. She punched me in the arm as she said it, then pulled her hand away and pretended it had been somewhere else. She cleared her throat, and stared straight ahead, through the glass at two rows of Victorinox knives. 'So, what should I be looking at?'

'Something medium-sized and multi-purpose, I reckon. That way you only need one. And I'm buying, remember. And the idea is to get you a good one.'

'You don't have to . . .'

'I know. But we had that fight two days ago, over oyster mushrooms, and you lost. So that's how it is. I'm buying.'

We settled on a thirteen-centimetre Global utility knife, exactly the same as the knife I had in my own kitchen. Mine had been a present, and I hadn't realised until now how well chosen it was. It had been from Jess, whose fingerprints were all over this shopping trip in a way I hadn't expected, and it had spent too long in the storage facility down the road. Jess was still a presence, in incidents and small things said, though that was it, mostly. I realised I had little that was stronger to hold onto, not from the past few years. We had become a succession of small details and then, in Louisville, stopped.

Kate weighed the knife in her hand and I could tell the grip felt right. She nodded. She looked closely at the blade, as if she could see its sharpness.

'I'm buying you lunch,' she said. 'If lunch is feasible for you in a place like this.'

'Feasible? Sure. People might talk to us. Or they might not. They're better when you're eating. It's toilets that are the worst, men's toilets. "Hey, aren't you . . ."' I mimed the instinctive mid-stream half-turn. 'And then it's all over your shoes.'

'Men urinate on you?' She looked horrified, and glanced down towards my shoes, as if the tell-tale splatter marks might still be in evidence.

'Not with my consent. And not at all now that I stick to the cubicles.' Where, occasionally, you hear them talking about you at the trough. Was that Curtis Holland that I saw in the foyer? Was that that guy from Butterfish? No, that guy's too fat. Etcetera. How shit was their third album? Yeah, how shit were the other two? Ha ha ha. All the while with one hand on it, thrashing urine messily against communal stainless steel, standing in the piss of previous customers.

'I know a place,' she said. She led the way to a down escalator and into the nearest café at the bottom, past diners and the counter and all the way to a booth at the back. 'Everyone sits at the tables outside. No one sits here.'

We were next to the kitchen doors and I could hear trays clattering, water pounding into a sink. The doors swung open and a waiter came out with two plates of white-bread sandwiches dressed up with alfalfa sprigs. Outside, a spruiker worked the crowd a few shops down, selling discount shoes.

We put our orders in and I fetched us glasses of water from the water cooler.

'Annaliese came home buzzing last night.' Kate said it as if it might be good news, or might not. 'She was

124

singing in her room, probably the song you were working on.'

I thought straight away of the email from Norway. 'She did a good job. I'm glad you played me that DVD.'

'I don't think she got a thing done on her history assignment. But there's always the weekend for that.' She was holding her water glass in both hands, like someone about to read tea leaves. 'I'm glad she got to do it. Could you make a copy for her? Whatever happens?'

'Sure.' I planned to already. I would burn her a CD. Gunnar and Øivind were missing a chance for something good, but I didn't think I would talk them around. That was a conversation I had to have with Annaliese though, not with Kate, not today. It was Annaliese's singing on there, and she would expect to have it treated as her business. I knew her well enough to know that.

'Her history assignment's the least of my worries.' Kate was following a train of thought. She reached down into her bag and pulled out a crumpled sheet of paper. 'This was in the bin. I'm pretty sure it came from Mark's room.'

She handed it to me to read. The writing was double-spaced Times, and the piece described the brutal killing of a pig using two dogs and a hunting knife. Some notes had been made on it, in small, meticulous, black capitals. 'Intestines' had been changed to 'guts'.

'Maybe the lesson is that I shouldn't go pulling things out of the bin. But what if he's . . . what if he's doing this?' She was holding her head in her hands now, looking out from under her hands at me as I read. 'Okay, he's not doing this. But why is he writing it?'

125

'I don't know. Maybe it's for school. Some kind of character monologue.'

'Yeah,' she said, not impressed with the only guess I had. 'From that Shakespearean play about the guy and his two pig dogs and the knife. One of those king plays, I'm sure.'

'King of Knives?'

She laughed, and it surprised her. 'That is particularly lame.' She was still smiling though. 'King of Knives . . .' Her expression changed again. She gave up the smile. 'He also − and this was for school − he once wrote a story in which someone . . .' She leaned forward. I knew why. '. . . did a shit in his father's car. A car exactly like his own father's new one.'

'I'm sure that's metaphorical,' I told her. 'Unless you know of a shit to the contrary.'

I wasn't certain why I was going into bat for Mark. He seemed at least as likely as anyone else I vaguely knew to do − or procure the doing of − a shit in his father's car. I could imagine him laughing his scratchy laugh long into the night, regardless of the consequences, the grounding for life, the binning of his games software, the loss of access to iTunes or whatever source he had for his preferred bone-shaking metal. I could see him fantasising about it being true, and his father forever approaching his fancy yellow sports car transfixed by the idea of the turd that had once been waiting for him on the passenger seat. So he would buy a new seat, a new car, but still the thought would linger and never again would his staff be trooped to the basement for him to show off.

'He used to teach himself magic tricks when he was

young,' Kate said, re-examining another, long gone, Mark. 'We still have the book. I found it the other day. It was part of a kit, but most of the bits got lost years ago.' I could see him, his bent little smile as he guessed the card you picked or drew the coin magically from your ear. 'And now look at him. I think it's a divorce thing. He's seen a therapist, you know. Not recently, but . . . He's borderline oppositional defiant disorder.'

'He seems okay to me.' He didn't, but he didn't seem a diagnostic distance from okay. He seemed like an archetypal Troubled Teen, but maybe that's what they were calling them now.

'Well, maybe you get a slightly different version of him. He thinks he has some kind of rapport with you. He's not exactly chatty around the house. And that's just the start of it. I can't have alcohol anywhere visible because he drinks it. He pierced his own ear with an ice cube and a needle, and then he got that pretend nail to go through the hole.' She seemed compelled to make her case. 'He calls his father Fletch, to his face. His name's Campbell Fletcher, and there's nothing about him that ever gets abbreviated. No Cam, no Cambo. And Mark calls him Fletch, and not in a nice way.' She tried not to smile, but failed. Mark had no smartarse name for her. 'I bet Campbell hates it.'

Our lunch arrived, a sandwich each on Turkish bread. She picked hers up, put it down again.

'He's pretty much opted out of parenting, though. Campbell, I mean. There's no consistency from him. He likes to think he's still a parent, when it's convenient. Annaliese was his biggest champion until she was about twelve. Then he just forgot one thing too many. Forgot to pick her up from school, forgot about turning up to a musical she was in, turned his attention somewhere else, yet again. Some new girlfriend. When he turns on the charm, you feel like the most important person in the world. When he turns it on someone else, you know where you stand. Did Annaliese tell you how she got her iPod? She did some filing for him, for about an hour. That's not parenting.'

'It can't be easy,' I said, and it came out sounding stupid and trite.

I started eating my sandwich. Kate looked at hers. I thought she was going to tell me to try a bit harder.

'I don't know her sometimes,' she said. 'Sixteen-year-old girls now? They're predators. More than one person has said that to me. Predators. I was at this party – parents were there too that time – and one of the fathers started talking about them fucking in the bedrooms. He actually said the word, and he said it twice, as though, suddenly, that was all fine and it was just what happened. And apparently they see oral sex as not sex – just a step on the way. That's what I've got to deal with.'

'Right.'

Did she know I had seen Annaliese topless by the pool? Had she seen her hand on my arm in the studio?

'With Mark that stuff is fine, or at least it used to be. He used to talk about everything. Once he said he was worried about waking up with erections, so I told him the main lesson from that was that he should never fall asleep at school.' She laughed, and finally took a bite of her sandwich. It didn't stop her talking though. 'With Annaliese there was no easy way. I left books in her room and she stormed out and slammed them down on the table and we had the whole "how dare you" thing. You've seen how that goes.' She swallowed the last of the mouthful, drank some of her water. 'I'm sorry, I'm ranting like a mad woman.'

'Well, I'm a couple of bites ahead of you, but . . .'

'Annaliese isn't like that. All those things people say kids do. I'm sure that's not her.' She fiddled with an alfalfa sprig. 'But she's sixteen. She doesn't want me to know everything. That's how sixteen works, isn't it?'

'Always has been.' I remembered the life I had lived in my head, the things no one knew, the need to shut my door and have a place that was just mine. She was waiting for me to say more, to reassure her that Annaliese wasn't dragging boys off to bedrooms. Or dropping into studios, telling stories, playing a cool kind of twenty-five and an unfinished kind of sixteen, both at the same time. I couldn't talk about Annaliese and boys, what might happen at parties, or might not. 'So what do you want to do with *your* life?'

She had taken a second bite of her sandwich and she stopped, mid-chew, as if she'd heard the question wrongly. She finished chewing, and swallowed. 'What do I want to do with my life? I'm living it now. I want to get these kids through school.' She smiled, and shook her head. 'I unload about my possibly psychopathic son and the sex-crazed world that's ready to suck up my daughter, and you want me to unload about *my* life as well? You're a brave man.'

'I think I can take it.' Most of my time was spent moving a cursor around a screen, clicking to make ever-smaller changes to the same songs, contemplating the next meal. I could listen to someone talking, listen to

129

Kate and her stories of this life I hadn't come close to living. If I hadn't been in a band, if I had instead studied music and taught it, would Jess be working somewhere across town, telling someone about my disregard for the kids and my misspent charm? Could I have been the other half of this life, the sad, despised man who pinned his virility on his car?

'Okay,' she said. 'Okay. Primary teaching. If you really want to know. That's what I'd do with my life if I could do exactly what I wanted. But it's complicated. I'd have to do an exam to qualify for anything, and the only way to do it externally – the degree – would be to do another degree first.' So, she had looked into it. 'I'd like to work on literacy with disadvantaged kids. But I don't know. I don't see it happening.'

'Why not?'

'Why not? A million reasons why not. Because those degrees don't fall conveniently out of cereal boxes. Because in the real world I have to have a job. I've got two kids with a lot to deal with. Two kids who have been fucked up to varying degrees by the way the divorce panned out, frankly.' Her own bluntness stopped her in her tracks. She glanced over to the counter, where milk was being frothed noisily at the coffee machine. 'Or just by being fourteen and sixteen.'

'Well, I hope the chance comes along. I think it's something you could be really good at.' I was so out of practice with real conversations that I had no idea trite was my strong suit. I meant every word of it, even if I had no artful way to say it. It would have to stand as it was.

'Thanks,' she said. 'But that's not likely.' She picked

her sandwich up again. 'And that's life in the suburbs. It's not like being in a band. Not like spending your thirties flying around having a wild time, getting to be Peter Pan and . . .' She stalled there, but I'd caught the thread of her logic.

'Go on, finish. Peter Pan and what? One of his Lost Boys? I think that's where that goes, assuming Derek's Peter Pan. And assuming you're not casting me as Wendy.'

'No. I hadn't thought . . .' She stopped, corrected. 'It's not what I meant.' Her look said it was exactly what she meant.

'It's okay. You just weren't supposed to know me that well yet.' I pitched it as a joke, however true it felt. I couldn't keep *all* my secrets from her, I realised. Didn't want to.

'Hmm.' She smiled, looked at her sandwich and put it down. 'So, what made you come back here, Lost Boy, when the obvious place to keep working with a bunch of Norwegians might be, say, Norway?'

'It was time.' My brother. We had no father, no parents. I had no anchor if I didn't have my brother. Was it as clear as that? Some secrets were still mine, still being worked out. 'I'd been on tour forever and I needed to sit down.'

'So, is Derek sitting down too?'

'Only for lap dances, I'd imagine. Derek bought himself a West Hollywood apartment with a spa for three, and then upgraded to a spa for five. He showed me the catalogue. Romance Two, it was called. It's his own mini Playboy Mansion. Derek buys Hef's fantasies off the rack.'

She laughed. 'And what about you? I can't see you hanging around in that granny flat forever. What are you looking for from life, if it's not Hef's fantasies?'

'I haven't worked that out yet.' I'd had Derek stories ready, but the focus was back on me. 'This is a chance for me to think about it, I guess. No playmates though, probably no stripper spa parties, and no lounging around in silk smoking jackets with bunny logos. Maybe it's time for me to embrace my inner Kenmore and see how it works for me.'

'Hey, don't sell Kenmore short,' she said. 'I'm sure there are spas all over this suburb happy to swing like it's the seventies at Hef's place.' Her expression changed. 'We used to have a spa.' She shook her head, as if it couldn't have been true. 'Back at the old place. Back in the old life. We had this house at Indooroopilly. It was . . . competitive. It was a statement house. If you drove up the driveway and parked at the front and got out, chances are it'd stop you and you'd gaze up at it and you'd think, "They're richer than me." That was the look it had. It's not me to be in that house. I don't know why it ever was. Annaliese had a friend out where we are now, and it was different, and I had only half the money I'd had before, so . . .' She shrugged, as though she'd been backed into the house she was in now. 'It's better though. Campbell can have Admiralty Towers. I'm happy.' She nodded, still testing it in her own mind to see if she believed it. 'We never had the chance to work out that we liked different things.'

She told me she had started uni after finishing school, but that it didn't go so well. She began an Arts degree and met no one. Every class was a room full of hundreds of

132

people, and they all seemed to talk to each other but not to her. One day, she caught the bus home, and left her textbooks on the seat, knowing she wouldn't be back. For weeks she left the house in the morning, pretending. She went to daytime sessions of movies and came home in the early afternoon and watched soaps. She ended up as a legal secretary, met Campbell. Annaliese came along quicker than they had planned. They hadn't planned, in fact.

'It's just like they say it is.' She was up to the other end of the relationship again. 'The only people who get rich out of ugly divorces are lawyers. Divorce is a chance to show that it's possible to divide something in two and both walk away convinced you've got less than half.' She was off in the thought for a moment, then suddenly back, looking at me, stuck for the next thing to say, as if she had stepped somewhere she shouldn't have.

I was divorced too, and far more recently. She knew about that. She had read it in papers and magazines, earlier in the year. We had crossed over to my story again. Even in this conversation, I was preceded by the two-dimensional more difficult, more fascinating version of myself.

'I'm sure it's different with kids,' I said as our way out. 'I'm sure there's more to it.'

🎧

'MY MOTHER LIKES TREES,' Annaliese had said to me. 'That's why we live out here.'

Maybe Kate did like trees. I knew that she ran on the bush tracks on the back of Mount Coot-tha early in

133

the morning. I couldn't picture her in the statement house, or the life that went with it, even if she had downsized unwillingly to get where she was. Annaliese had a better version of the story. I could see Kate saying it, however many years ago, as they drove along Gap Creek Road, past caramel-coloured cows and landscape gardeners, high eucalypts and dense bush, signs advertising horse poo for two dollars a bag. Maybe it was a dollar back then.

'Look at the trees, look at the trees, and we're still close to everything.'

She was finding the best way through for all three of them.

She phoned me later in the afternoon. 'I'm on the back verandah,' she said, in what sounded like a harsh whisper. 'It's cordless. The phone.'

I rolled my chair forward and looked up through the studio window, but couldn't see her through the bushes.

'I'm in the studio,' I whispered back. 'Phone with a cord. Old school.'

She laughed, and said, 'All right. What I meant was . . . I was just about to put some laundry on and I found a bank slip in Mark's pocket. I've just seen how much money he's got.' So she was outside, hiding from him to make the call. 'I don't know where it's coming from and I don't know what he's going to do with it.'

'Well, unless it's a middling two-figure sum, it's not all from me.' I stood up, and walked as far as the cord would let me. My back was stiff from sitting.

'No, I figured that. But thanks for confirming. It's not a two-figure sum. More like a four-figure sum. We all know he's ripping you off, but he's not ripping you off that much.'

'All? Who's all?'

'No one. It's . . . I can't ask him. I haven't even been into his bedroom this year. I just demand his sheets fortnightly. And don't think I didn't try for weekly. I assume he puts the clean ones on when I give them to him. I've got no idea how he could have so much money.'

'So, you want me to go undercover and find out?'

'Yes. Yes, I do. That'd be great.'

It had been a joke, and then suddenly it wasn't one. It was a straw, and she was clutching at it. 'I'm not sure that I do undercover.'

There was nothing from Kate in reply. Nothing. Maybe a small 'Oh'.

'But maybe I could have a word with him.' And what would that word be? I had no idea, but every other thing I could think of to say next – every way out – failed me, didn't form itself into anything I could decently say. 'I'll do what I can.'

I heard her breathe out, and then she said, 'Good. Thank you. Don't feel you have to though. Only if it comes up. I was just a bit surprised by the amount of money he's got. Don't go thinking I'm totally crazy.'

'Not totally.'

She laughed. 'Thanks. That's about the best I could hope for, I guess. If you need any help with the undercover thing, call me. I've got years of costume parties behind me, remember.'

🎧

'IT'S ABOUT STURT TRAVELLING inland to the desert with a whaling boat and two crew, missing the inland sea by millions of years.' Patrick had taken a closer look at our father's opera notes. 'He'd done quite a bit of work on it. Would you have thought there'd be an opera in it? I guess Voss became one, so there you go. It's a genre, explorer opera. What possessed Dad to wade in I just don't know. Did you know Sturt had a whaling boat?'

'No. All that explorer study at school, and no mention of a whaling boat.' We were on Patrick's balcony. He was back in town and about to sear trout. 'How bizarre must that have been, if you were some indigenous person out there, watching this caravan come through the mulga with their cocked hats and their horses and dragging their whaler?'

The dark mass of the park lay in front of us, with its rose gardens and poinciana canopies and the wide dry lawns where families played on weekends. The buildings of the CBD, most of them still full of lights, stood up over the treetops and seemed closer than they were. A breeze wound around from the river, but sluggishly, heavy with warm, humid, salty air.

Patrick had put bowls with three kinds of olives on the glass table, and he had opened a riesling because he had suddenly had enough of sauv blancs. I had brought a sauv blanc. He sat back in his chair, the light from the cream-and-beige loungeroom angling across his face. He took an olive stone from his mouth and dropped it into the saucer in front of him.

'Well, exactly,' he said. 'That comes up. I don't know if they did the actual exploring in cocked hats, but the rest of it. It's all there. He wanted – Dad wanted – them to build an actual boat, full size. It would have been like Fitzcarraldo, Herzog's Fitzcarraldo.'

'I haven't seen it.'

He picked up his wine glass, and wiped his hand across the ring of condensation it had left on the table. 'Well neither have I, but it's about this guy who takes a big boat over a mountain, I think. It's one of those stories of grand folly.'

'As far as you're aware.'

'As far as I'm aware, yes. You're not telling me you have to have actually seen something to reference it? I'm sure that's not how it works.'

'So Fitzcarraldo could be a whimsical cartoon musical about a vainglorious yet eccentric mouse who rode in Don Quixote's saddle bag?'

'Well, it could. But I would have seen that, obviously. You know that's my genre, the whole rodent-Quixote-musical-cartoon thing. Right up there with outback explorer opera.' He leaned forward towards the olives, took a large green one from the middle bowl. 'Where the fuck did you get an idea like that from? Shrek? You must spend a lot of time alone.'

'I do now. And it's good, mostly. It got noisy there for a while.'

'Yeah. Come in and I'll do the trout.'

He led the way to the kitchen, which was at the far end of the large open-plan living area. The water in the saucepan had come to the boil.

'I just bought these . . .' He struggled for the name, then picked up one of the two new bamboo steamer baskets he was referring to. '. . . things. Blaine took

137

his. So I may trash the greens, but you'll have to bear with me.'

He picked up the recipe, which he had printed from the internet. His salsa verde was in the blender, his organic veges were cut and in piles. He studied the page as if the recipe were in a tiny font, or another language in which he knew a few phrases but no more.

'Right, trout,' he said, and went to the fridge.

He dribbled oil in the frying pan, turned the heat up to high and lowered the two fine-looking pieces of trout in with tongs. He loaded the broccolini, beans and snow peas into the baskets and set them on the boiling water. For more than a minute he was calm, watchful. Then everything happened at once – hot oil spat from the fish, smoke started to rise from the pan, steamed billowed. I moved forward.

'Don't help me. I need to . . .' He waved me away. 'All right, fuck it, help me. What are you holding back for?'

I turned the heat down, took the tongs and turned the trout, and I steadied the baskets. 'Just fine-tuning. That's all.' I would be buying him a knife next.

'Oh god,' he said as he shovelled it dispiritedly onto plates. 'You don't realise how dependent you are. Bloody Blaine.'

He gave me knives and forks and took the plates himself and led the way back out to the semi-darkness of the balcony. Dependent. I hadn't been dependent. Blaine going was like Patrick having an organ removed. Jess going put me in a haze, but it wasn't the same. I played that night. I cooked in the next town without catastrophe.

The salsa verde was great, and I told him so.

138

'Did I tell you how it ended with Blaine?' he said. 'Did I tell you that?' He hadn't. He knew he hadn't. 'We had a friend – she's still a friend – and she asked us . . . she asked if Blaine would give her his sperm. She and her partner decided they'd rather do that than go to a lesbo-friendly sperm bank. They said they would have asked me but, you know, heart disease and cancer, what can you do? Dud family history.'

'They'd be smarter genes than Blaine's.'

'I like the catty stuff, you know?' he said, mock-seriously, pointing at me with his fork. 'I like the catty stuff from you about that dumb arsehole with a family history of long life, long tedious life. Anyway, I thought he should do it. Worse than that, way worse, I made the mistake of saying, "It'd be great to have a child in our lives".' He measured it out word by word as though it was the most categorically stupid thing he could have said. He made his non-fork hand into a pistol, held it to his head, and fired. 'Well, didn't that open up a can of worms? A lot of ridiculous dog and fence talk, and the screech of commitment-phobic tyres as Blaine and his worldly goods left the scene.' He took a pause, to allow the image to settle. 'All right, it wasn't quite that quick. But you get my point.' Patrick with a child in his life – I had never contemplated the possibility, never thought he had either. The child would have been well dressed at least, or expensively dressed anyway. 'I read that you heard by email. From Jess. I mean, I know we talked at the time, but I didn't know that. That can't be a good way.'

'I heard it got some coverage. I didn't look. I don't think anyone, any outlet, had the actual email though.'

He didn't contradict me. 'There *was* an email. So the story might have had some truth to it. But it wasn't one email. Nothing's ever that simple.' It didn't make a lot more sense to me now than it had on that kerb in Louisville, looking down at the gravel and the bottle tops in the gutter, reading her half-dozen hurried sentences properly for the first time. 'I think it was just . . . a necessary thing for Jess to do. Someone had to make a move, a clear move. It was the right thing for both of us. I wasn't really doing my bit. I got married in the wrong state of mind. Dad had just died and . . .' Nothing was certain then. Nothing. That fucking clown stole my watch and put it in a balloon. 'We got married in a stupid wedding chapel in Nevada.'

'I would have liked to have been there.' It came out sounding oddly formal, like a written RSVP in the negative from someone who, try as they might, couldn't make the date work. It was his way of sounding less angry than he was, or had been.

'Yeah. And if it happens again, you will be. I'll need some style advice. It was sorely lacking on the day. We got married after the soundcheck. Jess lodged the papers while we were doing the show. Derek announced it to the audience, naturally.' To a perplexed silence, then cheering. I had to take a bow. 'When I came back here, a month ago or whatever, I flew in via Sydney. I had one of those annoying transfers where you have to pick up your bags and re-check. So I changed to a later flight and I caught a cab to Balmain and I stood outside her door. But I couldn't think of anything to say. So I left. I went back to the airport. She was probably there, in her house. It was early.' It was a terrace house, about a hundred years old. All the curtains were closed. It had a Brunswick green fence with a matching mailbox. We had bought furniture together in Brisbane but not a house, though we had talked about it. Whenever Jess pushed the idea, it was never the right time. So she rented some storage space, let her job go and joined the band on the road. 'I didn't really have a plan. We just hadn't had contact for a while. Most of the sorting out had been by email, and it had all been very decent, but . . .'

'But you'd know she's getting married again. You would have heard that from her.'

I felt like I was falling, a long way and into something dark. It was hard to breathe. Married again. He had really said that. 'No. No, I haven't heard from her for a while.' I was looking at the table, at an ant that was crawling across the glass. Even my own voice seemed like it was coming from far away.

'Oh. She sent out a group email, but I figured she'd talked to you separately. That was a couple of months ago. I don't know the details. I think they met through touch football, right after she moved to Sydney.' He was talking quickly, shoving information in front of me in case it helped. 'He had one of those names like Jason, or something like that. I've probably still got the email.'

'Don't send it.'

☊

I REALISED I DIDN'T want to be with Jess, that the best of our relationship was long gone, and had been in

141

a different part of our lives. That was the time I missed, and it was years ago. We both married out of desperation, out of fear that we had lost our moment but had a last chance to grab at it by the Nevada roadside. I think she had been waiting for years, and I hadn't been noticing. She had set herself to outlast my ambivalence, to ride with the band for as long as it took for the wheels to stop and for me to see a long uncomplicated future with her. She settled for an impulse instead.

'Let's have a big party when we get home,' she said, her mind all the time on the wedding she wasn't getting.

We bought matching platinum rings from the first store we went into. Hers didn't fit, so she wore it on a chain. I was dashing her hopes with every step we took, and putting it down to spontaneity.

So, now she was getting married again. She would be planning this one, getting it right. She would speak at the reception about marrying me, because no one else would, and because they would all know. She would say something funny that would take all its power away, pull the fuse right out of it. 'Honestly, that whole being on tour thing . . . we had to get married, just so we had a bit of paper to tell us where we'd been. It's all quite disorientating.'

I hoped for Jason's sake that was the Jess he was ending up with. Not the one with the migraines, who was usually unhappy. I knew both of the Jesses pretty well, one from long ago, one more recently. I didn't know why she hadn't told me she was getting married.

In Patrick's garage, in the space previously occupied by Blaine's car, there was now a lot of our father's junk.

The notes and drafts of Captain Sturt's Whaler were in two unmarked boxes.

'There's another one you should take as well,' Patrick said as we were loading them into my boot. He went back inside for it.

It was a collection of media articles about Butterfish, and me.

I opened it in the kitchen when I got back to my house. I couldn't remember my father talking about any articles, after the first one or two back when we had no record deal and our only coverage was the occasional gig plug from Ritchie Yorke in the Sunday Mail.

'Any time you're in the paper,' my father said as he sat with the Sunday Mail open in front of him, the first ever reference to Butterfish there in a column running down the right-hand side of the page, 'you should cut the article out of one copy and buy another whole paper, so you've got the context when you look back on it later.'

I don't know where that rule came from, but it was clear neither of us had stuck to it. Ever since, he had been clipping articles from a diverse range of sources without me knowing. From the way it appeared, he had even gone looking for them. Some of the magazines he had were international. There were pages printed from websites, and photocopies people had sent him. And he had Curtis Holland Regrets.

I opened a Stella and sat down in front of the TV, and I read it for the first time. It was late and every commercial channel was plagued by cheap ads for dating services.

The article opened with the journalist's recollection of his question, 'So, Curtis Holland, do you have any regrets?' It had apparently come up deep into an otherwise unremarkable interview. In fact, he had me down as sluggish before then. I took to the question as if I'd been waiting for it all day, and lost in a torpor of talk about success. I came across as chronically shitty about interviews in which people said they had no regrets. Have they learned nothing? My hands became expressive at that point. Regret was normal, human, inevitable. Without regret, how would we ensure that we made each of our worst mistakes only once? On I went, into a riff on the subject, practically a lecture. And the journalist had his title and his article, and whatever else we spoke of barely rated a mention. Well before the end, I was tried and convicted and put away as intriguingly deranged on the strength of his minute observations – twitches, tics, a narrowing of the eyes, a long-lost gaze.

I have no recollection of the twitches and jerks, or the interview, or the journalist, or even the city. The photo gave me nothing. I was up against a stone wall. It could have been a city hall or a museum or a cathedral. It added some weightiness to my load of regret.

And despite my lack of memory of the whole event, the article seemed to have me quoting my much more recent conversation with Annaliese, reciting the same catechism.

I took a look at the date, and went back to the box in the kitchen. It appeared to be the last article my father had clipped, and the interview must have happened early in the tour for Supernature.

So, my approach to regrets preceded my father's death and my precipitous marriage. I never saw the article in the press-clipping file after the tour, and I couldn't say I was surprised at that.

I opened the lid of one of the boxes containing Captain Sturt's Whaler. A silverfish ran away from the light. On top, there was a scrap of paper on which my father had written 'this for bassoon at reveal', with notes dotted in on five hand-drawn lines below. I closed the lid again, and settled for the TV.

I could see him, in his car, having this small brand new idea, grabbing the paper and pen from the glove box at a traffic light. How long had this opera been in his head? Perhaps for years of music lessons and clumsy student assaults on Für Elise, perhaps all the time he listened to his Deutsche Grammophon records in the seventies. He had dozens of them, works for symphony orchestras along with half a shelf of operas and operettas, some jazz and some carefully selected pre-war blues, which he viewed as modern music. My mother's records had gone to a cousin of hers, with the exception of an original cast recording of the songs from the musical Hair, which had been misfiled among the operas and operettas and didn't surface for a year or two. Patrick played it often. Our father never did.

When the cast sang about the dawning of the age of Aquarius, I confused it with Atlantis and imagined a lush tropical island rising out of the sea, with our mother on it, young and well and in a big hat. I thought we might go there some day, and then I knew we couldn't.

Our father's musical tastes got no closer to contemporary than a white-haired Arthur Fiedler coaxing a breezy Tiger Rag out of the Boston Pops. 'Brilliant,' he said, enthralled as the venerable conductor worked his orchestra and kept the tune skating along. It was from the twenties, from the sound of it, and for two of us in the room it might as well have been musak from the ark. By the late seventies, punk had taken hold in the UK, Abba had toured Australia in triumph and Countdown had claimed our house every Saturday and Sunday evening.

Patrick made a list of preferred gifts for his twelfth birthday and put Fleetwood Mac's Rumours at the top. Lindsey Buckingham was probably his first crush, though it was never put that way. He talked incessantly about how great he was, how talented. He stared at the photos on the sleeve, but never at the album's front cover, which featured Stevie Nicks and Mick Fleetwood but not Lindsey. Some of it rubbed off on me. I wanted to *be* Lindsey Buckingham. If he was so great that he had such a hold on my big brother, I wanted to be him. I wanted to pose for black-and-white band photos and pout and wear a guitar rakishly and date the chaotically glamorous Stevie Nicks. I wanted to be that comprehensively famous.

Then one of my friends at school wanted to be a neurosurgeon, and I wanted to be a neurosurgeon. I didn't know what a neurosurgeon was.

It was a few years until I listened to the album properly. I think Patrick wanted Phil Oakey from Human League by then. Lindsey was, by the early eighties, someone he had once had a thing for, but they had managed an amicable separation. I was twelve and Patrick was sixteen. I was learning piano and playing his early Billy Joel records. He put Rumours back on one day and told me to listen to Songbird, closely, and he said, 'You could play that.' He told me it didn't matter that it was sung by a girl. And although part of me still wanted to be Lindsey Buckingham even then – the Lindsey Buckingham who, implausibly, could find himself in a position to write a song about being dumped, like Second Hand News, and then could make it brilliant and complicated – Christine McVie singing Songbird was the track I needed to listen to. There it was, recorded live in an empty auditorium, a brilliant choice. The rest of the album was recorded in a studio, but Songbird was entirely without fuss – grand piano and vocals and little else, with a big big space for the sound to swell in. I could imagine the room. It felt almost dark, as though one small light had been left on for the song to be played, and the notes rang across the polished mahogany floor of the stage and off into the air. A song sung for the sake of singing, for a personal truth it might contain, not for an audience.

I played it on the old upright in our loungeroom, gave it everything and sold it short as the carpet and the close walls sucked it up. Years later, whenever Butterfish turned up at a two-thousand seater with a grand on stage, I'd play a few bars of Songbird before the roadies wheeled the piano away and set us up.

There was still a lot of junk in Patrick's garage. I might have borrowed the opera and taken the clippings, but there were boxfuls of relics left behind. He had shunted them somewhere when our father died, then brought them to his flat once the second car space had no more car to go in it. Patrick made all the arrangements for the funeral, sorted out everything that needed it, tied up our father's loose ends. Months after, he told me he was still getting mail, our father's mail, and I hadn't thought about that. He had a redirection organised, since people don't

147

automatically know. Your place in the world isn't instantly and entirely surrendered. Tracks lead back to where you once were, and still the mail comes, for a while at least.

It didn't need to be said that I should have been more involved. Patrick had taken it on without complaint, but I had sensed a couple of times that he resented my disengagement with the details. I turned up, but I didn't do a lot more.

I put the article back in the box, and I imagined our father's hands over the years scissoring the edges of the clippings, finding and cutting and filing. Reading, and seeing what I had made of myself. The media's version of it anyway. The first surge of sales in America, the ride we went on. Derek's embrace of it all, my turn as the recluse from the parallel universe, better off shut up in a room, tinkering away. Each of us made the other look like a freak, Derek desperate for applause, me desperate for peace.

There were no articles, though, about getting married and divorced, about the walls falling in with Written in Sand, Written in Sea. Perversely, I wanted my father to have read about those too, and to be around when I came out the other side of it, crept out the other side, away from the light, and found whatever turned out to be next. But Curtis Holland Regrets was the last he saw, and I wasn't happy that he had seen me face regret like a twisted sideshow oddity. I had hoped my approach was more subtle and reasoned, more real and less of a carnival, than the journalist had made it out to be.

I wanted to let my father know I would be okay.

☊

ON SATURDAY MORNING I wrote an email to Jess, then several emails to Jess, then trashed them all. The last address I had for her was gmail, and I didn't know if it was still active.

I couldn't describe the part of her I missed, or the part I had lost long ago, or adequately wish her well. I couldn't edit out enough apology to get the balance right. Some things run their course. That was what had happened to us.

There were days when I could have given her more thought, more time. Regret. Here was another one perhaps finally starting to take its proper shape, and that was fine by me. I was ready to put a name to it.

But Jess getting married – I wasn't sure I was ready for that. It kept coming back like a new idea and I pictured the day, and me erased from her history. She would have a service in a garden with her sisters as attendants. She would make her parents happy. Jason's best man would tell the story of his friend talking about this new player at touch football, and how quickly she had captivated them all. The bride would beam, sit there and beam in the way she had always wanted to, shelving for the evening her own regrets about a few wasted years. Jason would give her a ring that would fit her finger.

There was a knock at the door just after ten. I was deep in a patch of wallowing and first thought it was Jess, come with a forgiving version of home truths and a wish to tell me face-to-face where her life was heading. But it was Mark.

He was wearing a crumpled non-black Westside Walk volunteer's T-shirt with the sleeves torn off. He had a sizeable new acne cyst over his right eyebrow. 'Mum said you wanted the lawn done again.' He said it as if the idea caused him wry amusement. On all sides the grass was straw-coloured and quietly struggling not to die. Growth was not a priority. There were a few new stalks, but they were mostly weeds.

'It's more to do with the trees around the back,' I told him, realising this was Kate sending him my way for the talk I'd agreed to have. 'All the bark and dead leaves on the ground that could be a fire hazard. I'd like to get that all raked up in case there's a bush fire.'

'No problem. Where do you want it to go?'

I had no idea. I was making it all up on the spot. 'I thought I might get your input on that.'

'Really?' He made a noise that might have been a laugh, or a nervous tic of the type invented by journalists in the interests of painting a better word picture. 'Well, you could put it with the grass clippings for now, but you probably need a plan for all of it, since it's still a fire hazard sitting there.' He looked over towards the previous week's pile of dried grass. A bush turkey had scratched through it for bugs and one side of it was strewn across the nearby ground. 'Are you up to composting it, do you reckon? That'd take a bit of effort.' The delivery was deadpan but the cracked smile was back. This was the rapport Kate thought we had.

'Enough effort to pile it up in something, then walk away and leave nature to take its course? Yeah, it's a bit much.' I was working on keeping the rapport up near the high-water mark. 'It's probably something I'd outsource. Is it within your areas of expertise?'

'I wouldn't say that, but the landscaping guy down

the road'd probably sell you one of those green plastic things they do it in and he could tell you how to do it. After that, you know me, I'm a gun for hire.' Also said with a delivery as dry as the grass.

A warm gust of wind blew in, sending leaves cartwheeling along the rutted driveway and flapping the stretched front of Mark's shirt.

'So where does all this money go to? This money you earn as a gun for hire.' It was his mother's question, jammed into the conversation at a point where it didn't quite fit. I told her I'd try, and this was it. 'It doesn't look like it all goes on T-shirts.'

He looked down at his shirt front. 'Hey, I had to work for this. I had to rattle a tin. I had to shake loose change out of people for all these charities. It got my class out of school for an hour. Or in my case the whole morning.' He was implying there was a story there, of him wheedling his way around the system again.

'So what do you do with it? The money?'

He looked me in the eye, as if I wasn't to be trusted. 'What are you? A spy for my mother? Most of it goes on bourbon and hookers, the rest of it I waste.'

☊

GOOGLING 'BOURBON', 'HOOKERS' and 'waste' gave me lots of John Lee Hooker references, but failed to reveal the original author of the line. I was sure I'd heard it, or something like it, somewhere before. But, whatever its origins, there was no going back to the money question a third time, so I wasn't turning out to be much of a spy.

I would pass on Mark's bourbon and hookers line to Kate when the chance arose.

I resisted putting my own name into Google to see how I was faring. In the early days of Butterfish I ego-surfed regularly but, by the time The True Story of Butterfish had yielded two hit singles and some good sales, too many scabby youths with time on their hands were happy to take a swing at us and it stopped being fun. There were fan sites too, and fights in chat rooms, and plenty of lies and exaggerations. There was simply too much being said. I had heard that some Chinese college students had posted something hilarious on YouTube featuring lip-synching, Still Water and a beaker containing a liquid that may have been urine, but I hadn't seen it.

I was sure we had been thoroughly done over throughout the blogosphere following the release of Written in Sand, Written in Sea. Derek would know and, in two days' time, he would probably drag me through every detail he could recall. I checked QF176 on the Qantas website. I had been assuming he would come via Sydney and arrive mid-morning, but it was LA–Brisbane direct and getting in at 6.05 a.m., a detail he had conveniently omitted to mention in his email.

I got off line, and went back to Captain Sturt's Whaler. My father had made extensive notes about the plot and the music. Even his notes had gone through drafts. Key points were underlined, and in the margins he had written 'YES!!' or 'clumsy – fix this' or 'needs to be more forceful?' as he had gone through and edited himself. He had made some rough sketches of the set, and of costumes, with notes about colours. He had photocopied lithographs of Sturt and soldiers of the time, but his costumes looked more frankly operatic, more stagey. They were costumes that would be worn by people who you would expect to sing, not uniforms battered and grimed by the desert. There was a chorus of convicts in stiff yellow suits with arrows on them. He had made notes outlining his concerns about chain drag, and the impact of the noise as the convicts moved about the stage. He thought he might settle for manacles and dispense with leg irons.

At one time he had written letters to possible librettists, and he had kept copies and all replies. All had declined, some after what seemed to be genuine consideration. He had been turned down by established librettists and playwrights, and then by novelists and poets, then by a music journalist, an academic and someone who had once taught with him at a school and who had gone on to edit an obscure journal about calligraphy. After that he had pressed on regardless. There was a zeal to his mission. If the obstacles preventing him staging this opera were immovable, he would be the irresistible force to counter them.

He wrote his own libretto. He knew Sturt like a brother by then, and had taken a three-day bus tour out of Alice Springs to see what salt pans and endless parched red dirt looked like. He had a voice from Sturt's correspondence and he could use that, and he also had copies of his reports. He tried to turn report extracts into song – Sturt writing them by candlelight in his tent – which may not have been such a good idea. As a librettist, Sturt made a great explorer.

In later drafts my father reworked the lines, and they were more song-like though never exactly magical.

153

The convicts sang about their lot – about how they had stolen a pound of lead from a church roof or a loaf of bread and ended up with seven years' hard labour. 'Hard labour, hard labour, hard labour' the chorus went, with different voices taking different parts and each line to be delivered in a decrescendo. There was a corroboree scene which, in all but the most gifted hands, risked ending up looking rather distasteful, or at the very least patronising in a 'noble savage' kind of way.

The two whaler boys were from Liverpool and missed the girls they had left behind. In most versions they were clean cut and close to identical but, in some, one of them was older, a drunkard and a thief. He had a livid scar across his face from a tavern brawl and he spoke more like a pirate. 'Contrast,' my father wrote in the margin, 'contrast'. He looked like he was one draft away from giving him a hook for a hand, and an eye patch. Then he abandoned contrast and reverted to the fresh-faced youth he had started with. He always had Sturt – ambitious, determined, enigmatic, misunderstood Sturt – for colour and movement.

I looked at the music, and found myself humming it, then singing a line or two. At its best it wasn't bad, but it was never memorable. That's what I had to accept. Here was my father's last big adventure, and it would have ended up with nowhere to go. Captain Sturt's Whaler could have turned from two boxes of notes and drafts into three boxes, or four, and into fully developed scores, but still it wouldn't have ended up on a stage.

My father was a quiet man who kept to himself – what was he doing writing an opera? There could hardly be a bigger dream. It was for the music, clearly. The music and the story. I'm sure it wasn't about glory. Or fame.

And I could see some melody lines running through there that had some strength, and something going for them, even if nothing stood out. His lyrics were rudimentary though, self-conscious drafts that I could see he had laboured over.

Writing operas and dating Russians – when the Ten Stupid Questions interview got around to his favourite things to do with his time, would these have been the answers? But there wouldn't be any interviews. There wouldn't have been any interviews, however much work he might have put into it. Favourite Indulgence, Guilty Secret, Six People Living or Dead You Would Invite to a Dinner Party. All with a publicist going, 'I know you've done it a million times before, but people read this section . . .' He would not have been a good fit with that world and, if anyone had put the millions of necessary dollars behind his opera, it's where he might have found himself.

One song was about Sturt's first sighting of the desert pea that came to bear his name. I thought it had one of the stronger melodies, and I took the notes to the studio and played it on the keyboard so that I could hear what it sounded like outside my head. My father had sketched out some string parts, so I found a synth string sound and worked with them too.

I opened a new file on the Mac, and I started to record. I brought in woodwind and brass and percussion, and fleshed out a few bars to an almost orchestral sound. It felt really competent, but not better than that.

I still wished he had heard it though, even if it was just a few bars.

♩

I PUT SHEETS ON the spare bed for Derek on Monday afternoon. I had bought multiple sets of identical sheets online from Svolvær and had them delivered to Patrick's work. I bought a lot on line, actually, until I got the email from him saying, 'For fuck's sake, I am not a storage system. Some things can actually wait until you arrive. Happy to look after the essentials, but calm the shopping binge or we'll be putting you in therapy.'

I had been imagining settling in, having guests. I wouldn't have expected that Derek would be the first. I didn't want it to be a student house, or some austere minimalist place. I was thinking a mid-scale non-chintzy B & B look. The manly version of that, obviously, where everyone says the place looks okay but no one openly likens it to a B & B. Patrick was right. I should have been buying the essentials, then focusing on the rest once I'd seen the place.

With the bed made, I put away the last of the groceries. The place looked okay, so my plan was on track. Not that Derek would put a lot of time into noticing, and not that I particularly cared about whether he did. But there were no wall hangings with hokey embroidered aphorisms, there were no teddy bears on the beds and none of the furniture was an assemblage of milk crates. The pitch was right.

I had gone out for eggs and bacon and authentic maple syrup. French toast was Derek's breakfast of choice. Many an argument had been fixed over the next morning's French toast. Well, some anyway.

I put the eggs into the fridge, and headed for the studio.

As I walked out the back door of the house, I could hear the hum of the studio airconditioning unit. I assumed I'd left it on inadvertently when I went to the shops. But the door was unlocked as well.

I slid it open, pushed past the curtain, and there was Annaliese.

'I was hot,' she said. 'So I had a shower.' She was leaning on the edge of the desk, wearing the white robe we had talked about the previous Thursday. My white robe. Her hair was wet. She stood up, away from the desk. 'You don't mind, do you?'

She had left the light off, so the room lacked its usual harsh fluoro brightness. Daylight glowed faintly through the cream curtains behind me and the curtains over the window, which she had closed. She took a step towards me.

'Curtis,' she said, in her husky low voice and in a way no one had said it for a long time. Her tongue touched her lower lip, and she gave a hint of a smile.

She reached out and put her arms around my neck, stood up on her toes and kissed me on the mouth. I lifted my hand, to keep some distance between us, but she took it when it hit her sternum and slid it under the edge of the robe and onto her left breast. She made an mmm noise, and her mouth opened. I could smell my shampoo in her hair.

As her tongue touched mine I pulled my head back

and stumbled half a step away from her. My hand slipped from the robe and her soft skin, and back into the cool air. The robe hung open for a moment, and then she gathered it up with one hand and bunched it closed in front of her.

'What?' she said. 'I thought you . . . we . . .' She frowned.

'I really don't think . . .' I began an explanation without knowing where it went after the beginning. I was about to patronise her, offend her. 'I'm not going to say, for a second, that there isn't something between us. But it can't be this.'

Behind her, the bathroom door was still open, the light still on. Steam hung around in there and misted the mirror. She was sixteen, in my studio, wearing nothing but my robe.

Her cheeks went blotchy. She looked at the window. 'Oh god. I feel so stupid.'

'No . . .' My instinct was to reach out for her, but I held back.

'What an idiot.'

She took a big breath in, then ran for the door, yanking it open with the hand that wasn't holding the robe. Before I could stop her, she was gone. I stepped outside, and watched her run all the way to the hole in the hedge that was near the pool, with the ends of the robe flapping as she ran. She pushed through the gap, bumped the banana lounge with her shin and then I lost sight of her. I heard the back door shut as she went inside. I could still taste her mouth.

I felt exposed. I felt like someone standing at the scene of an unsolved crime, someone who had done the wrong thing, sent reckless signals, kissed the wrong girl. Done something bad and left DNA and fingerprints all over it and stayed fixed to the spot while Kate and the police and the media strode across my dead grass to confront me. But there was just me standing there, and no crime. An incident, but no crime.

I stepped back into the studio. I reached to turn on the light, but then decided not to. I shut the door behind me. There was no sound but the forced breeze of the air-conditioning. I followed Annaliese's wet footprints back across the cheap carpet. In the small bathroom, the shower screen was still beaded with water, still warm to touch. The towel was back on the rail. I picked her clothes up from the floor. They were still warm too, as if she'd soaked up the heat of the day and just now slipped out of them. A singlet top, a mini skirt, and practical underwear – a strapless bra, boy-leg pants. She had been waiting for me wearing just my robe, and she had left wearing nothing more.

In the kitchenette, I had some balled-up plastic grocery bags ready to use as bin liners and I put her clothes in one of them, locked the studio and went to the house. I went to my bedroom and I pushed the bag behind some jumpers that were piled on the top shelf in the wardrobe. A longer-term plan would come to me, but not right now.

What was she doing next door? Who else was home, and had they seen her running in wearing the robe, wet from my shower?

The phone rang. Kate was home. Kate was home and had seen Annaliese run in and had just heard a warped version of everything. All hell was about to break loose, Annaliese's underwear was hidden at the back

159

of my wardrobe, and touring a dying third album while my marriage was crumbling was about to look like one of the better times in my life.

The phone kept ringing, three times, four. It went through to voice mail.

'Chubs.' It was Patrick. 'Surely you're there. You aren't out having a . . .' I picked it up just in time to hear him say 'life.'

'No. I was . . .' What was I doing exactly? What worthy respectable thing was I doing? 'I was just on my way back in from the studio.' I sounded flustered, I knew it. 'I was taking a look at some of Dad's work.'

'Oh, great.'

'I've recorded some of it. Just a few bars. I wrote parts for some other instruments.'

'You've been working on it?' His tone had changed, and not for the better. 'You've been writing bits and recording? I really don't know how I feel about that.'

'No, it's . . .' I had done another wrong thing.

'I didn't know that was what you were going to do when you took the boxes.'

'No, no, it's just . . . it's a few bars. So we could both hear it. Rather than just reading it.'

'Really.' I wasn't forgiven yet. 'Well, I was calling to say I found that email from Jess, and it's Justin who's the new guy, not Jason. I think I said Jason the other night. And I also wanted to tell you I sent an engagement present, just something small, but I didn't go to the party. I thought you should know that. About the present.'

'That's good. It's good you sent something. You've known her for years and . . . I'm glad you did that. And you could've gone to the party too, if you'd wanted.'

160

'Chubs, they looked like very dull people. Not my kind. Not even yours.'

And with that final piece of sibling feedback, the call was over. I sat in silence and watched the phone but it didn't ring again. There was no noise from next door, nothing. I made myself a cup of tea and sat and watched it go cold. I took a chair into my bedroom and I stood on it and pushed the bag all the way to the back of the shelf.

Did anyone, anywhere, know anything? Should I talk to Kate? How would I start it?

And Annaliese, what about her? I should have handled the recording session better. I shouldn't have let it end with thoughts of anything else still lingering. She had a spark, and a way about her, and I had played her the Billy Joel song, the Billy Joel *love song* that sounded as if it was about just such a girl.

But she was older. Billy Joel's girl was older. She was a woman, and it could be different.

♁

ON TUESDAY MORNING, FOR the first time in weeks, I turned on my mobile. Messages pinged through during the early part of the drive to the airport, and then stopped. With the near complete absence of traffic – since it was 5.30 a.m. – I was ahead of time, so I pulled over and worked my way through them. Patrick, our manager in London, Derek – most people who had tried the phone had then resorted to email. There were journalists wanting comments for articles that had long ago been written and filed. I was listening for Jess, I realised,

161

but she wasn't there. And then I thought of Annaliese, who didn't have the number, didn't even know about the mobile that had spent the whole time I had known her in a drawer. There would be no message from her, nothing to fix the mess of the day before.

As I had turned out of the driveway, heading right, I had looked left and seen Kate in the distance, settled into her stride, running away from me and towards the Mount Coot-tha bush. Her day was starting in its usual way. There had been no revelations next door. Not yet.

It was up to me to deal, somehow, with what had happened. That wasn't Annaliese's job.

I had stopped on the verge of the Western Freeway, just near the Botanic Gardens and the cemetery. The sun was still low enough that the tall eucalypts on the far side of the road cast shade across my car. Two taxis sped by, probably on their way to the airport with passengers bound for Sydney or Melbourne on commuter flights. I pulled out and moved in behind them, and we passed through the roundabouts and onto Milton Road. Annaliese was still in bed, still asleep, with my robe somewhere in her room. I turned the radio on. Someone was interviewing Evan Dando, who had put together a new Lemonheads line-up after a long hiatus. There was a new album on the way. He was talking about the Reading Festival in 1997, when he broke the band up on stage without anyone expecting it, and then kept the name on the shelf for nine years.

'I think I just did it for shock effect and I was high, you know,' he said. 'The band didn't know anything about it either. Everyone looked at me and went "Huh?"'

He had toured hard during the mid-nineties, melted

down famously on a number of occasions that had caught the media's eye, and had decided to take his life offstage for a while.

I drove along Milton Road, right into the glare of the rising sun. There were enough cars now to amount to traffic. Steam gushed from a tall chimney at the brewery.

I had begged for a break before Written in Sand, Written in Sea.

'What would one year off cost us?' I said to the execs at the meeting in New York. Our manager looked across the table, like someone trying to show his open mind all over his face. Derek swivelled in his chair and kept his eyes on the floor. He wasn't on my side that day. Down whichever avenue was in front of us, and through the haze, the sun glinted from the top of the Chrysler Building. It looked like a fender on a fifties car.

'Momentum,' one of the execs said. 'Someone once had this same conversation with Axl Rose about Chinese Democracy.'

One way or another, they all pushed. It was done openly and it was done subtly. A new album would be for the best. One more album before the break. So I should pull my frayed ends together and get up and do the job.

'We'll send you somewhere nice,' they said, but we ended up in LA.

And then the album tanked and there was no resistance to calling it quits. The company, in fact, embraced the idea. Our dumping hadn't been made public, and a band break-up was an easier way out. As soon as our manager told them, they had us cancelling the German tour and on a flight to New York. Just Derek and me. The others had already stopped being part of the story. We left them in Düsseldorf, working out where they wanted to go. 'They'll get tickets,' the person on the phone said. 'To wherever.'

By the time we were picked up from JFK, the company had switched fully to executive out-placement mode, drafted the media releases, booked in the interviews. Vice President Karl – who had flown out to LA, eaten doughnuts and squeezed my hand hard at the end of the day and said, 'Remember, it's a big company, and in it I'm your champion' – was nowhere to be seen. He was being someone else's champion that day. The PR team worked through our answers with both of us, answers that were without blame or malice or reference to the collapse of the sales figures. The decision was mutual. It was time. All the best brush-off statements came out, lined up and said their own versions of next to nothing.

Then, after holding firm for a full two days or so, Derek took the wrong tablet at the wrong time, or was struck by a fit of the malice we'd been keeping at bay, and he stuck it to me in a print interview that got syndicated and quoted and changed the story.

'I never said . . .' he said, and they told us they had quoted him verbatim and kept the recording.

'It was all true anyway,' he said. 'You *did* break the band up, you arsehole. We *did* have creative differences that made me fucking want to slap you. You spent a whole year sulking. Everyone wanted to slap you.'

Derek, like a teenager in detention, then had to sit down with the PR people and craft the next media release, the one that took back what he had said and

164

most of the truth in it, and that stated unambiguously that he wished me nothing but the best. We were still friends, he said, on the day in our lives when we both thought friendship was furthest from a possibility.

And I sat down and did my homework too, and the next round of interviews. I said I needed a break. I was ready to spend some time doing other things, behind the scenes.

Our radio play numbers flared, there was a brief spike in sales of our first two albums but not the third, I slipped quietly away and Derek set up camp in LA, showing the world his B-grade bad-boy side.

So, that was it. Months ago. And no contact since, until the email that began 'Fat Boy, do you ever turn your phone on?' as if we were walking along a street and mid-conversation and it was the old days.

I was on Airport Drive when a new text message came through. I didn't need to look at it to know that Derek had landed.

I hit the roundabout at the Kingsford-Smith memorial and swung right, and up the ramp marked 'Departures'. This was my plan to get him out of there quickly, and I'd sent the text suggesting it before I left the house. On my way up the ramp, another message came through. I pulled into the two-minute parking area and picked up my phone. The message read 'I patted a beagle.'

There was almost no one around, since 6.30 a.m. wasn't a big time for international departures. Some backpackers were clambering out of a van, looking dusty and sounding Nordic. A middle-aged couple stood near a Landcruiser, running through an unwritten checklist a final time before hugging their daughter and choking up as she headed off on an adventure. Her father turned away, took off his glasses and rubbed his eyes. Behind him, way in the distance, the city skyline was stamped on the hard blue edge of the sky, like a barcode.

Derek strode through the doors in a black leather jacket and aviator sunglasses, with a backpack over one shoulder. He waved, and headed my way. He walked like he was shooting a video, or as if his balls were too big. He looked immaculately shabby.

I got out and opened the boot, and he slung his bag in. I saw myself reflected in his glasses, squat, Shrek-like. Shrek after a season of banquets.

'So, you got through the baying crowds unscathed.'

'I've changed my hair,' he said. 'Surely that's obvious.' If there was anything self-mocking about it, it was running too deep for me. His eyes and a third of his head were mirrored out by the sunglasses, so that probably wasn't helping. 'You're looking well nourished.'

'You know me, every year waiting for the call for the Twenty-Five Most Beautiful People shoot.' I walked around to the driver's door, and he got in on the passenger side. 'Actually, I'm holding out for Most Intriguing. I think they always had me down as the intriguing one.' He wasn't listening. He was fiddling with his seatbelt and making it look as though it was something other people usually did for him. 'And I know you're shitty that they don't have an edition for the Twenty-Five People Most Likely to Accidentally Marry a Porn Star.'

'I haven't, have I?' He lifted the glasses to look at me, and I saw his eyes for the first time. 'No, I'd remember. Or there'd be paperwork at least.'

I pulled out from the kerb and drove down the ramp towards the road.

'So, how was your flight? That's the first thing I'm supposed to ask, isn't it?'

'Yeah, that's good. Very civil. I had a bed, so I slept.' The glasses were back in place, and he had turned his attention to the seat adjustor. 'We're going to the Wesley, yeah? I told my mother I'd go straight there.'

'We'll be there about seven if we go right now. Is that . . .' Early. Surely it was well before hospitals like seeing visitors.

'I said I'd go straight there.' He was still adjusting himself in the seat, and he cleared his throat. 'This jacket's going to be too hot, way too hot. I don't know why I wore it.'

'Leave it with me. I'll take it back to my place. With your bag.'

'Yeah. Good. Thanks.' He looked out the window, in the direction of the new factory-outlet stores and the building work that was going on.

'I'm sure they'll be glad to see you. Your parents.' This was not the time for French toast, I could tell.

'Yeah, well. It won't be the biggest thing on their minds.' We swung onto the Gateway Arterial, and merged between two semi-trailers. To our left was the car auction yard with hundreds of clean cars in rows, and then the road rose and the factories and warehouses were below us. 'Hey, I've made a start on the solo record.'

'Yeah? I thought that was just a rumour.'

'It's mostly a rumour. But I've got some ideas down. I don't want to rush it though. Plus, there's a few distractions.'

He was back on a better topic, away from illness and back to business and to his hazardous life. He had stories

167

to tell. A party at the Playboy Mansion, where people sat around the grotto and the game room and anticipated lewdness but nothing much happened. Lollipop-bodied girls he had met who were so hungry they had stopped making sense. His first, and last, colonic at the instigation of one such girl.

Sure, I could say to him. Don't we all have that kind of life? Why, I had a wet near-naked sixteen-year-old's tongue in my mouth just yesterday. But that story had layers and Derek's, in my experience, didn't. He followed the line his body chemistry took him on, and he got a result or he didn't.

We hit Coronation Drive and he went quiet again. As we drove along the river bank towards the Wesley Hospital, I almost pointed the rowers out, just to break the silence, but I had nothing to say about them. It would have come out sounding like a line to a child. Look at the bird – what noise do birds make?

At the hospital entrance I gave him a key to the house. 'Call me if you want me to pick you up.'

'I can get a cab.' He undid his seatbelt and opened the door. 'But thanks.'

'You don't know where I live.'

'Okay, you've got me with that.' He looked out through the windscreen, at the neatly clipped bushes and the red brick walls and the bust of John Wesley. 'I actually have no idea, do I?'

'That's right. So I'll text you, and that way you'll have it on your phone.'

'I'm jet-lagged,' he said. 'I'm not into the time zone yet.' He looked up at the building in front of us and the floors of windows that might be wards or operating theatres or administration. His father was in there, somewhere. In one of these buildings, with a hole about to be made into his skull. 'Shit.'

'It's good you're here,' I said, but he wasn't listening. His mind was already off in the hospital corridors, on its way to whatever was about to show itself, his moment of reckoning with his father's disease. 'I hope it's okay.'

☊

I TOOK DEREK'S BACKPACK to my house and spent the morning working. I kept my mobile in my pocket, but there were no calls. I hoped that was a good sign, but I knew it was no sign at all.

In the afternoon I went out to buy a new portable hard drive, and I came back to find Derek and Mark drinking my Stella on the verandah. It had not gone well at the Wesley.

Derek had lost any composure he had managed in the morning, and jetlag and fear and beer were all taking a swipe at him. 'How long do you stay at hospitals?' he said. 'I've got no idea. I don't do hospitals. I had sandwiches wrapped in plastic for lunch, egg and lettuce. Everyone just hangs around. All day. I left while my Dad was having an X-ray. I wrote him a note.'

He looked ragged and his tan had turned sallow. There were half-a-dozen empty stubbies next to him, one on its side. I couldn't remember how many I had put in the fridge. Mark was slumped back in his chair with a stubbie cradled on his lap, and a cap pulled down casting a deep shadow over his eyes.

169

'I met your friend,' he said. 'He has a more . . . liberated attitude to alcoholic beverages.' He smiled a smile with a lazy bend in it, and took a mouthful.

I looked Derek's way and he said, 'Hey, just beer. It's just beer. I'm living by that email.'

'Sniffer dogs. Ha.' Mark laughed, in a derisive kind of way.

'Glad I gave you something to bond over.' I could imagine Derek starting to tell stories a couple of beers in, and they wouldn't have flattered me. I set the hard drive down on the table and took a seat.

Derek said, 'Hey,' and stuck his hand in his pocket. He pulled out a lip balm. 'I got this at a garage sale at Tori Spelling's place. For a buck. I was high, obviously.'

'Shit, are you serious?' Mark sat up, pushed his cap back and reached out for it. He pulled the top off and rolled the end out. 'So, the last lips to touch this were Tori Spelling's?'

'Well, no,' Derek said, as if his story was already losing air. 'I've used it. But it was definitely from her garage sale. I turned up with a few guys and we all went looking for the best thing we could get for a dollar.' He went to drink more beer and nearly missed his mouth. It was more important to invent this pointless story than to get his aim right with his stubbie. 'This was the best thing.' Could there have been any doubt?

'It's still killer material. I can use this.' Mark continued to scrutinise the lip balm closely, as though a few molecules of Tori Spelling might remain.

'Yeah,' Derek said. 'Yeah.'

'Use it for what?' I still wasn't moving at the right

170

speed for this conversation. I'd stepped in too late and too sober.

Mark put the top back on. 'You don't think I just mow lawns, do you?' He gave the lip balm back to Derek, and they clinked stubbies to toast the triumph of owning an intimate Tori Spelling cast-off for a dollar. 'I write things. For money. I could write about that. I do pig-killing stories for Bacon Busters. I do a fair bit of porn. Picture pays twenty bucks for a joke, and you can get them from the internet. Twenty bucks for a hot website as well. Too easy. Fifty bucks for a True Confession. That's good. FHM just said they'd give you free stuff, but the only time they specified it was for best chick's confession and you got a dildo, so . . .' He shrugged. He was in it for the cash, not for dildoes. 'S'pose it could do for a birthday present for Mum. She hooks up with dildoes often enough. She might as well have one she could rely on.' He laughed, then pulled his cap back down so that his eyes were again out of the light. 'It's the True Confessions I like. You can write in as a mobile phone salesman who goes to the chick's door. I've done one as a dishwasher repair guy, one as a seal-a-fridge guy. Anything other than a pool cleaner's still fair game.' He cleared his throat, like someone about to recite verse. 'I saw her for the first time in years when she was waiting tables at a restaurant in the Cross and the first thing she said to me was, "You wanted to fuck me since the day we met at art school." Etcetera, etcetera. And he's now a panel beater but that's okay, and they go back to her place and she likes it dirtier than he's ever dreamed of.'

So now I had my fourteen-year-old neighbour drunk on my verandah adlibbing porn, exactly a day after I

171

had kissed his sister in the studio behind the house. This was not the impact I had meant to have on the neighbourhood.

'I've got a plan, you know,' Mark said as Derek's eyelids sagged and closed, jerked open, then closed again. 'I'm not just about the writing. My father, when he was, like, ten, was in London at a zoo, and he saw these piranhas, two in a tank, with a thick glass wall between them, facing off. Did you know piranhas can strip a two-hundred kilo capybara to the bone in minutes?'

'What's a capybara?' Derek struggled for a moment out of the deep hammock of jetlag and ethanol and perhaps other chemicals that had made it past his beagle friend, then relented and slumped again. Gravity had called all hands on deck, and he was defeated.

Mark looked at him, at the struggle now lost. The capybara question hung there like someone's famous last words. 'I don't know. I got it from the internet. I did a talk on piranhas years ago at school, and that was one of the facts.'

Did people learn anything any more? Take on facts in a context and make anything of them? Were we all just caught in a drift of internet factoids?

'I think it's like a cow-sized guinea pig. Or at least the big end of dog-sized.'

He turned to me, twitchily, as if I was some kind of oracle. I had redeemed my tedious sobriety and latecomer-to-the-party status with a perfectly shaped factoid. 'Cool,' he said, looking closer by the minute to following Derek down the hatch of drunkenness. 'Why don't we have those here?'

172

'Well, we do, but they're just wombats.'

'Oh.' That was obviously much less exciting. 'Well I couldn't just write what I know.' We seemed to have dismounted from the piranha tangent and found ourselves back on the topic of writing. 'Everyone says "write what you know", so what would I write about? "There's this guy whose sister gives him the shits. Meanwhile grass grows in their backyard. Sometimes he is sent to mow it. For a pittance."' He shrugged as if, with those few words, his whole life story had been despatched.

'Good. See, it came together for me at "pittance". There's feeling there, something at stake. Clearly that part doesn't apply to my yard though.'

He nodded, smiled knowingly, as if I was a third party and we were talking about his other dumb rich neighbour who threw money his way for next to no work. He raised his stubbie in a one-sided toast.

'But it's not just about the writing anyway.' His eyes were on Derek again, though Derek was lost to us.

'It might be time to be getting you home, I think. And we'll see if we can make this slightly less bad before your mother arrives.'

'She's on a late. She'll be hours. Nine something. That's half a day away, practically.' If it was an argument for more drinking, it petered out pretty quickly. He blinked hard, and refocused on me. 'Ah, fuck it. I'm guessing that's it for the beers.'

'Good guess.'

He set his near-empty stubbie carefully on the ground and clambered out of his chair. It was Annaliese who was on my mind as we walked across the grass to the hole in the hedge, Annaliese who would be somewhere

173

next door right now, not expecting to face me. In my head I cycled through things I might say, and each one of them felt fake and forced and wrong in its own way.

Mark was telling me about a plan, though not coherently. It involved fish, Siamese fighting fish. His shirt snagged on the hedge as he went through, and he stopped to disentangle himself, leaving me standing next to the banana lounge on which I had seen Annaliese lying topless.

'Well, I might be heading back,' I said. 'I might see if I can get some coffee into Derek to keep him awake for a while. Get him over the jetlag.'

'No, come in. I've got to show you. I've told you, now I've got to show you.' He threw a handful of leaves aside and clumped his way up the back steps with me behind him. 'Hi honey, I'm home,' he bellowed in a friendly drunk way as the screen door clattered open. He clumped down the corridor, towards Annaliese's room. 'I've brought your friend Curtis.'

Annaliese shrieked and her chair rolled forcefully across the floor. 'Go away. Go away.' Her door, which had been ajar, slammed shut. 'Leave me alone. I've got really bad cramps.'

Mark turned, stuck his fingers in his ears and scrunched his eyes shut. 'Aargh, women's business.' He shrugged, as if women were a mystery not worth the trouble of trying to solve. 'Come and I'll show you.'

He opened his door and led me into his room. It smelled fetid and closed up. There was junk all over his desk, and Rammstein and Donnie Darko posters on the walls. He had embraced the archetype, with one notable exception. Near the window was a tank full of bright fish, with veiled tails trailing behind them. They looked like the aquatic equivalent of Bratz dolls.

'Hey girls,' he said, and the fish seemed to flare up, moving skittishly around the tank and taking on more vivid colours. 'It's you. They don't know you. You might be a threat. And that's just the girls.' We walked further in. 'You can keep up to ten of them in one tank – the females – as long as you have plenty of weed for the non-dominant ones to hide in. Not the same with the boys though. They go crazy.' The buckled drunken grin told me he liked the prospect of crazy. 'Fancy goldfish. That's what Mum reckons they are. She thinks I've got about three of them. And over there's what she doesn't know.'

He led me across to the far side of the room. On the floor, on a trolley base that could slip under his bed, were another dozen fish, each in its own small compartment. They whipped around when they saw us, and puffed up and flared.

'That's the boys. It's a barracks, a betta barracks.' The consonants fell over each other on the way out, and he stopped to steady himself. 'Betta's the genus name. That's how you keep the males.' It was one large tank, with dividers marking out each fish's territory and keeping them apart. 'They'd rip each other to bits if you put them all in the one container. Like, totally to bits. There'd be nothing but fin debris.'

He was impressed by the fury pent up in these small bright fish. Facts started coming out of him. He talked about their labyrinth organ, and how it made them halfway to a lung fish and meant they could survive in a small amount of stagnant water, even the water in a water

175

buffalo's hoof print. He told me the males made bubble nests when they were happy, and for breeding. One digression stumbled into another, with varying degrees of coherence. He opened a cupboard and showed me his stores of fish food, freeze-dried bloodworm, brine shrimp and a box labelled Hikari Betta Bio-Gold Bites.

'Bloodworm,' he said vaguely, squishing it around in the unopened packet. 'They love their bloodworm.'

I asked him who fed them when he and Annaliese were with their father and he said, 'Oh, that's never more than two nights, usually one. He's, um, disengaged. I think that's what we call it. I'm oppositional defiant – which covers all kinds of bad shit – and we call him disengaged. Because somehow the word cunt went out of fashion.' He said it in a tough-guy way, but half choked on the big word and started to go red. He cleared his throat and his voice came back scratchy. There he was, a sneaky fish breeder who could barely swear, boasting about his badness and the label someone had given him. 'I fast them then, when we're with him. You've got to, anyway. Weekly. Give them the inside of a pea – one each – and then fast them. Constipation's death to a betta. That's a quote. I read it somewhere. A website, so, you know . . .'

I didn't know. The idea got stuck. I asked him what he did when he went on holidays with his father. He was gripping the back of his chair and leaning heavily against it. He stared in the direction of the female tank, but probably past it. His mind was off dwelling on some point connected with fish maintenance or trying to catch it as it drifted away in the boozy haze.

'Hmm? That's not how he is with holidays. He

takes holidays *from* us, not *with* us. Disengaged.' He was mustering up the courage to revisit the word that had made him blush. '*We* might go on a holiday though. Mum and Liese and me. That could be a risk. I haven't had them that long though, the bettas. I was hoping we'd get the right kind of new neighbour. Old man Novak wouldn't have remembered, or done it right. Or kept his mouth shut. We go for weekends to my grandparents at the coast sometimes, but I pea the fish on Friday after school and we're home by Sunday and they're good with that.'

In the next room, Annaliese was typing hard. She would be able to hear voices, but not any of the content. I was being enlisted as an accomplice to the secret fish farm.

'It could all get a bit complicated when I start breeding though. That's the plan. Breeding.' He gazed down into the barracks at his boys. 'The big plan. I need breeding tanks and vinegar eels and brine shrimp eggs. I'm not there yet. But I've got a buyer who'll take them. A shop that'll take them for five bucks each minimum. Reckons he can sell as many as I can get him.'

Outside, at the front of the house, a car engine revved as it came closer. There was a squeak from the brakes, and the engine stopped.

'Mum,' he said, matter-of-factly. He smirked. 'Now it starts.'

'What about her roster? I thought you said she was on a late.' I could hear Kate's feet on the wooden front steps, her key in the lock.

Mark drifted out of his room, his smirk now a see-sawing smile. 'Yeah. I must have read it wrong.

177

Sometimes you have to follow the line practically all the way across the page.'

Kate called out 'Hello' as she swung the door open and, as she looked Mark up and down, I noticed again how drunk he was. I'd got used to the sway, the unusual amount of self-disclosure.

'Annaliese,' she said loudly.

'Leave me alone.' Annaliese's voice came out still sounding angry, and she didn't open her door. 'I'm doing my homework. I'm having really bad period pain.'

Mark stuck his fingers in his ears and went 'La la la.'

Kate frowned and said, 'No you aren't. It's not . . .'

'What? Now I have to prove it to you?'

'No, no, sorry.' Kate backed down. 'It's just that I thought . . . doesn't matter.' She was now giving Mark her attention.

'Special occasion,' he said, slurring it more than he needed to.

'Derek, Derek from the band, is back and staying at my place.' I felt obliged to try to broker the best peace I could. 'And the special occasion is that it's not every day you meet a dickhead as big as Derek.'

Mark went 'Woo' and punched the air, as if he'd accomplished something. He turned pale, quite abruptly. 'And now I'm going to the toilet.'

He crossed the room at an angle, moving quickly and like a worried crab, his right hand coming up to his mouth.

'And you,' Kate said, sizing me up as if I was a candidate for a TV show called When Good Influences Go Bad, 'You seem sober.'

'I was out of the house for an hour or so. I had no idea

this would happen. Somehow, Derek and Mark found each other. Low-level mayhem ensued. I hadn't had the chance to talk the special-occasion rule through with Derek.'

She gave it some thought. 'I need a cup of tea. We should have a cup of tea.'

She put her bag down on the sofa and walked with purpose into the kitchen.

'I think it'll be okay.' I couldn't work out why I'd said it. It would do no good.

'Oh, really?' She stopped, yanked open the pantry door. 'Because you're the expert when it comes to okay in these sorts of matters?' She pulled out a box of tea bags and held it out for me to choose.

'No, I mean, I think Mark will be okay.' I pulled a bag out without looking. Another fell on the floor. 'That can be mine. I mean with other things.' I lowered my voice. 'The money. Mark's money. It's essentially legitimate, and so is what he plans to do with it.'

'What's *essentially* legitimate? Why do you sound like a politician dancing around a big fat lie?'

'Okay, fair point. It's all legal. He writes for magazines. Pieces on a range of topics. For money.' It was a trade-off. Put one issue to rest while another took its turn front and centre, show Kate things weren't all bad. That was the rationale, though it was all about me, really, and Kate walking in to see me as an agent of disarray. 'And some of the topics are, well, maybe fine. And others of them are a bit more like porn. Or pig killing.'

She shuddered. There had been no good way to put it. 'And the okay bit of this would be?'

179

'He doesn't kill anything. Or do the porn stuff. And he's got a great imagination. That could take him a long way.' Dance, politician, dance. Dance around the big fat lie. 'And the money's just for a hobby.'

She unplugged the kettle, and took it to the sink. 'A hobby? So, not some money-making venture? That's not like him.'

'Okay, it's a hobby that crosses over into a money-making venture. Or may do if it works out.'

'Mmm . . .' She had her back to me as the kettle filled, but I was no less under scrutiny.

'And it's possible he may not go to a lot of trouble with the tax paperwork, but other than that it's all okay. Right up there with cake stalls and garage sales. And that's all I can say, or it'll be a complete breach of trust.'

'Okay,' she said, 'okay,' perhaps relieved, perhaps not. She was thinking it through, actively wishing porn, pig killing, delinquency and jail out of his future, wanting to mother him out the other side of adolescence to something better. 'He just . . . His father does nothing with him, so this is what happens. There's nothing acceptably male in his life. And then along comes Derek, and that works out really well.'

Metres away, behind the half-closed bathroom door, Mark had started heaving his guts up into the toilet.

'Well, maybe when Derek's gone I could . . . do something. Some non-drinking acceptably male thing.' Annaliese was hiding in her room because of me. Mark had his head in the toilet because of me. It wasn't much to offer to do something, though I had no idea what it might be.

180

Kate looked past me towards the bathroom door. 'Don't feel obliged.' She plugged the kettle in and pushed the switch down. Mark heaved again, and moaned. Kate opened her eyes wide, and shook her head. 'I might go in there and check up on things. Such a good parent. It can't all be down to Campbell, can it? One inexplicable tantrum, one too drunk for homework. It's a great day on Gap Creek Road. Why don't we all just put Child Safety on speed dial?'

♩

'YOU'RE WORKING ON THAT?' It was Derek's voice, a cracked version of it that wasn't ready to start the day. 'That's going to be really good. What are you going to do with it?'

I was in the studio and Lost in Time, the song sent overnight by Gunnar and Øivind, was playing. I could see their point about getting Annaliese to do backing vocals, but I wasn't sure now that it was ever going to happen. And that was a story that could not be explained to them by email, or ever.

'Hey, this is me listening to it for the first time.' I had ideas and I didn't want to lose them. I was making notes. 'I might have to give it some more thought. And shut the door or you'll let the heat in.'

I heard the door rumble and clunk, my attention still on my notes, and Derek came and sat next to me. For about a minute, he said nothing while I wrote. He swivelled the chair around a couple of times and then stopped and stifled a groan. I put my pencil down.

He was, predictably, dishevelled, and in the clothes he had fallen asleep in the previous afternoon. His face was creased and his tan now appeared chemical and unhealthy. He was looking around the studio, seeing what I'd got for myself.

'Hey, fuck, Space Invaders,' he said, his voice still with a rasp in it, but not the sluggishness of before. 'I'm going to kick your arse at this the second I'm in the time zone.'

'The time zone? That'd be the place where you don't drink all those beers, would it?' If he was going to boast about kicking my arse, I was going to call his hangover what it was.

'What?' he said, not listening or not understanding. Or not caring.

He rolled across to the game console on his chair. He gazed down at the glass, his hair hanging in front of his face. I wasn't certain if he was going to play, sleep or vomit. I picked up my pencil and tried to go back to work.

He fumbled around, and I heard a switch click and then the familiar blast of electric alien noises that said the machine had come to life. My ideas for the Splades were rapidly losing their clarity, and they disappeared completely as his game began in a clatter of erratic knob work and klutzy firing. It all went wrong fast. He took the aliens out piecemeal and they descended and monstered him.

'Fuck it,' he said. 'It used to last longer, right?'

'I think you forgot the key level-one tactic about knocking the aliens out in columns.'

'Yeah, whatever.' He was staring down at the screen as the sample game appeared and started playing. 'It's the chair that's the problem. You shouldn't do it on a chair with castors.'

'Well, you just let me know when you want to kick my arse, okay?'

It was as if we had found ourselves straight back on tour. I could hear my own smugness, but I couldn't seem to stop it. All this over a twenty-cent arcade game from the late seventies.

'Mitchell Froom's place is a bit more settled than this,' he said, looking at the unruly cables and the boxes I hadn't yet unpacked. 'But I guess you've just moved in.'

'So, he's producing your new stuff?'

He looked non-committal. That meant the answer was almost certainly no. The mere name drop was to put me in my place. Mitchell Froom was a legend, I was the newbie being tried out on the Splades.

'I don't know yet,' he said eventually. 'It's early days. Early days in this new post-band-implosion life.' He pushed some streaky hair out of his face, and yawned. 'He's got a great set-up though. None of that big-studio shit. You get to use, like, the actual kitchen. He's got great snack food. You could learn a thing or two from Mitchell Froom about snack food. There's this almond thing . . .'

Weariness meant that he lost interest, and let the self-aggrandising anecdote slide. He gave another big yawn, and stretched his arms up in the air. His hands settled on the back of his head. His eyes looked watery.

'And, just like at Mitchell's place, here you get to use the actual kitchen. In which I could make you some French toast for breakfast, if you happened to be so inclined.'

'Yes,' he said emphatically. 'Yes. French toast. Definitely so inclined.' He stood up, as if his body had new anti-gravity energy already. 'I knew I was staying here for a reason.'

My notes were scrawled, I realised. I'd written them too quickly, and didn't know if they'd make sense when I got back to them. Derek pulled the door open, stepped into the glare with his hand up to his eyes and led the way to the kitchen.

He sat at the table while I whisked.

'Mmm, it's that cunning blend of herbs and spices,' he said rustily, his chin on his hand.

'I think you'll find that's KFC. But thank you. Vanilla, cinnamon and a pinch of nutmeg, and then a good long soak.' My Delia Smith side came out of nowhere, flushed out by Derek's haphazard way of putting it. Even when he really liked something, he would only half-try when it came to turning it into words. I had never been able to resist correcting him, however prim it made me sound. I lowered the first piece of bread into the egg mixture.

'That Splades stuff . . .' He was gazing past me, out the window. 'You could go well with that. With a bit of luck.' He swirled his coffee around, picking up foam that had caked to the inside of the cup. 'I liked the kid next door.'

'You don't remember the kid next door.' I turned the bacon, swirled the bread in the mixture.

'Sure I do.'

'What's his name?'

There was a pause as he gave it serious consideration, his eyes as blank and defocused as a doll's. 'You know I'm not a name person. And I'm waking up very slowly.'

'Mark. His name is Mark.' The bread hit the pan with a sizzle.

'Mmm. French toast.'

'Okay, Homer. We're only minutes away now.' I made room for the second piece of bread and dropped it into the pan. 'You should remember his name because we've been invited around there for dinner tonight, unless you have other plans.' It had been Kate's idea at a time when Mark's vomiting was reaching a crescendo, and I would have said yes to anything. 'Mark was hurling so much when I left yesterday I could have sworn I heard his pancreas hit the bowl.'

'Mmm. Sweetbread.'

I put the tongs down and laughed. Derek's creased face smiled.

'The point, Homer, is that havoc was wreaked. Young Markie brought up internal organs, and tonight we're showing him it doesn't have to be that way. Try to imagine it – you, sober, substance-free and behaving like a decent human being.'

'Or what? I get time on the naughty step?' He gave another yawn. 'Geez, is there no caffeine in this coffee? We're not starting the substance-free thing now, are we? I can be quite dislikeable substance-free.' There was a free shot on offer, and this time I was going to be the good host and decline to take it. 'Do we really have to? Is this, like, locked in?' I wished it wasn't. I wished guilt hadn't got the better of me. It seemed like the worst, most dangerous way to spend an evening, dragging Derek next door to try out his smarm-and-charm routine on a wounded Annaliese and a shitty Kate.

'I had to do something to calm his mother down.'

185

'Oh really? And calming mothers is a thing you do now?' He pushed the coffee cup across the table away from himself and then slouched back in the chair. 'It sounds like you've got yourself a great substitute for a life here. I wish I could be you. It was just a few beers. He's got to learn how to drink a few beers.' He stared blankly, dumbly, at the wall. 'My father, he was fucking cross-eyed. And no one told me.'

I turned the French toast. I didn't know what to say. I wanted to backtrack. I was stuck at 'I wish I could be you', but nothing could be said about that now. There was a fine line between glib and contemptuous, and I told myself he had meant to be glib.

'It's the way it's pressing on his brain. The tumour.' He said it Schwarzenegger-style, more like 'too-ma', and he made himself smile. It was a forlorn attempt to consign it to fiction, to make it as powerless as a sub-plot in a movie, over which the action hero would invariably triumph. If you could say it Arnie-style, it couldn't be entirely real. It couldn't be that serious. 'One eye is kind of stuck looking down and in. It's like he's got a bug on his nose and he can't stop watching it.' His chair scraped back as he stood up. 'Okay, I'll come. Tonight. It's not as if I have plans. And it sounds excellent.' He said it as if it was the biggest burden imaginable. 'Hey, don't burn that. I've waited months for this French toast.'

I slid it onto the plate just in time. I sliced a banana over the top and put the bacon on the side. His father was propped up in a bed at the Wesley, two pictures of the world coming in and not fitting over each other – two bed ends, two views of the garden – as the mass in

his head pressed out and forward, compressing complicated strands of tissue and rendering them useless.

I put the plate in front of Derek and he said, 'And the
maple syrup would be . . .'

I fetched it from the pantry. He took a close look at
the label.

'Genuine article. You are living well.' He poured it
zigzag across the French toast and a slick of it collected
near the bacon. 'So, they do the thing today. The biopsy.'
He was cutting the toast, loading up his fork. 'The hole
in the head. After that it's probably radiotherapy. It's not
an easy area to poke around.' His voice had started to
go shaky, and he put the fork down. 'Some more of that
coffee would be good. I can make it if you tell me how
the machine works.'

I took his cup and said, 'No, that's fine. Eat the French
toast while it's hot.' I took the coffee from the freezer
and emptied the old coffee grounds into the bin. 'So
how was it yesterday, seeing him there? How was he?'

'Oh, he was in and out. In and out of the room, I
mean. He had tests. He can't read properly. That shits
him. But, you know, when the tumour size comes down
that'll hopefully be different.' He pushed the first corner
of French toast into his mouth, chewed mechanically.
'It's, you know, weird. He's better with buttons if he
closes his eyes, or the bad eye at least. He's got an eye
patch, but he won't wear it. It's this flesh-toned plastic thing. And this is my father, right? Never needed
help in his life. He's got these really ugly pyjamas. He
never wears pyjamas. And my mother's fussing around,
annoying him any chance she gets.'

I scooped new coffee into the metal cup, tamped it

187

and locked it into the machine. 'It must have been a long day.'

'Yeah,' he said. 'Yeah, it was. Sorry I drank all the Stella.'

'Hey, it's for drinking. I hadn't quite anticipated it'd all go in an afternoon, but I hear they've made some more.'

I sat down opposite him. He was crunching bacon, and blinking. He rubbed his eyes. He cut another large piece of French toast and ate it. He made an mmm noise and pointed approvingly at the plate. He chewed and chewed, and sniffed, and looked like he couldn't swallow. Then it was down.

'Man, good,' he said. 'I think I made you do the third album for the food.'

'I knew there had to be a reason.'

'Hey, that was a good record. A really good record. You know it was.'

'It was.'

He snapped a bacon rasher with his knife and pushed a piece onto the next mouthful of toast. He liked his bacon crispy.

It was as if I was watching a tour breakfast, any one of dozens of tour breakfasts on a methodical city-by-city advance through the US Midwest.

'Have you heard from Jess lately?' I wanted Derek not to know about her engagement, to be as in the dark as I had been. I had to ask.

'Yeah,' he said. 'Once or twice.' He stopped eating. 'So you know then?'

'Yeah.'

The coffee machine hissed, and as coffee started to drip into his cup I poured some milk into a jug and went to froth it. Out the window, I could see washing on the line next door.

'You know I wouldn't have slept with her in St Louis if it hadn't been over, right?' he said behind me, through a mouthful of food. 'And she'd had a lot to drink. An awful lot. And I was kind of wasted, of course.'

Milk was spilling all over the counter before I could take the words in.

'You didn't know. Oh, fuck, you didn't know.' He was out of his chair, coming forward. 'She said she'd tell you. She told me she'd . . .'

Milk was running from the edge of the counter. He grabbed a tea towel and I said, 'Not a tea towel. There's a cloth in the sink . . .'

'It was just one time,' he said, tea towel clamped to the edge of the counter, sopping up milk. 'You've got to understand that.' He was looking panicky. The milk was beating him. 'In St Louis, two days before she left the tour in Louisville. She was upset. It was just . . . it just happened. We met in the bar, before the show.'

'No, she went for a walk before the show.' I was back there, working hard on every memory I had of that particular day, looking for clues, looking for it to be untrue. 'I told her to be careful. She said she always was.'

'Well, she came to the bar. It was just to talk. She drank scotch. Way too much. I already had some pills on board. She started crying, and then my arms were round her, and then I guess I just kissed her, or she kissed me . . .'

'For fuck's sake – you think I want to hear this?' I wanted him to stop. He was on his knees, mopping milk, rushing through this story that was cutting into

189

me. 'You think it's not enough that you slept with her? Do I have to hear every goddamn detail?'

'It was . . . She was . . .' Milk ran over his hand and down the cupboard door.

'I know what she was. I know how shit things had become between us. We could hardly talk. She didn't exactly mention in her last email that she'd fucked you but, from the spelling, it was clearly written in a hurry and it wasn't meant to be comprehensive.'

'It was like a video. It wasn't like it was really happening. It just kept going. From the bar, to my room . . .'

I pulled the tea towel from his hands and threw it into the sink, hard. It was sodden with milk and it hit with a clang.

'Could you at least have the decency . . .' I was shouting down at him. He was crouched on the floor and I was shouting. I could hear myself, but the words and the force of them felt like they came from somewhere else. He recoiled against the low cupboard. I made myself take a breath. 'The decency to stop squirming around trying to tell me that you aren't responsible at all?'

He steadied himself with his hands. I stepped back, and he stood up slowly.

'I'm sorry,' he said. 'It was just that one time.'

He went back to his cold French toast. He sat there, but he didn't eat it. I poured more milk into the jug, and then just stared at it. St Louis. There had been no change there, no signal, nothing I could recall that stood out on any part of that day. Nothing other than Jess and me peeling away from each other, and I already knew about that. We had got our relationship down to terse loveless conversations about the practicalities. She read books, listened to her iPod, retreated. I focused on business and factored her in nowhere. Derek had warned me, he had even warned me. Earlier in the tour he had pointed it out to me, said she seemed lost.

I didn't know it, but she was talking to him then. Emailing home, running up phone bills, testing out the idea of leaving. Of course she was. There was nothing out of the blue about what happened in Louisville.

The shock of it was through me, I thought. I couldn't put the scene out of my head, couldn't stop myself picturing it, but it was landing on a dead spot now.

'I'd better take you to the Wesley,' I told him, as civilly as I could manage.

'You don't have to. I can get a cab.' He looked wary.

'They're not quick out here. So stop looking at me as if I'm Ivan Milat and I just asked you for a shovel. I'm doing this for your parents. You should be there. And right now you shouldn't be here.'

I told him he might want to put some shoes on, and I went to find my keys.

I couldn't find and name the one point where it had gone wrong with Jess. I couldn't grasp the point when it had been right, though I knew there had been one. I wanted to show him his actions were not as powerful as he thought, that I wouldn't be hurt so greatly by what he had told me, or by what he had done. I wanted him to sit in silence, guilty silence, as we drove to the hospital. I wanted to be better than him. And at the very same time I wasn't, since his father's skull was about to have a hole put in it and a piece of tumour taken out, and my intentions were all about punishing Derek for stepping in when Jess was vulnerable and lost and our relationship had already faded till it had no colour left in it.

☊

THERE WAS NO SUGGESTION of remorse remaining by the time he got back from the hospital. I had wasted a day staring at the walls. I had driven down the road to the Gap Creek Reserve carpark and tried a walk in the dry bush, but it had been too hot and I had lost the stamina for hills long ago.

Derek came back in a cab, and walked through the door saying, 'I should have got wine for dinner. I forgot about dinner.' I reminded him about the substance-free theme of the evening and he said, 'Oh, yeah,' without really listening. He was already walking past me, on his way to the kitchen.

He stood at the coffee machine, trying to work out how to use it. I told him to sit down and I would make it for him. He sat in the chair where he had eaten breakfast. I frothed his milk, and there were no revelations this time. The earlier conversation wasn't mentioned. I had a picture in my head of him leading Jess to his room, his VingCard in his hand, ready to unlock the door. That stupid drug look on his face, Jess's eyes down.

'His head was shaved,' he said. 'They had to do half his head but he made them do it all. He was gone on the Valium when I got there. Just ten milligrams and he was wasted. I guess it's lack of practice. Then we just sat there for two hours once they took him away. My mother does sudoku. I didn't know that. I didn't really know what sudoku was.'

I put his coffee and the sugar in front of him and concentrated on finding him a spoon.

'And he came back and his mouth was hanging open and he was really pale, with this big bandage round his head. He was sleeping it off. They brought his lunch in and took it away again. I thought they'd knocked one of his teeth out with the tubes, but apparently it's been gone for years. A canine one, or something, one of those ones on the way to the molars.'

'And the biopsy? How did that go?'

He was talking around the margins, telling me nothing, skirting around it himself perhaps. I didn't need to know about his father's teeth, or his mother's sudoku habit.

'Oh, we'll know more tomorrow. It's a tumour of some kind. They're pretty sure of that, but they need to know the type. So, that's it for now.' He shrugged, putting distance between himself and the bad news that could turn horrible, and he finished stirring his coffee. 'We'll know more tomorrow, maybe.' He tapped the spoon on the side of the cup, then looked around for somewhere to put it. I took it from him. 'And he should be out tomorrow too. It wasn't a big hole. So, tonight, should I go and get wine?'

'Same answer as before. Let's skip the wine.'

'Good,' he said. 'Right.'

And Jess? What about Jess? What about St Louis? For much of the day I'd rehearsed our next conversation, but his head was still at the Wesley and it wasn't the time for it.

He went to check his email while I watched the news on TV. I expected him to come back in from the studio with more big-noting stories name-dropping new famous friends who had emailed him, but then I heard him in the shower. He came out in a towel with his hair standing on end and nothing to report. He went to the fridge and poured himself a glass of water. He had a top-heavy body, more so than the previous time I'd seen him, gym arms and pecs and spindly legs.

I imagined him padding around hotel rooms, light on the balls of his feet, striking poses in the mini-bar mirror, loving his own bulky shape among Pringle tubs and mini-Scotches. Behind him the hotel bed, sheet turned back: St Louis. In my head, it was still St Louis.

☊

THE SUN WAS BEHIND the hill when we set out for next door. Its light still caught the treetops and the top of Mount Coot-tha, but down at ground level the cicadas were switching on.

'This is great,' Derek said. 'Going to the neighbour's place for dinner. It's so . . . neighbourly. I don't know who I live next door to in LA.'

'Could be LA, could be you – who's to say?'

He laughed, but just enough to acknowledge that the line was a joke. 'Mark, right? The kid?'

'Yeah.'

He seemed to take pride in remembering, as if I'd sold him short and he had the stuff of neighbour-liness after all. LA – it was all LA that was to blame for the lack of it in his life across the water. He was okay.

'And his mother's Kate and his sister's Annaliese,' I told him, 'but obviously you won't be expected to know those just yet. I'm just telling you so you can practise them a few times now and get ahead of the game.'

'Kate, Annaliese, right,' he said. 'Test me on them before we get to the door.'

A car drove past. Dust kicked up and billowed in its wake. Annaliese's bedroom light was on. Derek kicked at a stone that he could barely see, his Converse sneaker sending it skittering along the road.

'They're pretty good, the Wesley people,' he said. 'Once I'm in Dad's room, they give us a bit of space. I have to send Mum out for the sandwiches, though. You know how it is. I just can't do the chat when I'm there.'

'Yeah.' There was no ego in it. It was just Derek's reality. He was the lead singer, so there was no peace for him, anywhere. He couldn't buy a sandwich without someone wanting a turn, wanting their own Butterfish anecdote, of which he had plenty – mostly riotous stories of high living and decadence gone wrong. 'That's good. That's a good thing. It's not the time for all that.'

The verandah light came on as we approached the house. I must have slowed down. Derek was ahead of me, and then stopping for me to catch up. I was one conversation short of ready for the night – the straightening-out conversation with Annaliese that I kept not having.

I wished I had kept her in the studio a few minutes more and found her a better way out. An end to the encounter that she could have walked away from, rather than fleeing. It was as if there was some magic good thing I should have said, but I still hadn't found it.

I led the way up the steps and knocked on the door. I could hear a TV on inside, then Kate's voice and the murmur of Mark's in reply. A chair rumbled on castors, nearby, and the door swung open. Annaliese was wearing leggings and a loose T-shirt, and her hoop earrings again.

'Hello,' she said flatly, as if it took more effort than it could possibly be worth. She looked at my chest, and then past me. It was as though my face was pixelated and couldn't be seen.

'Hi, I'm Derek.' He stepped forward, around me. 'You must be Annaliese. Curtis was telling me about you.'

'No I wasn't.' The answer snapped out of me, right at Annaliese.

'Okay,' he said slowly, with the caution reserved for the dangerously mad. 'Well, that's weird.' He had a coy smile, as if he was onto something. 'Let me be clear.' Still the slow careful voice of the hostage negotiator. 'Curtis has told me nothing about you. Nothing. Just the name. And even that was on the way here.'

'Right,' Annaliese said. 'Well, hello.' She shook her head, as if we were both old fools, but harmless in the end. 'Come in.'

We followed her, with Derek mouthing 'What?' and signalling confusion, and me trying to wave his gesture away. None of it made sense to him. She was sixteen and she hadn't fawned. She had played the whole thing tough and given no hint of welcome. And I, of course, had behaved like a freak. Mark was standing near the dining table, and he half-lifted his hand to acknowledge us. He was wearing a black Sepultura T-shirt with a semi-nude Viking-style wench contorting under the band name. Kate stepped out from behind the kitchen counter with a large spoon in her hand.

'Oh, hello,' she said, taking a good look at Derek, the real Derek Frick, here in her loungeroom. This was more like it, more like what Derek was expecting.

'Mum, Derek. Derek, Kate,' Annaliese said, dispatching the introductions with efficiency. 'And I believe you know my brother, Mark.'

Derek's gym-built body swaggered forward on his undersized legs. Kate reached out to shake his hand as if he'd just been dipped in pheromones and all her receptors were jangling. I could have done without it. Annaliese glared at her, but Kate wasn't noticing.

'Welcome,' she said, with a hint of a nervous flutter in her voice. She cleared her throat. 'It's very good to meet you.'

'You too,' Derek said, shaking her hand and shamelessly looking her up and down. 'Yeah. Pleasure's all mine.'

He finally released her hand, and then encouraged his hair to fall forwards over his eyes so that he could brush it slowly aside in a gesture that a cheap body-language paperback had told him was particularly alluring. I knew his playbook, and I knew it all too well. Most of his moves were as sophisticated as a chicken scratching around in a barnyard, but they worked far more often than they should have.

'Curtis has told me so much about you,' Kate said, her eyes still drawn to Derek. It was my turn to feel like the speedbump. Then, like a boat righting itself in a storm, the better Kate, the real Kate, was back. 'But it's okay – I'm sure at least half of it's not true. With the exception of you making this impressionable young boy ill yesterday.' She was smiling, making something of a joke of it, while at the same time not letting him off the hook.

'Ah, yes,' Derek said, on the back foot, pheromones evaporated without good effect. 'Yes, sorry about that.'

She laughed, and asked him how he was enjoying being back.

Annaliese turned to me, and in a tough whisper said, 'What have you told him?'

'Nothing. Nothing.'

She looked into my eyes, angry with me anyway, even if I had truly said nothing. 'Whatever.'

'No, not whatever.'

'Drink?' Kate said, looking my way.

My mind was blank, but she held up a bottle of mineral water and I said, 'Great. Thanks.'

She filled a glass and set it on the counter for me. She pressed a button on the microwave and said, 'Right, now we're in action.'

An electric wok was sitting on the bench top. Next to it were boards piled with chopped chicken and capsicum and shallots. Kate twisted a dial and a red light came on, and she picked up a bottle of oil. I noticed she had a Band-Aid around the tip of her left index finger. Her new knife was in the sink.

She glanced back my way and said, 'Someone's going to get a fingertip, and that's just how it is.' She held her hand over the wok to check the heat. 'Any suggestions, Curtis?'

'Get it really hot. Hot and quick is the way to go.'

'I'm still at the fingertip part,' Derek said.

Annaliese stepped in. 'Curtis bought Mum a knife. A really sharp one. So this was kind of inevitable.'

Kate slid the chicken from the board and it hit the wok with a hiss. She recoiled, then started moving it around with the spoon. Mark went to the fridge and kept his back to us while he drank Coke Zero from the bottle. He opened the freezer door and did a ripping gassy burp into it before shutting it – his own private comedy, hanging out on the other side of the kitchen freezing his burps.

'So . . .' Kate said, her eyes down on the wok as she skidded the chicken around on the hot black surface. The end of the fob-watch chain she was wearing as a bracelet kept clinking against the edge but she maintained her focus on the contents. 'Do you wok much, Curtis?'

We talked through it, step by step. I resisted the urge to ask for the spoon. Derek leaned against the counter with his mineral water, watching us as if he'd walked in on the second episode of a TV series and was trying to work out what had happened in the first. I hadn't mentioned the knife to him, or the salmon recipe tutorial. I hadn't prepared him for Annaliese at all.

'Call me when it's ready,' she said, and made a move towards her room.

'Liesie, I was hoping you could serve the rice.' Kate glanced up from the wok only briefly, but her look held every maternal hope for peace, decorum and a reasonable night.

Annaliese sighed and pushed past me to the drawer, where she found a large spoon. She stood watching the numbers on the microwave fall and the rice cooker turning on the plate. Mark muffled another burp with his hand, and then sorted through the letters magneted to the fridge until he found a second D and could spell the word 'DILDO'.

Kate scraped the vegetables into the wok. The microwave pinged and Annaliese swore as the steam billowed around her when she opened the lid of the rice cooker. Kate added soy sauce and set her face into a look somewhere between uncertain and fraught as the cooking reached its climax. Mark rearranged his groin in his large shorts. It took both hands. Derek had a look of restrained glee, as if I had taken him from celeb world and the world of brain biopsies and gifted him a peephole into some kind of mad house – a place where nothing was false and every petty, scratchy thought was instantly ventilated.

The meal was served, and we took our plates to the table. Someone had set a fork at each place, rolled in a coloured serviette.

'Now, I'm a bit uncertain about all this,' Kate said. The rest of us were poised to eat. 'I got the wok as a present a while ago, but I haven't used it much.'

Mark dug in and, through his first mouthful, said, 'Hey, it's not bad. It's really not bad.' He speared another piece of chicken with his fork.

The tension that had hung in the air in the kitchen seemed to abate. With the meal made and signs all around of some success, Kate relaxed. I caught Annaliese's eye, quite by accident, and she almost smiled before she remembered I wasn't a candidate for any of that. Derek was answering a question of Kate's and found himself in a well-worn anecdote, but he didn't seem to mind. At the end he slipped into a story about a Berlin hotel we'd stayed in, which had set out so seriously to be cool that it, as he put it, 'lost its head up its own post-modernism' and was so oddly designed that we had each separately locked ourselves out of our rooms, semi-naked, when trying to find our bathrooms in the early hours of the morning. He had been standing in the bright light of the corridor, wondering what to do, when I had walked out of my own room six doors down.

He was warming to his preferred task of being the centre of attention when Kate asked him why he was home. It threw him for a second, since he'd slipped into performance mode and had forgotten his real life might be a topic here.

'Well, I hadn't seen . . .' he started, and then corrected himself. 'My father's having some medical tests. That's it mainly. But he'll be out of hospital tomorrow, so it looks like I'll be going back to LA on Friday.'

'So, does that mean the tests have gone well, or . . .' Kate stopped before offering the alternative. 'Sorry, it's not my business.'

'No, no it's fine. We still don't really know. We'll find out tomorrow.' He picked up his fork and rounded up some of the stray grains of rice on his plate.

LA on Friday. It was news to me.

The CD that was playing came to the end of its final track. It was Wilco's Summerteeth. It had come out the year before The True Story of Butterfish. I had played it a lot then, and I'd wanted to be half that clever. These were pop songs with wryness and wit, and stories that sounded like they came from real broken hearts, but they never gave up being pop songs. I could remember a conversation in a hotel bar with a journalist who had loved it as much. It was morning, the lights were up and a cleaner was flicking stray peanuts into a pan with a brush. The bar was closed, but that made it quiet and perfect for an interview. The smell of the previous night's drinks, beer and bourbon, leached from the carpet and upholstery.

We were on the rise then. Jess was on holidays from uni and along for the ride, my father was in deceptively good health.

And now Derek was going back to LA in just two days. There was his father, biopsied and bandaged and lopsided as his almost-certain tumour pushed his brain around, and Derek had his exit plans made.

'Why don't you pick the next one?' Kate said to him, and he ducked under my gaze and headed for the stereo.

He chose Billy Joel's Songs In the Attic, which was surely an old CD of Kate's from the eighties. 'This one's for my good buddy Curtis,' he said in an old-time American radio DJ voice, 'a big fan of the Joelster who regrets only that you don't have his earlier work more comprehensively represented. As far as I can tell.'

Annaliese smirked and looked down at her dinner. Derek came back to the table and we proceeded to argue about the merits, or otherwise, of Summer, Highland Falls. I was for the merits.

'It's got a comma,' he said. 'Right in the middle of the title. So that's elegant, at least.'

🎧

'THEY DON'T EVEN ALPHABETISE their CDs,' he said as we bumped our stone-cold-sober way through the night, heading back to my house.

'It's not all about you, Derek.' He had been looking for the Bs. He always did, and never discreetly enough.

'I bet they don't have Written in Sand, Written in Sea. Arseholes.' He stopped, as if listening for something. The night was close to silent. He shook his fists at the sky in mock fury. 'Why didn't anyone keep the faith?'

But there was no faith. We were just a band. A band that panicked and fought and overcomplicated its third album. Somewhere up the road, through the trees, someone's front verandah light went on. Derek didn't see it.

'There were people who loved that album,' he said, tripping over his own feet in the dark. 'People who got it and thought it was brilliant.'

'And by now you've probably slept with both of them.'

'Oh, probably.' He said it as if it was wearily self-evident. It was a performance that straddled the fine line between parody and his vast but precarious ego-driven notion of himself, as usual. 'Hey, how about those neighbours? I totally get it now. I totally get why you'd be saying yes to dinner. I think I've got a mother–daughter thing going on. If that's the kind of crazy wrong thought that crosses your mind in the clean world, I should have brought some pills.'

'You mean, you and the two of them in some romp situation?'

'That's the one.' He was pitching it as if it was a great idea, one that amused him and maybe stirred him a little at the same time.

'I don't think that's how it works even at the Playboy Mansion. It's not the same as twins, Derek. Or miscellaneous busty faux-lesbians drenching each other in Cristal. Frankly, I think it's problematic with the twins as well but, you know . . . unless the mother and daughter thing is just about one of them holding the hose in your arse while the other one turns the tap and gives you the wash out?'

'Man,' he said unflappably, 'I worked out my colon's not a sexual place. Nothing that far in is. It just doesn't have the right receptors.' He stayed somewhere off in the thought for a while. It sounded wise, the way he put it, but it wasn't. He was irritating me with the way he was dragging my neighbourhood into his glibness. 'Are you, you know, with the teen, in any respect? Surreptitiously showing the schoolie some adult life?'

Anger surged in me, biologically. My heart jumped into my throat at a gallop and his head looked like a small but easy target. I wanted the dumb provocative look off his face. I could make it out in the moonlight, but also from memory.

'Look, just . . .' I got stuck there. I wanted to tell him to grow up. I wanted to tell him his father might be dying, and it was not an event to miss. I wanted him to stop drilling down to the thin seam of story that concerned the glitch in my relationship with Annaliese earlier in the week. 'Just stop being Derek Frick for a second, will you?'

'Hey, I was only checking to see that the way was clear. Didn't want to step on any toes. Who doesn't love a chick in uniform?'

Derek Frick was back in my life and trampling all over it. I'd had years of his smug pronouncements from his patch of amoral high ground, the harm he caused with a bleary feckless smile across his face. He stumbled on a rock and I grabbed him by the collar, pushed him back hard and our feet tangled and we crashed to the road. I landed on him and my head hit his face. His mouth opened and shut like the mouth of a fish. He gripped my shirt front but he couldn't breathe. I pushed myself up from the bitumen, and he lay there winded.

'How long before you fucked my wife did you stop being my friend?'

He blinked up at me, and gasped. He slapped the road with one hand and, finally, the air rushed in. He took big heaving breaths, and then pushed himself onto his side and up into a crouching position. He steadied himself with both hands and his breathing settled. He coughed, and spat onto the road.

'You wouldn't even know.' He said it quietly, still looking down at the road, but I heard it. 'You're such a shit communicator, you wouldn't even know.' He stood up slowly, and turned to face me. 'Is that blood?' He opened his mouth to give me a look. 'I think it's blood.'

'It's just spit.'

'It tastes like blood.'

'It's not blood.'

'Did we just have a fight? Did we just have a two-second piss-weak version of a man-on-man fight out here on the road? I think we did.' He laughed, and I thought I saw some blood run between his teeth.

'It's the picture all the magazines wanted. They just weren't here at the right time.' I was less angry. My heart was still flying along, but my muscles were spent. One lunge and a fall was all they had in them. There was an apology I owed him, I thought, but it was stuck in my throat waiting for an uncounted number that he owed me.

'And it wasn't about me stopping being your friend or being anything,' he said. 'The business side of it swamped the fun side of it. I found new ways to have fun, you stopped having fun. You didn't even tell Jess you'd stopped. You didn't tell her anything. The rest of us didn't know what to do when you got married. It was such a crazy bad decision. You know what I regret? More than the St Louis incident? Which I do regret, by the way, contrary to what you might think of me. I regret that I didn't stop you that stupid day beside the road on the outskirts of Reno when the two of you got married and she ran around getting the paperwork right while you went on with the job as though it hadn't happened. "Best day of my life" – that's what you should be saying about your wedding day. And you went through it like a fucking zombie.'

'Yeah. I'm not exactly proud of that myself.'

'I should have had the balls to stop you. That was the day I should have been your friend, but I was just another guy in the band.'

In the distance, an engine hummed. Ahead of us down the road, the air filled with a diffuse light and a car came over the crest of the hill. The pool of its head-lights fell closer to it as it tilted down the slope and came towards us. We stepped off the bitumen. It picked up speed and caught us, fleetingly, in its lights as it drove by. Derek was wiping blood from his chin.

We both turned to watch it go, as though it was something to marvel at, something rare and not often seen, a four-wheel-drive like all the others, its red tail-lights heading towards the forest.

'My parents want us both to go over there for dinner tomorrow night,' Derek said, as if a new start could be made to the conversation. 'They told me they hadn't seen you for ages. Didn't even know you were back. I said we'd cook. Which means you, obviously.'

With the camber of the road, he was standing a little below me and looked smaller than he was. There was none of his smugness now.

'Obviously,' I said. 'Well, I think I'm free. And the poor guy deserves something other than a plate of your nachos on his first night out of hospital.'

He laughed. 'Hey, how well is this visit going? I thought we might get to fix a few things if I stayed with you. That was seriously part of my plan.' He shook his head, wiped his chin again with the back of his hand. 'Let's get back to your place. I want to see where all this spit's coming from.'

🎧

'SO, YOU LINED THIS up to tell me you've finished the opera?' Patrick said when he came into Harveys and found me at a corner table. There was a cautionary tone to his voice.

207

'No. That didn't seem like such a good idea.' I folded the newspaper and put it down beside me.

He sat and picked up the laminated menu, glancing at it without reading. He turned it over in his hands a couple of times and tapped its edge against the glass table top, as if he was straightening a handful of loose pages. 'I'm sorry about that. For the strange reaction. I just . . . It had been in my garage and suddenly it was like it had slipped away from me, this crucial piece of Dad. And then it was becoming something else. He was gone but you were working on it together. You'd blown back into town and managed to find a way to him that I didn't have.' He stopped, and smiled. 'That sounds like I've been in therapy ever since. Which isn't the case – I have far too much self-belief for that. But my shitty reaction was about me, not about you. That's my point.'

'Thank you. And I'm not working on it, just so you know. There's a few bars I could play you if you ever wanted, but that's it.'

One of the staff came up with a notepad and we put our orders in. Patrick put on a glum face when I went for a plate full of fat and carbs, but this time he kept his thoughts to himself.

'So, the opera,' he said, leaning forward in his seat. 'What's it like? Is it any good?'

He was frowning, as if his expectations were low. Which meant he wanted it to be good, better than good. He wanted our father to have left us a great surprise that we could take out to an awe-struck world.

'It has its moments,' I told him.

The waiter arrived with a carafe of water and two glasses. Patrick didn't look up.

'It's bad, isn't it?' he said. 'That's what that means.'

'No, it's not bad. And I'm no real expert when it comes to the genre. Opera in general, not just the outback explorer sub-genre. There are some good ideas there, but I don't know. No hits. Maybe that's what I'm saying. And maybe that's not the way to think about opera. I've had too many conversations about music with the wrong people.'

He put his hand on his thigh. His phone was buzzing in his pocket. He pulled it out, looked at the number and said with a weary dismissiveness, 'Of course it's you. I'm going to have to take it.' He flipped the phone open and held it to his head. 'Miranda, what's happening?' His tone was breezy now, fake but convincingly so. 'Well, if you don't like it in orange we can try it in something else . . . If it's the shade that's bothering you we can go more tangeriney . . . Look, I'll be back in the office soon and I'll call you from there. This'll be easy to sort out. Really.' With Miranda duly placated for now, he finished the call and closed the phone. 'Bloody clients. I thought it was going to be a real issue.' He pushed the phone back into the pocket of his tight-fitting pants, and glared at the counter as if our meals were intolerably late. 'So, no hits,' he said. 'And there were all those letters from people who didn't want to help him.'

'It takes a lot to get an opera up and running.'

'Yeah. Opera. Why would you try it? And Sturt, Captain Sturt's Whaler. It sounds like a book that would win the Miles Franklin but that only about ten people would read. Why couldn't he have just got a few friends together and written some songs? He knew people, whiskery old jazz drummers, and all that. They could have played the Story Bridge Hotel on Sunday after-noons, surely.'

I could see them, veteran music teachers on their afternoon out, playing for beers and loving every second of it. But instead he'd shut himself in with a cocked-hat captain and the fantasy of an inland sea.

'He dreamed big,' I said, 'and I guess there's nothing wrong with that.' And then, inside his zipped-up chest, a scruffed-up old artery tore and blocked and his dream was boxed and put away.

'So, how's Derek?' Patrick said. 'How's all that going? Has he disgraced himself yet? How are the two of you?'

He knew there would be something to tell. Derek left stories in his wake wherever he travelled.

'He's fine. He's not coping at all with his father's brain thing which, from the little I know of it, seems like a big deal. He's at the Wesley now, or maybe at his parents' place since his father's getting discharged today. He's . . .' I was going to ramble and say something safe, drop in a few of Derek's LA stories, but I stopped myself. 'Did you know he slept with Jess? A couple of days before we broke up, before she left? That's been the big piece of news.'

His phone buzzed in his pocket again. He looked at me as if he was half a step behind and just catching up. His mouth was open. 'No. No. My god.' His phone stopped buzzing and, after a pause, a message came through. He honestly didn't know. I was more relieved than I'd expected to be.

'And then last night he made it sound like I made it happen. I'm a shit communicator, apparently.'

'Wow. I didn't think we said that. Not that directly

anyway.' He was fully caught up now, and ready to be himself again. 'But, really, how does that lure the dick out of the man's pants and on its way to his best friend's girl? I think there's a bit of responsibility to be accepted by a couple of other parties here, regardless of how you happened to be communicating.'

'Yeah, well, I showed him a thing or two about communicating last night. I sort of knocked him over onto the road. So that was sophisticated.'

'You knocked him onto the road? He's lucky he didn't steal your marbles or you might have stuck his head in the toilet or emptied his lunch box into the bin.' He pushed back in his chair and laughed. Behind him, our waiter served salads in high white bowls to the two women at the next table. 'But, really, I can't believe he and Jess did that. And then he puts it back on you and your communication skills when, to be honest, it's just that you're like Dad. And I don't mean that in a bad way at all. Things stay in your head and you don't even know it. You don't know that people haven't heard them while you've been thinking them. I did eighty percent of the talking in that house when we were growing up. Sometimes I talked just so there'd be noise other than Deutsche Grammophon.'

He was being straight with me, nothing more. I had spent much of my childhood wishing he had kept more in his head, without having any idea of how the silences were nagging at him. He enjoyed the clamour of advertising, the lunches, the pitches, the incessant talk. I had always thought they'd be the worst parts of his job, all of them competing for air and pulling him away from the quiet times when ideas come. Not for him. He had put

211

a name to this difference between us, and I had never seen it for what it was. Maybe that's what happens when you come along second. You don't notice those things. Perhaps he was like our mother. I wanted to ask.

He topped up my water, and then his own. The glass door swung open and a new group of people came in from the heat. They were led to a nearby reserved table for six. Four of them looked like ad agency people – funky frames to their glasses, spiky hair, shirts by industrie or someone similar – the other two were steely-haired middle-aged men in matching chambray shirts. Perhaps they sold cars or made nails or had a timberyard that had traditionally shot its ads on a handycam and featured a big-chested average-looking girl in a bikini getting memorably worked up about a pallet of four-by-two.

'Come back to me,' Patrick said, waving a hand in front of my face. 'Give me a bit more than twenty percent. Even if you're pissed off with me.'

'I'm not. I just hadn't seen it that way. I'm not pissed off with you. I don't even think you're wrong.'

I couldn't see our mother's features in his face, though I had only a few photos of her to go on. He was already older, I realised, than she had ever been. That was a new thought, and my breath stuck in my chest. I looked away from him, to the lengthy description of Harveys' version of osso bucco written in white on the pane of glass to his right.

'Look,' he said, 'someone should have pushed Derek into the dirt years ago. It would have been character building.' He reached out to his water glass, holding it with the tips of his fingers and thumb and rotating it like someone trying to crack a safe. It was a habit and I'd seen it before. It was nothing to do with drinking, and he was probably unaware of it. 'And very wise of you to do it deep in the anonymity of Kenmore. It would have been the wrong look entirely if you'd done it in midtown Manhattan when the band was breaking up.'

'My thoughts exactly. They hardly gave me a chance to anyway. They had us in adjacent rooms with two different publicists, drafting statements which they then swapped – the publicists actually met in the corridor to swap them – and we each took the red pen to whatever the other had written. I could see his back through the frosted glass. He always leans back in his chair. Sometimes I could see his shoulders pressed against the glass.'

'So, decking him in your own street I'd call a kind of progress. You know what I think?' It was rhetorical. He was going to tell me. He was winding up to tell me in a big brotherly way. I was up for it, up for some brothering. 'I think plenty of people's lives come unstuck. Weirdly, Chubs, yours came unstuck in a rockstar kind of way, and we all got to read about it, not that what was published was necessarily the true story. And in the end, it's not that much of a rockstar story anyway. It wasn't about drugs or any of that, any of the Derek shit. It was about Dad, and Jess, and the ride of a lifetime going off the tracks. So, suddenly there's this vacuum. A lot of people hit that vacuum, get a bit lost – a lot of people who are thirty-something. I tell you this as someone who has months of thirty-something left.' He put on a face that was meant to look wry and wise. He would be forty soon. 'This is just your mid-life crisis, Chubs. Everyone's entitled to one. Even you. Even the poster boy for dag rock. And, like Dad, you just put your head down and try to push through. Unobtrusively, no histrionics, with the exception of decking Derek. I'm assuming you haven't been dating Russians or writing operas . . .'

'No.' After talking about myself in thousands of interviews, I had finished every one knowing I'd be reconstructed paper-thin in the article. That was all I had given them – a paper-thin version of me – all I had let them notice. Occasionally a crack had opened up but that was the extent of it. Yet Patrick, my brother, knew me to my magma after all, knew some deeper hidden strata. And we were still here, still talking, and what he saw looked okay to him. The strongest part of what I felt was relief. 'No Russians, no operas.' I was thirsty, I needed water. I drank half a glassful. 'But I am getting my cabin cruiser refitted with a mighty pair of twin outboards . . . Actually, there was something I wanted to talk to you about, on the subject of cabin cruisers. Sort of.' I could hardly have made the link sound less natural if I'd tried. 'The young guy next door, Mark. He's fourteen and sarcastic in a clever way, and deafening himself with metal, and somehow I ended up telling his mother I'd do some kind of men's thing with him.'

'And you're calling on me because that's not what you're into?' He laughed. 'I don't think I do fourteen. I think there are laws about that. And I don't think I even do it in international waters, if that's where the cabin cruiser comes in.'

'I don't think it was that kind of men's thing she was thinking of. Though I'm sure she'd be fine if, one day, etcetera etcetera . . .'

He laughed till his head rocked back and he slapped the table with his hand. 'Excellent. Bake a big cake for his eighteenth birthday and leave room for me to pop out of it.'

The older of the two chambray-shirted men looked up from the laptop the agency people were showing him. He stared at Patrick, looking over his glasses and frowning as if he couldn't quite bring him into focus.

'His dad's a bit of a non-performer. His parents split up a few years ago. So Kate – his mother – wants some kind of positive male influence in his life. So far, Derek's got him stupidly drunk and – surprise, surprise – turned out not to be it. And I've got him over a couple of times to work on the garden, but that doesn't count for much. So I thought about manly things, like climbing a mountain, and then I realised that he'd hate it and I'm about half a lifetime undertrained. So how about the Powerboat club?' It sounded like a bad idea as soon as I heard myself say it. 'You've wanted to take a look at it since you found Dad's membership card. I think we both do. You, me, Mark, a drive to the coast and dinner at the Powerboat club. He's with his father this weekend, but they get back on Sunday afternoon.'

'The Powerboat Club? This Sunday?' he said, not immediately telling me I should just get myself less fat and kick a football with the kid instead. 'Is anyone . . .' He chose his next word carefully. 'Expecting this idea? I mean, I'm up for it – you know I am – but what about him? And anyone else. What's this actually about?'

'What am I supposed to do? Hire a stripper? I'm struggling for options here.' It would be time away from Campbell and Annaliese and his festering room, at least.

A pressure valve. A chance away from the dramas to eat at someone else's expense, evade homework, deride whoever he needed to. Not that I could honestly say it was entirely about Mark. From where Kate stood, I could easily look like nothing more than a lesser version of Derek, rolling in with a thoughtless kind of harm on offer. I didn't want that. 'If Rammstein's ever in town, maybe I could take him along, but there's nothing like that coming up. Not that I can see. And aside from the metal, his main interest seems to be online war games. And, confidentially, fish. Tropical fish.'

'What's confidential about fish?'

'He's a complicated boy.' Mark needed to be experienced, rather than explained.

Patrick emptied the last of the water from the carafe into our glasses. 'Sounds fascinating. Sounds well on the way to being thoroughly fucked up. Let's do it. Let's show him the most manly night the Caloundra Powerboat Club has to offer.' He laughed, at the prospect of Mark watching the two of us drink mid-strength beers while old people went mad for keno. 'I can't imagine you helping out the neighbours like this. No offence, but I'm not used to you as the "neighbourhood guy" yet.'

'I don't think anyone is. I'm not. If there's ever an official ceremony as part of it, I'll let you know.'

'Well, in the meantime I'll make do with a good look around the Powerboat Club.' He settled back in his chair and ignored the water he had just poured. 'I should have seen him more, you know. Dad, I mean. I was in the same town. There shouldn't be all these mysteries, even if they're nothing.'

216

'We've all got stuff we keep to ourselves,' I told him. 'It's all right. You could have seen him every week and there'd still be things you didn't know.'

'Yes, but somehow it brings out the Miss Marple in me.'

Our meals arrived from the kitchen then, his salad with the dressing on the side, my gnocchi gamberi with sage butter. Maybe there would be something of our father to find, maybe there wouldn't. If there was, I wanted to know it, and Patrick seemed to need to know it. It was a gap in *him*, rather than just a gap in our father's history. That's how it looked. He lifted his fork and picked through his salad. 'Oh god,' he said, rather dramatically. 'I think I'm over rocket, all of a sudden.'

♁

I SAW KATE DRIVE in from work while I was in the kitchen making coffee. I was waiting for Derek to arrive or call from the Wesley.

I wanted to listen again to the vocals Annaliese had recorded for my unfinished verse and chorus, but I couldn't have Derek walking in on that. He would have nothing to say that I wanted to hear.

Annaliese and Mark were in their pool and fighting in the usual way when I went down the back steps. She was shouting loud enough for her voice to carry. 'You could break my back, dickhead.' His reply was a bomb dive.

I shut the studio door behind me, put my coffee down on the Space Invaders console and called Kate.

217

'I'm going to the coast – the Sunshine Coast – on Sunday for dinner with my brother,' I told her. 'And I thought maybe we could take Mark. I know it's not a classic guy thing, but . . .'

'All the better,' she said right away. 'He'd sneer all over a classic guy thing. So, you know, if you and your brother took him to the footy and tried to talk about chicks, I think we'd all be in trouble.'

'Fortunately, none of that's likely.' I didn't mention the cake, the surprise Patrick had offered to hold back for Mark's eighteenth.

'He's with his father from tomorrow to Sunday afternoon. Hang on. Let me just do the right thing and run it by him – Mark, I mean, not Campbell. I'm sure he'll think it's a great idea. Not that he'll tell you in a conventional way, of course. But you know that.'

Through the phone, I could hear their back screen door open, and then slap shut as she went outside. She was saying something, but not to me. The pool gate clanged as it swung shut on its safety hinges.

'Why are you taking me to dinner?' It was Mark's voice, close to the receiver and loud, sounding rude but doing it as a game that would annoy his mother.

'It's a front,' I told him. 'I'm actually going to harvest your organs for sale on the black market.'

There was a pause. 'Okay. Dinner's a bit of a bonus then, I guess. I thought you were just supposed to get me wasted and leave me in an ice bath with a note telling me to get to dialysis right away.'

'You were wasted the other day and I missed my chance.'

He didn't hear me. There was more talk in the background. His hand muffled the phone as he snapped at Kate. Then he was back with me, all his usual atypical ironic charm in his voice. 'Just Mum,' he said. 'Worried about the kidneys. If you could leave me with one, that'd be cool.'

'Sounds like a fair deal. One kidney should more than cover the meal for all of us.'

'Hey, one other thing,' he said, his tone completely different. For the next few seconds all I could hear was his breathing, and a question of Kate's receding in the background. I looked through the studio window, but all that was visible through the gap between the bushes was the end of the pool and the banana lounge, which had been tipped on its side. 'For some reason I've got to go to Dad's for two nights, not the usual one. Friday and Saturday. Could you pea the fish for me?'

'Pee? That sounds kind of wrong.'

'No, remember what I told you? You give them the inside of a pea, one each.' He was almost whispering. 'I'll write it all down. I'll stick it in your mailbox. Okay?'

Annaliese pushed herself up onto the edge of the pool then, lifting her upper body out of the water. She looked right at me – through the gap – and I stared back her way, her brother's voice in my ear. Then she dropped from view again and, through the phone, I could just hear the steady rhythm of her freestyle strokes as she swam away.

'It'll be in your mailbox,' Mark was saying. 'Did you get that?'

219

DEREK WAS HOVERING NEAR the bust of John Wesley, as we'd arranged. He had his sunglasses on and he was looking down at his phone as though a very important text message needed his attention. I pulled up next to him, and he flipped the phone shut and got into the car.

'Thanks for coming to get me,' he said, and he swung the sun visor down and studied himself in the mirror that was on the back of it. He rearranged his hair, but it didn't seem to go where he wanted it to.

'So, how's it all gone in there? Should we be giving your parents a lift home?'

'No, they've got a bit to do yet.' He pushed his hand through his hair one more time, then flipped the visor up. 'Appointments to make. And they've got to mark him up for radiotherapy. That's how they hit the same spot each time.'

He was looking straight ahead, keeping his sunglasses on.

'So, what is it exactly? What did you find out?'

He opened his phone and glanced at it, then shut it again. 'It's not the best but it's not the worst. It's a big word ending in oma, but isn't that usually the way?' He said it as if he was trying to remember the name of a song or a cheese or a beer, something he had tried and moved on from, without much to report.

'And how are your parents about it?'

'Oh, you know.' He exhaled – it was almost a sigh, but not quite – and he shook his head. I sensed that some serious truths were circulating in there. 'They're just planning the next step. Irritating each other with slightly different understandings about what every bit of it means. So what are we making them? What's the dinner plan?'

I turned the car left onto Milton Road and joined the westbound traffic.

'Soup. A recipe I got from a TV show.'

'Soup is good. Not a big ask when it comes to the vision, and all that.' He leaned forward and started pressing buttons on the stereo. 'What have you been listening to? What stations have you got it tuned to?'

We drove up and over the hill, and put the Wesley behind us. We talked about music, but briefly and only out of habit. I told Derek in some detail about the soup because I knew he couldn't take one more mention of his father. It was Antonin Carême's, or my take on one of Antonin Carême's – a soup he had devised for the Regency banquet of 1817 to celebrate the visit to England of a Russian Grand Duke. I told it like a fable, like Scheherazade, keeping a death at bay. I remembered every fragment of the story that I could manage – Carême inventing the chef's toque, the absence of garlic since it hadn't yet arrived in France, the gold leaf on the edible sugar model of the Arc de Triomphe or some other triumphal arch, one hundred and forty different meals all laid out at once.

Derek even asked questions, took flight from his life, all the way to the shops at Kenmore. He remembered the time when we had been friends with backpacks and had made it to St Petersburg, and the moment of stillness on a grand staircase in Peter's palace when the guide had pointed out a feature on the huge stained-glass window and, into the hushed appreciation, a British tourist – who we didn't much like – let slip a far-from-silent fart.

'The look on his face was the best bit.' He was still laughing, just imagining it. 'It was like he was somehow *near* the fart, but not responsible.'

The band was on hiatus then. We had an EP behind us that had done pretty well, and Derek and I had been working on the demos that would ultimately be the nucleus of The True Story of Butterfish. My relationship with Jess was on one of its hiatuses too. Outside the palace, Derek bought a medal from an old, bent Russian woman who looked like ET in a scarf. It cost him five US dollars. He wore it most days and called it an Order of Lenin. We answered to no one back then. No one took photos of us or looked at us twice. Three years later, he wanted to wear the medal at a photoshoot in Boston. He had found it on a trip home. 'I can give you fifty reasons why that won't be happening,' the publicist said, as she steered him away from the photographer and took the medal for safe-keeping.

Derek had bought the unit for his parents a few years ago, when they had been on the brink of retirement. His father had owned a service station, but had been done over by the multinational that put petrol in his tanks. He had hoped to sell it and live off the proceeds, but instead it had ended up surrounded by cyclone fencing and covered in graffiti, with the remediation of the land set to cost almost as much as the block was worth.

They wouldn't take money so Derek, without saying a thing, bought them a unit on the river at St Lucia. Three or four bedrooms, city views from a long balcony, secure basement parking – I saw the flyer in his hotel room when he was lining it up, though he didn't tell me then why he was buying it. He got a designer in and had the place made over, and on a brief trip home he drove his parents there and handed them the keys. It was a gift, and their old house had become their superannuation.

We were on our way to St Lucia, with me in the driver's seat and Derek nursing a half-made soup on his lap, whole chicken breasts floating around in Antonin Carême's fragrant broth, or my version of it at least. The cooking pot sat on a folded towel, and Derek complained about the heat radiating through to his thighs.

The soup had required an hour of simmering, which Derek had said had to be done at my house. I had imagined a few hours with his parents, and making the soup there from scratch, but Derek had insisted the visit couldn't be long. He told me a nurse had made that clear at the Wesley, although I had my doubts. So I had chopped and fried the onion and garlic, added the spices and the chicken and the stock and set it all simmering, while Derek paced around my kitchen, drank three Stellas and asked me if I had any scotch.

'It's one of these,' he said, peering out into the dark and up at the tall buildings as we drove slowly along Macquarie Street. 'They all look the same at night. I think it's on this block anyway.'

Beside the road, people walked in pairs on a pavement tilted by the roots of drought-stressed poincianas. A Malaysian or Indonesian couple, probably students, pushed a baby in a stroller. A group of joggers streamed by, flicking sweat. Most but not all of the buildings were big functional yellow-brick edifices from the seventies, and it was in front of one of them that Derek stopped us.

223

'Yeah,' he said, still staring out the window. 'This is it. Be ready for them to be a bit . . . off. Okay? Be ready for that.'

'It's been a big few days. I'd be a bit off too.'

He went 'Hmm,' but said nothing. He sat, gripping the pot by both its handles even though the car was safely parked.

'So let's go then. Let's feed these people.'

He led the way past the yellow-brick bank of mailboxes and along the concrete path, carrying the soup while I brought the Tupperware box with basmati rice, coriander and chopped celery. He buzzed on the intercom, then buzzed again when there was no reply. On the other side of the building, the long bass note of a CityCat engine passed, heading downstream.

'I'm going to have to call them,' he said. 'My phone's in my pocket.'

He was about to hand me the soup when the intercom crackled and his mother's voice came through saying, 'Hello.' She sounded positive and strong, but it was just one word.

'It's me,' he said.

'Hello Me,' she said back to him. 'I'll just check if we're letting in people by that name.'

'We have soup. But you can only have it if you're not going to be embarrassing.'

'I can't promise that,' she said, keeping up the sprightly tone. 'But come on in.'

The door lock clicked and buzzed, and we pushed our way through.

'Bloody parents,' Derek said, half to me and half to himself.

The foyer was bright and clad in a light polished stone. Three fake grass trees stood in pots in a bed of smooth white pebbles. Derek walked over to the lifts and pressed the up button with his elbow. It had slipped his mind for now that I had no bloody parents.

The lift took us to the eighth floor. His mother already had their front door open.

'Curtis Holland,' she said. 'Let me see you.' She was smaller than I remembered, and her hair was wispier and whiter. She was wearing a blue dress with a hibiscus pattern – the kind of dress you never saw advertised but that older women never had trouble finding. She faced me and put a hand on each of my biceps and scrutinised me as if I were a hat stand or a tall appliance and she was a customer willing to be persuaded. The Tupperware lunch box was stuck between us like an inauspicious offering. 'Well,' she said, and left it there, because no one knows the decent way to say you've stacked on the kilos and started to sag.

She led us inside. Derek's father was still nowhere to be seen. The balcony doors were open and the city lights stood in a clear row in the distance, behind West End. The bone-coloured curtains lifted a little in the breeze and flapped down again. Other than a few signs of human habitation – a newspaper, a ball of wool with two knitting needles lancing through it and making an X – it looked like a magazine photo. It was all taupe and bone and beige, with subdued downlights, and the TV was in a Balinese teak hutch, with shutters.

She took us into the kitchen and said, as if it were an instruction, 'This island bench – it's beautiful, but not for food.' It was a big polished slab of grey stone, with flecks of white and cream and pale yellow. 'It's Persian limestone, so acid does it no good. But there's a lot of space on the other benches. Enough anyway.'

They were stainless steel, and she steered us over to an area she had prepared next to the cooktop. There were chopping boards and a knife block, and more downlights set unobtrusively into the underside of the cupboard above.

'I'll go and see what Bill's up to,' she said. 'He was having a bit of a lie down.'

Derek put the soup on the Miele cooktop and lifted the lid. Three sizeable chicken breasts bobbed around in the brown stock. Further down the bench sat an elderly toaster oven, a jar of instant coffee and a container with old spoons and ladles jammed into it, like too many flowers in a vase.

'Jesus,' Derek said quietly. 'It's not like I didn't try.'

He leaned over and lifted a roll-up screen that concealed a built-in plush-matt-steel Gaggia coffee machine that showed no signs of use. I realised that all the new appliances I could see were designer brands. At the far end of the kitchen even the dishwasher was Miele, though near it a pair of pink rubber gloves hung over a sleek European mixer tap at the sink, with a bottle of cheap green detergent sitting behind them. I took the lid off the Tupperware box.

There were noises from down the hallway, voices and a door shutting. 'Here he comes,' Derek's mother's voice said, coaxing us all to feel upbeat about it.

I thought I heard Derek say 'Fuck' as he breathed out, but I couldn't be sure.

His mother led the battered Bill Frick into the kitchen, and he went with my whole name as well. 'Curtis Holland,' he said, a little louder than he needed to. He reached both his hands out and made his way forward carefully so that they could take my hand and shake it. They were bony, veiny hands, cool and dry. He was smiling, in a wizened but genuinely happy way. His head was gripped by the white gauze that wrapped around it, holding wads of dressing in place and sticking up above his shaved scalp like a Christmas-cracker crown. It didn't quite hide the purple lines marking out the upper margins of the radiation fields. The striking feature, though, was his jet-black glimmering eye patch. 'How do you like the new gear? Pretty flash, isn't it? Carmel made it. Said she'd make me a parrot to put on my shoulder to go with it.'

'Jesus, Dad,' Derek said before I could reply. 'Don't people usually wear hats or something? It's all a bit on show.'

'I'm inside. Why would I wear a hat inside?' His one rheumy eye turned towards his son, who had nothing more to say. 'And now, me hearties,' he went on, in a voice that had gone all pirate on us, 'who be the designated driver? There be drinks to be had by all as can have 'em.'

Carmel laughed. 'He's no Johnny Depp. But at least he's not that one with tentacles on his face either.'

'I'd better get to the next phase of dinner,' Derek said. 'Curtis, shall we?'

I let him tear the chicken breasts into pieces, while I tipped the other ingredients into the soup and brought it back to a simmer. He worked on the chicken slowly, then stood stirring the soup with an old wooden spoon.

227

All the credit for it came his way when it was served, and he didn't even notice. Bill sat opposite him, repeatedly losing pieces of chicken from his spoon. Derek looked past him, at a bad watercolour painting of flowers that I knew his parents had won as third prize in a raffle years before.

Carmel offered to help and Bill said, 'Oops, splashdown,' as a chunk of celery landed back in his soup. 'I'll soldier on,' he said to her, 'as long as you're okay with a bit of mess.'

She looked sad, brittle for a moment. She made herself smile. 'It'll all come out in the wash.'

She glanced across to Derek, who was blinking, holding his spoon halfway to his mouth.

'Fuck,' he said, but not loudly. 'Stop being so falsely cheery. Not everything . . .' It came out of him as though it was on a spring, and then it just hung there.

'No,' she said. 'I know that.' She put it firmly and clearly, as if she'd known it for a while. She stared him down.

'That's star anise, isn't it?' Derek said, his eyes back on his bowl of soup. 'I'm sure I can taste it.'

'Beats me,' his father said, his good eye turned Derek's way. 'But it's great. It's delicious. And I'd better make the most of it. I'll lose my sense of smell with the radium, more than likely, and that knocks out most of your taste.'

Derek stirred his soup with his spoon, as if looking for something quite specific and hard to find.

'Right,' he said.

☊

HE BOUGHT TWO BOTTLES of red wine on the way back to my house, and he sat in the passenger seat with them clunking against each other on his lap as we turned onto Gap Creek Road.

'Jesus,' he said. 'Pirates. Mad old people.' He stared straight ahead and held each bottle by the neck, as if he was steering something. 'See what it's like? I've had days of that.'

Days of not quite engaging, days of gazing at the bad art set just beyond the ugly life in front of him. Days of thinking that a real world was waiting for him an ocean away. His parents had taken real life as far as pantomime to make him see it, and he had kept on fighting them. And he would be gone in under twelve hours.

'It's probably just that they're not strong enough to take you by the collar and wrestle you onto the road when you shit them,' I said, in a way that I hoped sounded friendly.

He laughed. 'We're not going to have to do that again tonight, are we?'

We passed the landscape gardeners and the paddock where the two caramel cattle spent their days. The moon was ahead of us, above the trees. Derek reached forward and flicked between radio stations, dismissing each one on its first burst of music or word of conversation.

'You should rig your iPod up in here,' he said. His other arm stayed around his wine, cradling it.

I turned the car into the driveway and the front of the house glowed brightly in the headlights. I didn't have an iPod, never had had one. Most of his conversational repertoire relied on shots in the dark, and the goodwill of the listener.

Derek carried the wine up the steps and I followed with the empty cooking pot and Tupperware box.

'Now, I want to get properly drunk,' he said as I worked through my keys to find the right one for the front door. 'There's a total of fifteen point three standard drinks in these two bottles.'

He found a corkscrew and two glasses and we sat on the verandah with moths batting their soft wings against the light. Night settled in all around us. He inhaled the wine as I sat nursing a glass of it, and he fidgeted as if death might be in the next shadow and set to tap him on the shoulder.

'Jesus, wildlife,' he said, looking up at the light and all the bugs it had called in. 'Wildlife just getting on with it.'

A gecko jumped forward and took a small moth by the head, pulling it back into its mouth in jerks, crunching on the slender struts of its wings. Pieces of wing fluttered to the floorboards.

'I think, when my father died, I didn't really process it,' I told him. 'It was too big and too ugly. And I ran away from it and got back into work.'

'Hey, I took your interviews for a week when you went to the funeral.' He had been about to pour the last of the first bottle of wine into his glass, but he stopped. 'We divided up your interviews for a week and I took most of them.'

'Yeah, I know. I know. And that was really helpful. This is about me. I didn't fix anything. Beneath the surface nothing got dealt with. That's my point.'

There was a movie-style confrontation that I was avoiding, one in which I would accuse him straight out of doing the same, of dealing with nothing, though in his own spectacularly bad way. A way that involved rarely having sex with a person enough times to know their full name, and using whatever substance came to hand to obliterate any connection to the dangerous real world, where consequences abound, and good luck and bad luck do too, both of them needing dealing with. Then he would take offence and we would square off in the dust at the foot of the steps where the light ran out and throw a few witless punches at each other, his mouth would bleed again and nothing would be fixed.

'And that made a mess of a whole lot of things.' I was keeping it about me, for now. 'Or contributed to it. Plus, you have to factor in that issue about being a shit communicator and keeping everything in my head. That, I realise, didn't help.'

He studied me carefully to get a proper reading of how I was saying it and, when he realised he was supposed to, he gave a small laugh. He noticed the bottle was still in his hand, and he emptied it into his glass.

'Yeah, look about that . . .' he said as he put the bottle down on the table.

'It's true enough.'

'I'm glad it's over too, you know. The band. I had a year there when I thought my head might literally explode. I'd be walking behind you thinking if this gets any worse, Curtis'll be wearing brain on his back. It may have affected me a bit.' He stopped, and thought about it. 'Okay, understatement. I may have been an arsehole from time to time. *Was* an arsehole from time to time.'

He put on a tired wine-stained smile, and shrugged. St Louis, Jess. None of it needed to be put into words.

'So what have you got in LA, aside from girls who take you for colonics, and Mitchell Froom's biscuits?' He shrugged again when I said it, and he kept the smile as it was. It was just sort of stuck there now though, adrift from the thought that had started it. 'You won't have these people forever, okay? Your parents, I mean. Your father has a brain tumour. This shit is in your life now. So don't be a dick and work it out too late. That's all I'll say.'

He dragged another chair closer to him with his toe and put his feet up on it, crossed at the ankles. He wasn't going to make a contest of it.

'I can't stay here,' he said, as if it was a fact he couldn't dispute, and was resigned to. 'I'll go crazy if I stay here. I have to find whatever's next. I don't fit in here any more. I don't know what to do here. I don't totally know what to do in LA either, but it's LA. So it doesn't seem to matter. Whereas here? It might work for you, I don't know. I've got to get something happening, so I've got to be somewhere where it can happen.'

He had picked up the corkscrew, ready to open the second bottle of wine, but instead he set it back down on the table, its arms folded in to its sides. I wanted to tell him there were spas all over the suburb happy to swing like it was the seventies at Hef's place. I had no idea if it was true, and suspected it wasn't, but I liked the line. It was very Kate, in a way that Derek had no prospect of appreciating. He was welcome to the cleanest colon in LA, the best biscuits and all the strippers he could fit into his Romance Two.

'I've said my piece,' I told him, just to let him know I was finished and there would be no haranguing. 'This is me trying to have balls, trying not to be the shit communicator. You will regret this. That's what I'm telling you.'

'Yeah,' he said. 'Yeah, okay.'

And he turned away from me and looked out towards the road, following the ducking, weaving path of a large pale moth as it flew away from the light.

♎

I MADE DEREK FRENCH TOAST again for his final breakfast.

He sat with his phone flipped open in his hand saying, 'Are you seriously telling me there's no one I can phone to get some bacon? In LA I could make a call and there would be bacon.'

'There would not be bacon. You have never called anyone in LA for bacon.'

He groaned. Mineral water fizzed in the glass in front of him. 'But I know I *could*. See?'

He seemed to have forgotten that we had lived together in Malibu for months when we were recording the last album, and stayed in perhaps ten LA hotels at other times. I was not some groupie who would be impressed with boasts about dial-up bacon. I whisked the French toast mixture, though it was probably ready to go.

'Hey, neighbours sometimes have bacon, right?' he said. He pushed his chair back and stood up.

'This'll be fine without bacon.'

But there was no stopping him. 'I'm going to go and knock on their door,' he said. 'In tried and true neighbourly fashion. Then some time they can come to you for sugar, or whatever.' He was already moving, heading towards the driveway.

'Take the short way,' I told him. 'Go out the back and through the hole in the hedge. Everyone does at one time or another. If you're going to be neighbourly, you might as well get it right. And time's a-wasting. We've got to start thinking about the airport.'

I put the bowl down and started to make myself a coffee as I watched Derek stride out across the yard, the well-honed beefy triangle of his upper body carried along by his unworked legs. Tight pants, tight T-shirt putting it all on show, in a place where there was no one to appreciate it. He pushed through the hedge at a point where I couldn't see a gap, and I saw him go up the front steps towards the door. He was out of the house again in a minute, and turning towards me with a bacon rasher hanging from each hand, proud as a boy who had just landed two small fish.

I dipped the bread into the mixture, and I oiled the pan.

'They're good people,' he said as he came in the back door. 'You know, I think they liked it, the whole neighbour thing.'

It was a performance, still, for him, like everything else. On the table, his phone buzzed as he presented me with the bacon. He picked it up, looked at the number.

'Hey, it's Pia,' he said. 'Do you hear from her much?' She was the band's Sydney manager, and he wasn't looking for an answer. He was already taking the call. 'Hey

Pia, what's happening? . . . No, no, it's only a brief visit.'
I could hear her voice, explaining something to him,
but I couldn't make out the words. 'Okay, yeah. I'll talk
to Curtis. I'm at his house. We'll give you a call back
in a few minutes.' He flipped the phone shut and put it
down on the table. 'Someone's sent Who a photo of us
buying groceries yesterday. They want to give it a run.'

'Since they don't give groceries anywhere near enough
coverage, obviously.' I could have done without it, but it
was his last day here and we had only been buying food.
That could be public, if they wanted it to be.

'And, naturally, they want to know if the band's getting back together.'

'So, what do we say? Only for the purposes of meal
preparation?'

'Yeah, why not?' His hand reached down to the
phone again, and he gave it a spin on the table. 'I'd
happily tell them I was missing your French toast.'

'Good. So, no band. And they'll push a bit harder
and we tell them we remain friends and that you just
happened to be in town on a flying visit. And, guess
what, you've already flown. Nothing parental.'

'Too easy. Sounds like the dullest thing I've done
in ages. Perfect. And why don't I go back to LA and
create a diversion? Just to help you settle safely back into
suburban obscurity.' He smiled a cocky smile that I had
known some women to like. 'Now, get cooking. I didn't
finesse that bacon for you to just stand there with it.'

He left the room, finesse having not entered into his
day, and perhaps life, so far. I dropped the bacon into
the pan, and swirled the bread once more around in
the mixture. He came back with his backpack and set

it down on a chair, with his leather jacket folded over the top.

'Ah, LA,' he said, pretending to be wistful. 'It's already been far too long since I almost had sex with a D-grade celebrity.' He sat down, picked up his knife and fork and readied himself for the food. 'I'll come back,' he said. 'In a month or so. When he's doing the radiotherapy. It'll be shitty, and I'll be calling on you for soup. I'll sort the tickets out today, when I get to the airport. I've decided. So leave the sheets on my bed, okay?'

I turned the bacon, and dropped the first piece of bread into the pan. It hit with a sizzle and steam rose in a cloud.

'I might even wash them for you. I can do fresh sheets.'

ဂ

THERE WAS MAIL STICKING out of the box when I arrived back from the airport – a credit card bill, junk mail from two real estate agents who insisted they had cashed-up purchasers roaming the area and set to pounce on a place just like mine. On the bottom of the mail-box was a pile of folded sheets of paper, maybe eight sheets altogether. This was my fish-feeding instructions, printed single-spaced, and Mark had written 'Thanx' in black pen at the top of the first page. The level of detail was meticulous, and he had included several pages covering warning signs of illness and appropriate courses of action. Page one opened with the lines 'DO NOT LET MY MOTHER SEE THIS. DO NOT LET

MY MOTHER KNOW IT'S ONE PEA PER FISH OR LET HER KNOW HOW MANY FISH THERE ARE', after which he had added, in brackets, 'I think she thinks I've got about five and they eat their own weight in peas every Friday.'

The two pages at the back were held together by a staple. On the first, Mark had written 'A sample of my work' in the top left-hand corner in his characteristic precise capitals. The text was double-spaced, and nothing to do with fish. It was his piece about the panel beater who bumped into the girl he had once met at art school. Her nipples were hard from the beginning, and porn ensued quickly. At one point he actually used the expression 'gave her the old jelly necklace'. In a final flourish – though heavy with irony, I was certain – he had scrawled an autograph at the bottom of the second page.

I could imagine him, several suburbs away in a classroom, paying scant attention to the business at hand and smiling his cracked smile to himself as he thought about me working through the instructions and finding this.

I decided those two pages would stay at my house when I went to feed the fish in the late afternoon. I didn't know what I was supposed to do with them. Did he want feedback? Could I throw them out? If Who could end up with a photo of me buying groceries with Derek, was there even a minute chance Mark's porn might resurface from my recycling bin in a way that would do no good? 'It's okay. It was just written by the kid next door. He's very creative . . .' And soon enough my hard drive would be getting a good working over, and it wouldn't matter that there was nothing there to find, because that piece of news always comes weeks later and isn't news at all.

Before I put his story down on the kitchen table, I folded it so the words weren't face up. Then I put a magazine on it. Which made it look as if I was hiding it. So I pulled it out again, thought about shredding it. All of a sudden, Mark's story and Annaliese's clothes felt as if they were beeping like EPIRBs in some Child Safety crisis bunker.

I went into my bedroom and found the clothes at the back of the wardrobe. I lifted the bag out and, without opening it, bundled the clothes and Mark's story up in an old jumper that suddenly seemed as big as a bear pelt. Then I pushed it deep into an already full moth-proof storage bag, zipped it up, took my fish notes from the kitchen table, and I left.

Kate was still in her work uniform when she opened the door. She had her 'Kate' and 'Manager' badges in her hand.

'Oh, hi,' she said. 'I wasn't expecting you just yet.' Her hair looked as though it had just burst free, and she reached for it self-consciously and gathered it with her other hand. 'Not that there's any official fish-feeding time. Come on in.'

She took half a step back and I noticed she was barefoot. She put her badges in her pocket and gave her hair a practised twist with both hands and tucked it somehow into itself. She was looking at the folded sheets of paper I was holding.

'Notes. Instructions.' I didn't unfold them, since the capitalised lines about her were at the top of the first page. 'Mark's ten-point plan for feeding the fish. And thanks for the bacon this morning. Derek has this thing about French toast and bacon.'

'*Your* French toast and bacon apparently. He made a big deal of that. It's so nice that men can put their differences aside over the right recipe.'

'Well, you know, all those fist fights get tiresome after a while. And it's quite a recipe.'

'I'll have to try it some day. Try making it some day. I'm not expecting you to cook me breakfast.' Her cheeks started to redden and she went 'ha'. Her mouth was open and the sound seemed to fall out before she closed it. She turned away from me and began to walk towards the kitchen. Over her shoulder she said, 'You'll be wanting the peas then?'

Her feet had high arches and her calves were toned from running. Then came the blunt line of the bottom of the burgundy skirt. It didn't look right on her.

'It's all about the peas,' I said as I followed her. 'That's what the expert tells me.'

'They're in the freezer.' She led me into the kitchen and pulled the freezer door open, flapping the letter from school that was attached to it by a row of magnets. The largest magnet was a calendar from a local politician, and under his smiling face the letter tiles D, I, L, D and O had mysteriously taken the place of his name. DILDO, MP. 'I'm not sure why he can't trust me to handle a few peas.'

She swung the door shut and handed me the half-full bag. There was a note curled around the rubber band that kept it closed, Mark's writing: 'ONLY FOR FISH'.

'We just got talking about the fish one day. I said I'd help out, if he wanted.'

'I should be grateful, if he's putting his energy into fish instead of poo-in-the-sports-car stories. So, thanks for helping.' She looked uncomfortable, as if caught for a moment by the wish that his life wouldn't need all this analysis, and then she said, 'Oh,' and crossed the room and took a plate from the cupboard. 'You might need this for the microwave.'

I counted out the peas and added a few more in case any exploded or couldn't be peeled.

'They love their peas, don't they?' she said. She was leaning against the counter, one leg crossed over the other at the ankles. 'Are you done for the day? Work-wise, I mean. Do you want a beer after you've done the fish?'

I set the timer on the microwave and watched the plate start to turn slow circles in the yellow light. 'I can't think of anything better than a beer after this.' The house had the heat of the day closed up in it and my shirt was starting to stick to me. I could feel sweat running down my back. I had nowhere to be, nothing to do. A beer seemed like a good prospect, like a thing people with lives did. A beer with Kate, late on a hot Friday afternoon.

'Good,' she said. 'I needed an excuse to get started on one. And you'll do.' She put her hand to her collar and rearranged it. 'And since Mark's away I do actually have beer in the house. I picked up a six-pack on the way home.'

The microwave pinged. I tested the peas, and they seemed ready. Soft, luke-warm, not steaming. That's what the instructions called for.

'Well, here goes. If they're all belly-up tomorrow you can at least report that I got the peas right.'

'If they're all belly-up tomorrow I won't know, since I don't get to go into the room, remember?' She pushed herself away from the counter and stood to her full height. 'Now, go and pea and I'll get the beers out.'

I opened the door to Mark's room, bracing myself for the sight of dead fish, or fin rot, or a low-lying slow swimmer with swim-bladder disorder. I'd read my notes. All was well though. The fish danced and flared and made the kind of fuss they were supposed to. One pea after another, I split the outer case and dropped the soft inner mush into the tanks. How did these fish cope in the wild? How did they survive in the hoof prints of water buffaloes if they needed such delicate handling here? Did Thai farmers walk the fields squeezing luke-warm peas into hoof prints?

I heard Kate walking past down the hall, and her bedroom door shutting. With the girls done, I went over to the barracks to feed the boys, and they tossed and jumped and seemed more interested in scaring me than in the slowly sinking pea mush. Kate's door opened again, and her feet padded past along the hall. In the kitchen, she started singing softly to herself, then stopped abruptly and cleared her throat, as if that was what she'd been doing all along. The fridge door opened and shut. Two bottle tops landed on the counter, sounding like coins.

When I went out there, she was in a navy one-piece swimsuit, with her hair in a plait and a towel around her waist. She had another towel in her hand, and she held it out to me.

'It's stupidly hot,' she said. 'And the pool's right there.

Might as well have the beer in it. And I figured you could swim in your shorts if you wanted to. It's not as if you've got far to go afterwards.'

I took the towel, and the ice-cold Stella. A cockatoo gave a big scratchy squawk somewhere over the backyard. In the distance, a car or two trundled along Gap Creek Road.

'Why not?' The towel was a huge old-fashioned twenty-dollar note. I'd had one of the same design in the eighties. Charles Kingsford-Smith's head hadn't been quite right on it, and he'd ended up looking like my history teacher, but with a squint. 'If I was back at my place I'd sit in the airconditioning, which is in the studio. So that'd mean I'd work. Which I don't want to do right now.'

'Mmm,' she said. 'Good. To the pool then.'

She undid her towel at the pool gate and hung it on the fence. Kate had the Hollywood body of another era, when women had curves rather than angles, before anyone thought zero was a size.

She moved quickly down the three steps and into the pool, sending a wave out in front of her. She held her beer up carefully, and let the ripples hit the underside of her other hand as she held it out flat. She turned, half smiling. The sun was behind her now. High in a gum tree, the cockatoo squawked again.

I thought of Derek and his lollipop-bodied girls, Hef, LA, the grotto and waterfall and wishing well of the Playboy Mansion. The being seen, being noticed, being there. That odd unreal world with its stone façade like an expensive private school, its own set of airs and graces and its cheap-movie-set aesthetic out the back.

242

Everything was probably authentic, but the grotto in particular managed to look as though it wasn't, as if it was made instead of painted plaster on moulded chicken-wire, like a Disneyland ride, and would ring hollow if you rapped it with your knuckles.

Here the stinking heat was real, the woman in the pool was real. The smell of the parched bush, the bickering birds, all real.

'Come on,' Kate said.

I put down my beer and my phone, and pressed the face of Charles Kingsford-Smith between two black steel fence uprights to wedge the towel in place. I peeled my shirt up over my body and the sun glared on my white abdomen. There were whale jokes in my head, harpoon jokes, but I couldn't make them work. Kate was sweeping her free hand idly back and forth across the surface of the water. I wanted her to look away, but I couldn't find a way to make her.

I almost stumbled as I went down the steps, but turned it into a kind of surge that perhaps looked less self-conscious, and my bow wave washed across the pool and slapped into the dark blue tiles on the other side. With a couple of kicks, Kate drifted towards me, and I put in some one-armed breast-stroke that sent me her way.

We hovered at the shady edge of the pool, our bodies bright and distorted in the water. I drank a mouthful of beer, and set the stubbie on the pebbledash. We were half facing each other, maybe more than half.

The sun fell on Kate's errant hair as sprays of it drifted free from her plait, the end of which was now doused in pool water. She moved towards me as though to kiss me,

243

but I was stuck where I was and she stopped, checked her move. She gave me a look as if the light had fallen a different way and she had just noticed something for the first time.

'You don't want to break my daughter's heart,' she said, as though she'd outsmarted me, sifted through my thoughts and found that I wanted her, but found that one somewhere in there too.

She groaned, and splashed me, doused me with a faceful of water. She gave a wise laugh, and shook her head.

'I don't think I can explain Annaliese's heart,' I said. I wondered what she knew, what she thought she knew. My pulse clattered along. It rang in my head like heels on a fire escape. I was sure she could hear it, see it, and all the guilt with it too.

'She's got quite a crush on you,' she said. 'And you know it. And then you gave her that robe. I found it in her room. She said you gave it to her. I assume she didn't just take it. That wouldn't be like her.'

'No. No, it didn't fit me properly. I don't think it ever fitted me. We were recording and I told her the story about it . . .'

'Ah, yes, the hotel story. So that was true.'

'Yeah. All true. And I'm over that story now, so . . . So I gave it to her.' I let it finish there. It wasn't much of an explanation, but I could do no better. My heart rate dropped back to a brisk, harried walk.

'Well,' she said. 'I guess that beats a lot of the alternative scenarios. I've got to admit I panicked when I saw it. I wondered if it was Derek's work, and it doesn't take you long to join the dots there.'

There was still water in my eyes. I could feel the grip of the chlorine. I blinked and then rubbed them to make it go away. And the complicated people who were her children both perplexed me and drew me in in ways, different ways, that defied easy definition. They weren't children to me, and not quite adults either, and I couldn't explain even that. Their lives were full of negotiations and power shifts and forced trips across town, and hormones and wild ideas. Everything was to be tested – themselves, the inconsistencies the world offered to them every day.

'She would never have touched Derek,' Kate said. 'She's got too much, I don't know . . . class.'

She lifted her left hand from the water and pushed a strand of fallen wet hair away from the corner of my eye. Her fingers stayed on my cheek, gently, and then she let her hand fall quickly to the water again, throwing up a splash. A drop of water landed on my lower lip. Her hand bumped against mine under the surface, and our fingers interlocked.

I felt dumb, in the true wordless sense. Shit communicator. What were the words I needed? If this were a song, what would the words be? I held her hand.

My phone rang, on the far side of the pool. It broke the moment, let the world in. Her hand slipped away from mine.

'You should get that, if you have to,' she said. Her hand drifted away through the water.

'No, I'll . . .' It was Derek. That was my first thought. Derek, who needed three publicists to be able to get on a plane without distraction. Derek, who had got bad news from St Lucia before boarding, whose father had been found on the floor. 'I'd better get it. It might be important.'

I pushed off from the side, feeling like someone who had just failed a simple test. I hit the steps with my knee. I couldn't look back at Kate. I missed the call. I stood on the edge of the pool, water thundering out of my shorts, looking down at the phone. A voicemail message came through.

There was no crisis. And it wasn't Derek. It was Mark, checking on the fish. 'Dee Dee had some stress stripes this morning.' There was wind in the background, whipping a harsh sound over his voice, which was mumbling. 'And Lemmy wasn't himself.'

'Mark,' I told Kate. She nodded noncommittally and drank a mouthful of her beer. 'I thought something had gone wrong with . . .' I stopped. I was ready for her to say something that would let me off the hook, but she didn't. 'I thought there were problems with Derek's father. He just had a brain tumour biopsied. That's what he was in hospital for. I was worried something was wrong.'

Her expression changed. I was less of a disappointment for caring about the call. 'Well, I'm glad it wasn't that. It sounds bad. I didn't know. Mark and his fish – great timing, my boy.'

'Yeah.'

The last of the pool water was still running down my legs and across the pebbledash. Kate hooked her elbows over the edge of the pool and let her legs drift up in front of her.

'Go on,' she said. 'Make his day, if you want to. Call him back. Or call him back if there's urgent fish business, obviously. Or don't, if you don't have to.'

Dee Dee Ramone, Lemmy from Motorhead. I had no idea his fish had names, but of course they had the names of the gods of punk and metal, of the big players in the black T-shirt bands. The phone rang again. Mark was killing a mood he didn't even know about. I took the call.

'Yo,' he said. 'How are they?'

'They seemed fine to me.' Was that enough? Enough to count as a conversation? Could this be over now?

'So, fine? Everyone?'

'Well, they all seemed pretty lively. Nothing to worry about as far as I could see.' I couldn't guess who was Dee Dee, who was Lemmy. They were all just wispy bright fish to me. Mark seemed to be remembering a conversation we had never had, perhaps misremembering our conversation in his room after Derek had filled him with beer. There were random fish facts then, but no names. 'Do you want me to check on them tomorrow?'

'Yeah, actually.' Another rush of air scraped across his voice. I thought I could hear traffic too, in the background. 'That'd be good. Hang on a sec.' The phone clunked and I heard him, far away, saying something strident. Across the pool, Kate drank a mouthful of beer. Then Mark was back with me. 'Sorry about that. I'm on the balcony. But they're waving at me in there. Hannah is. She's made *mocktails*. I mean, what the fuck?'

I left him to be prised from the balcony and presented with his mocktail, as Hannah tried and failed and another Friday evening in Admiralty Towers turned quietly to crap.

I set the phone down, dropped into the water, and pushed out across the pool again.

'My boy and his far-from-simple life,' Kate said rue-
fully, as much about a moment that didn't involve her
boy, but that had now ebbed away. 'There's something
brilliant about watching your babies become people,
and then starting to have their own lives. I hope you get
that, if it's something you want. It's great when they're
three or four and they decide to begin every sentence
with "actually", or when you hear your logic coming
back at you but with their own spin on it.'

'Yeah, records don't do that. I could easily look like
someone who forgot to have a life. I know that.'

'That's not what I meant.'

'No, but it is what *I* meant.' I dunked my head under,
and the coolness of the water shocked my face. I opened
my eyes and saw my big hazy legs, like sunken tree
trunks. I had made false starts on a life, but stumbled.
I knew that. At least Jess was free now for the real thing.
She had wasted years with me, on and off. I shook my
head and pulled it out of the water. 'I've had some great
luck along the way, but you can ride it too long sometimes. It's what everyone wants you to do. So you do it.
And they all make it seem like such a big deal to kill a
band. It's not, really. Not if it's a relief.'

'I'm in danger of kissing you,' she said. 'But it would
be for the wrong reasons.'

'I didn't know there were a lot of wrong reasons for
that kind of thing.' Sympathy – was that the wrong reason?
Proximity? No, there was more to this than that.

'This is so much better than having old man Novak
next door,' she said. 'He barely moved.'

'Didn't kiss him much?'

'Not much. Cats have better breath than old man

248

Novak.' She deadpanned it, then gave me a hint of a smile.

Old man Novak – I had thought it was Mark's name for him. And maybe it was, borrowed by this version of Kate who could turn unkind remarks about a dead man's breath into something beguiling. I wanted our moment back. I gave half a beat of a kick and drifted closer to her.

'I'd invite you to stay,' she said, 'for dinner, but I've got a hens' night to go to. And I'm a shit cook, as you know. I'd better make a move. The hens' night's one of the girls from the shop. Mother hen at a hens' night . . .' She shook her head at the thought of it.

'Well, tomorrow I have to take a look in on the fish so, you know, I'd be happy to take my chances with the cooking then. Or maybe I could make something for you?'

She groaned. 'I've got family duties. Booked in a while back knowing the kids'd be away. My parents are downsizing. They live at the coast. I'll be there till Sunday helping them pack. I'm the junk nazi.'

Inside the house, the phone rang.

'Bugger,' she said. 'I've really got to get moving or I'll be late for the other hens. Come inside and I'll give you a key so you can check on the fish.'

☊

IT FINISHED ON THAT business-like note, with the key pressed into my hand as I stood in my damp shorts on the back verandah. I didn't make it inside.

'I'll see you on Sunday evening, I guess,' she said, meaning the Powerboat Club dinner I had planned for Mark. 'And thanks again for doing that.' She seemed to hover then, as if she might kiss me but, just as I edged forward, she clapped me on the arm with the hand that had given me the key and she said, 'Bloody hens' nights.'

She let go, and stepped back, and then I was on my way next door, through the hedge with the sun setting into the trees and the day ending and my shirt in my hand.

I showered the pool chlorine away and, when I got out, I caught myself in the mirror, flabby and shapeless. I imagined myself on the edge of the pool, beefy and bright white in the sun, water running off me and pounding the pebbledash. But she had almost kissed me. That had happened too. And I wasn't certain how to read it. How I felt.

All those years of being in a band, and during them I'd racked up a grand total of zero scenes like that, where you look back thinking 'Does she?', 'Doesn't she?' and taking it minutely apart like a teenager, bit by bit learning the outline of your own heart.

It felt as if I had turned sixteen some time in my mid-twenties, and by then Butterfish had come along and scooped me up.

I found Derek's unopened second bottle of wine in the pantry, eight standard drinks worth. I left it there, lying down, and went to the studio. I opened the folder labelled The Light that Guides You Home. Annaliese's voice came out of both speakers, clear and strong. There were sounds on there that the song didn't need, but none of them were hers. I had added and added, and now it was time to subtract. I pulled it back, right back, to piano and vocals. I split the verse in two, repeated the chorus. A bridge appeared, and looked like it had always been there. It lifted from the second verse as if on a current of air and then picked up a thread of melody that led to the chorus again. I played the whole thing through from start to finish and it played like a song, a two-minute song.

I picked the best grand piano sound I could find and closed my eyes and gave it all I had, seeing hammers on taut wires, sparks of dust caught by the light and humming in a vast empty space. Then I brought Annaliese's voice in and put the space in it too, drew it out until it rang off the hardwood boards and played to every empty seat. A song for two thousand people who weren't yet in the room, a song for the sake of the song. A song that felt thirty years old already, and that might have missed its time or might not.

It was done, in a way that it hadn't been before. It was a ballad after all, and a simple one. It was old-fashioned, and that was okay too.

I wanted to play it to Annaliese, and to my father. It felt like a song I owed them both.

Outside the studio, the night was still. Clouds had come in and I stood looking up at them, my head full of sound. Derek was almost back in LA. Kate's kitchen light was on. Perhaps she had left it that way when she went out.

🎧

LATE ON SATURDAY AFTERNOON, I went next door to check the fish. I walked down the hall and through the loungeroom and the kitchen, and saw how full of signs of life the place was. As deep as the grain of its timber, it carried the marks of the three people who lived in it, people who had filled it not with clutter, but with detail.

There were dead flowers in a vase, unexplained, scuff marks along the skirting board at the counter that separated the kitchen from the loungeroom, an eclectic array of cushions pushed to one end of the sofa. On the counter, next to the start of a shopping list, there was a basket of assorted junk – empty CD cases, mobile-phone rechargers, expired batteries and rubber bands. The fridge had vouchers and art and notes, and Mark's cryptic messages to no one. Vertically, along the very back edge of the visible side of the fridge, he had spelled out 'traces of peanut' in alphabet tiles.

I had the Mark line of logic ready for that. It was a time when one look at packaging would tell you that everything might contain traces of peanut, and now the fridge had traces of peanut too. It would be something like that.

The picture of Annaliese and Oscar the dog was gone, I realised. The note from school that I'd seen on the freezer door the day before was hanging askew in its place.

The TV guide was on the counter and opened to Friday, and a single wine glass stood in the kitchen sink with water in it.

I went to Mark's room, and visited the fish. I sat the wrong way round on his study chair, with my elbows leaning on the back of it, and I watched his girl fish lapping and dodging and hiding out under weed. There were more plastic tank toys than I'd realised – the pirate chest loaded with doubloons, the dry-suit diver in his helmet, the ruined castle. If I'd thought about it, though, I would have known they'd be there. Mark couldn't own fish without a sly joke about people who own fish.

I looked for Dee Dee and Lemmy in the boys' barracks, but not one fish there looked particularly like a Ramone or a hard-rocking seventies English bass player.

I sent him a text message that said, 'All good with the fish,' and I tucked his chair back under his desk.

Kate's bedroom door was partly open. I noticed it as I passed, and I found myself standing there, the fingertips of one hand on it, as if willing it to open further but knowing I couldn't push. I could see one corner of her bed, the single sheet turned back, two pillows, one on top of the other. A fat white paperback novel was splayed open and lying face-down on the bedside table. I knew there would be a ceiling fan, and I imagined myself looking up at it on a hot night. The fan turning, turning, swaying and clicking, warm air pushing over me.

I had talked to Kate about luck, but I didn't mean luck. You don't *feel* luck. Luck is part of the story, or it's not, but it isn't one of the living, breathing, beating human parts. There was something about her that made me want to explain myself, and something that made me want to explain nothing. To draw a line, make a start instead.

🎧

THERE WERE POOL NOISES when I opened the car door on Sunday – girls shrieking, a bomb dive. They were happy noises this time though. I could hear Annaliese's voice, but not the words. Then laughter, Annaliese and another girl laughing.

In my hand I had the CD I'd burned, but I put it back in the glove box. If there were friends over, it wasn't the time. I'd had it mapped out, most of the conversation anyway. I would walk in with the CD on show, Annaliese would clear the room to listen in privacy and we would have five minutes for me to tell her what I needed to. She would dismiss me with a 'whatever', I would tough it out and make her look me in the eye, and we would talk our way through Monday, put some kind of patch on the hole it had left in how she felt about herself.

And then I would play her the song, The Light that Guides You Home. I wanted her to hear it, and I wanted to be there when she heard it for the first time. I had run through that part of the conversation too in my mind as I'd driven next door, and now I wouldn't be having it either. Not yet.

More pool noise came from behind the house – big splashy freestyle strokes, another shriek.

Kate was at the open front door, and she waved when I looked up. She came over to the verandah railing as I got close to the steps and she said, 'He's just about ready. They haven't been home long.'

She leaned forward with both her hands on the railing. Her dress had thin straps that crossed her collarbones, but otherwise her shoulders were bare. I wanted Mark not to hurry, to go through his entire black T-shirt collection until he was satisfied he'd chosen just the right one.

'How was the packing?'

She wasn't dressed for packing. She looked as if she was about to go somewhere, or had just been somewhere.

'Pointless. My involvement anyway. I got fed every five minutes and they wouldn't throw away a thing.'

I reached the top of the steps, and stood facing her. She folded her arms and leaned against the railing with her hip.

'So, it's all in boxes,' she said. 'About a thousand boxes. Nostalgia rules.'

'Nothing wrong with that. I've been looking through some of my father's junk lately. He was writing an opera. And I had no idea. Do talk to your parents about their operas, if you get the chance.'

She nodded. 'You were teaching that lesson to Derek all week, yeah?'

'Yeah.' And roughing him up occasionally, and discovering he'd slept with the person I was married to. Not all secrets are operas. 'He's not an especially quick learner though. But there are people who might say I require some patience myself, so I'm sticking with the task.'

'So, now that he's gone, how does *your* life work from here? Derek still seems to be flitting around LA, but what about you?'

'I can't say exactly. But maybe I don't need to know *exactly*. I'm learning that it can be nice to discover a few things along the way, instead of living it like a tour itinerary. I've never been a flitter though. I'm not Derek.'

255

'Hey.' It was Mark, standing in the doorway, his hair slick and wet. He was wearing a shirt with a collar, a crumpled paisley-style mustard-and-black shirt. One end of the collar was bent up as if it had sat for months with weight on it.

Behind him, down the hallway and through the house, came more shouting from the pool. The music volume jumped, and I could hear Annaliese and another girl singing along.

'Lucky the neighbours are out for the next few hours,' Kate said, meaning me. 'That's Siobhan. The friend from school who lives down the road. She's here for dinner, since Mark's having a night out.'

'Just make sure you don't do mocktails,' Mark said, his sarcasm as unleavened as ever. 'I couldn't bear to miss that.'

'It's all I've been hearing about since they got back. Mocktails.' Kate glanced Mark's way, gave him a parental once-over to see that he had shoes on both feet, clothes fit for the public. 'I think it was the brandy-essence Alexander that was your favourite, wasn't it?'

'It was right up there. It was the one that was most like melted ice cream. And it's not like we've only been talking mocktails. You've been doing all that running around getting ready for Curtis to come over. Scrubbing the news print off your elbows, putting on your party dress.'

'Ha,' she said, with a look of horror crossing her face. 'There's no party dress. And if there was it wouldn't be this old thing.' She fixed her smile back on. 'Well, I think I have pizza to make.'

'Sure,' Mark said, giving us each a sly look, as if the three of us shared a secret.

He walked behind me down the steps, and I could feel a conversation brewing, a conversation I wasn't ready to have yet. We got into the car. He pulled his seatbelt around and clicked it into place. Kate raised a hand to wave as we backed away.

'Pizza to make,' Mark said dismissively. 'Everyone knows you *buy* pizza.'

'So, um . . .' I wanted to talk first, to steer the conversation away from Kate. 'So thanks for that article. The one that you left me with the fish instructions. It was . . .' Despite having two days to do better, all I could come out with was . . . 'nice prose.'

'Thanks,' he said, in a downplayed way that sounded close to sincere. 'I can send you a few more, if you like.'

'Sure.'

We turned right onto Gap Creek Road and headed for town. He fidgeted awkwardly, as if he had more legs than my car had room for. He pulled the seatbelt in and out a few times as though it wasn't quite right, whatever he did.

I asked him how his weekend was and he said, 'He's got cable. There was a Family Guy marathon. I haven't slept since Friday.' He gave a bear-sized yawn, as if proof was needed. 'It's quite cynical, that show. The dad has a butt for a chin.'

He pulled one of his boots off and looked in it for something. A rank smell, like a cheese gone wrong, drifted over my way, and I may have flinched. He reached down and hooked the boot around his toe and pulled it back on. He stamped on the floor to drive his foot in properly, and he held his fist up to his mouth to stifle a burp. His cheeks puffed up and the gas slid out of his mouth with a hiss. I assumed a good depth-charge of a fart would be next.

'Do you reckon it's true that if you get no sleep for two weeks you die?' he said. 'That's what I heard.'

'I don't know. I don't know who'd stay awake for two weeks.' It had the neatness of an urban myth about it. 'You'd get pretty scrambled though.'

'Yeah. Yeah, you would.' He seemed to find that an appealing prospect. 'I'm going to try a week, maybe ten days. I should be pretty fried by then.' He leaned forward, fiddled with the car stereo. 'Hey, you got your iPod hooked up to this?'

'No. I haven't got around to having an iPod. I used to be married to someone with an iPod, so I had iPod visiting rights.'

'You could buy your own,' he said. 'That happens.' It was a welcome, uncomplicated answer. 'So that's, like, fully over now?' He kept his eyes on the traffic in front of us, and asked it as if it wasn't much of a question.

'Fully. Courtesy of her impending marriage to another guy, from what I hear.' The traffic lights ahead went orange, and then red. We coasted to a stop. 'But that's a positive, I now realise.'

'Closure,' he said, in a Doctor Phil-style American accent, and he gave a big sniff that sent snot rattling around his sinuses.

'That's right. I was thinking I'd throw a mocktail party to celebrate my progress, but now I'm not so sure it's the thing.'

He gave a mucousy laugh. 'Well, I'm in, obviously.'

258

He was horribly sleep-deprived, and all secretions and stumbling pheromones and truncated half-sentences, but we had a thing going that was starting to look genuinely like rapport, and I didn't mind it at all. We drove through the city and the Valley, then down James Street past Harveys and Luxe and the Cru Bar, where crowds hung around looking beautiful and moody and sharp, next to blackboards with chalk descriptions of wines by the glass, the words spelled somewhere between phonetic and dictionary standard. Mark took it all in, and I wondered if he saw himself there in five or ten years, or saw himself somewhere very different.

The traffic slowed and stopped as a car pulled out in front of us and another backed into its parking spot. Two women who had been looking at the Cru Bar blackboards caught up with us and walked by. They both had short black hair and fringes as blunt as wide paint brushes. One of them pushed a red Bugaboo stroller, the other carried two brown paper bags of organic groceries. My London friends had a Bugaboo, given to them by one set of parents. They told me, jokingly, that anyone who was anyone had a Bugaboo or, if not that, a Maclaren. Celebrity stroller envy, and two brand names, was all I knew about children. When Kate had mentioned children in the pool, I hadn't known what to do, what to think. What got me most, though, was that I hadn't grown up enough to give the issue any thought. I was a blank page, without even the question on it until then.

Patrick was on the street outside his apartment block when we pulled up. He was wearing a snug-fitting semi-see-through white T-shirt and jeans so tight it was clear he dressed to the left. And was uncircumcised.

Or maybe that's just how I saw it, or how the light fell. He had a jacket in his hand. It had a cut that might have been nautical. I imagined anchors on the buttons. He waved, noticed Mark in the passenger seat and signalled that he would get in the back.

'The wardrobe's great,' I said as he opened the door. 'But you do realise it'll be kind of daggy.'

'It's a club,' he said indignantly. 'There'll be a dress code.'

'Yeah, like shoes after six. Men to wear shirts.'

He made a harrumphing noise and got in. Mark moved his seat forward a couple of notches, which brought his knees up to the dashboard.

'Men to wear shirts?' Patrick said. 'What kind of a club is that? I mean, why bother waxing?'

Mark looked straight ahead, giving nothing away. Patrick, whose performance was for him, reached forward, tapped him on the shoulder and introduced himself.

I did a U-turn and took us through Teneriffe, past the long solid buildings that had been woolstores but were now apartments, past old Queenslander houses with giant stooped Moreton Bay figs in their yards, past the site where the gasworks had been pulled down and which a few thousand more people might soon call home. We followed the river towards the bay, then took the Gateway Arterial north through the industrial buildings clustered near the airport, and the golf course and the wetlands, where wader birds bent down from their high legs to pick around in the shallows. Mark's mucus and gas eruptions settled down into more of an equilibrium. Patrick badgered him with school questions he didn't much like but that Patrick rarely had the chance to ask anybody. Instead of giving much in the way of answers, Mark came out with a marginally relevant story or two about his father, caricaturing his pomposity and self-absorption. In that style, the three of us travelled north as the sun sank down into the heat haze and settled into the low peaks of the D'Aguilar Range.

'Hey, Chubs, remember when Dad wanted to take us climbing?' Patrick said as the Glasshouse Mountains came into view. He had grabbed the back of Mark's chair and was leaning forward. 'And then he worked out we might need a rope, so it never happened.'

'Yeah. Where did he get that idea?' I could vaguely recall it. It was after dinner one night and we were watching TV. Not a show about mountains though. 'He wouldn't even climb stairs if he could avoid it.'

'We were slothful, or something. That's what it would have been. Some initiative to stop us slothing around.'

'What?' Mark said sluggishly, blinking hard as he pulled out of a nose-dive into weariness. 'I thought your generation was all about playing backyard cricket and stuff. I thought we were the sloths.'

'I'm sure you're extremely slothful,' Patrick said supportively. 'But we were sloth pioneers. You wouldn't know how to sloth if Gen X hadn't gone there first.'

We took the Caloundra turn off, and Patrick looked up the Powerboat Club on the map. We turned right off the main road into town, and passed a caravan park and blocks of holiday units. Then we were on the seafront, with the waters of Pumicestone Passage and Bribie Island to our left. With the very last of the daylight faded and

261

gone, families were packing up, stuffing towels into bags, bunching fishing rods for carrying to their cars. Pelicans hung around in the hope of scoring leftover bait or the last fish of the day, walking like drunks, eyeing off children who might, from nowhere, drop a bream or a flathead to the ground through simple clumsiness. But the cars were filling and hope was exhausted, so one by one all but the most optimistic of the birds were casting off into the night and flying like boats that skimmed just above the surface of the water, cruising back to wherever they slept.

'There it is,' Patrick said, pointing and staring out the window into the darkness.

The carpark was half-full and light spilled from the open foyer of the Powerboat Club. Patrick was looking for signs, for traces of our father, as we drove in. The air was warm and salty and full of mangroves when I opened the car door. I got out and stood on the bitumen and took a deep breath. Patrick was already out and scouting around.

'Hey, Sunday roast,' he said, as though it was quite a find. 'I knew it. How could you go past that?'

He was at a noticeboard just next to the entrance, with Mark ambling up behind him. Next to the menu and the special orange flyer promoting the Sunday roast were a page of dress requirements and a poster advertising an appearance in the coming weeks by some remnant combination from the legendary local eighties showband Wickety Wak. Our father had known someone who had played in their brass section back then, but that was surely a chance association, not any kind of link to the Powerboat Club. I thought of telling Patrick, but knew it would send him off on some unhelpful tangent that would end only with us googling people who were better left ungoogled.

'All right,' he said. 'Let's see how this works for us.'

Like a magician revealing the final card in a trick, he pulled our father's membership card from his wallet, and led the way inside. The foyer was brightly lit, with a display of promotional merchandise — club T-shirts, stubbie holders, sun visors — at the far end of the counter. A couple aged about seventy were signing in. The jangle of poker machines rang from a doorway to the right, and directly ahead of us was the bar and dining area. Patrick was studying the black-and-white pictures of past commodores and the boards of office bearers' names. There was no one we knew.

He stepped up to the counter when the couple moved away, and the laminated card made a snapping noise when he placed it confidently down.

'Great, Ted,' the staff member said. She wore a name tag with 'Shanae' on it. Her blonde hair was bunched behind her head and scraggy at the ends. She must have been about twenty-five. She glanced at Patrick and put on a smile. No recognition, no curiosity, none at all. Ted Holland was a name on a card to her. 'And you'll be signing these two guests in then?'

'Yeah,' Patrick said. 'Where do I do that? It's been a while since I was here.'

She slid the book along the counter. 'No worries.' She looked across to Mark and me. 'Now you guys just have to carry these passes with you, right?' She was indicating some slips of paper attached to the book. 'But make sure any food or drinks go on Ted's tab and you get the member's price.'

'So there's a tab?' Patrick thought he was onto something. 'Members get to run a tab?'

'Yeah. Like at the bar, and that. You can settle up at the end of the night. I think they've had that system for a while.' She tore our passes along their perforated lines and handed them to us. 'Youse all have a great evening, okay?'

Patrick thanked her and scanned the walls one final time for clues before leading the way into the dining-room. A family celebrating something had lined up three of the square laminated tables and were well into their burgers or fisherman's baskets or Sunday roast. Three men stood near the far wall with tickets in their hands watching a greyhound race on the wall-mounted TV screen. The couple who had come in ahead of us were down at the bain marie, giving their dinner options some serious thought.

'This is so not Dad,' Patrick said to me as he took it all in.

The dogs raced frantically but in silence. 'Ah, died in the arse,' one of the punters said as they crossed the line. 'Could have paid for my tea if he'd got up.'

'Well, Sunday roast, I think,' I said to Patrick, who was stuck where he was standing. 'That's got to be the way to go.'

'Sounds good to me,' Mark said, taking in the food smells and seeing nothing else in the room worth a second thought. He stretched his arms out, and yawned.

'And a brandy-essence Alexander with that?'

'Coke'd be fine, thanks.' He glanced around in case someone had heard, but no one was looking our way. 'Whatever one they have that's got the most caffeine. It

264

hardly touches me any more, and this is day three of my awakeness marathon, remember?'

We ordered our meals, then went to the bar for drinks. Both times the Ted Holland card came out, both times the service was friendly and blank. We took our number to a table on the deck outside.

'So what do you reckon?' Patrick said. 'Mystery? Complete mystery?'

On the TV inside, the dogs were about to be released for the next race. A sea breeze came in and flapped the plastic screens that were pulled down around the edges of the deck. Juice Newton's Angel of the Morning played from a speaker above my head. I noticed Patrick scrutinising Mark's ear-wear properly for the first time, working out that it was a faux nail rather than a stud, with the flat scored head of the nail in front of the lobe and the bent tail hanging out the back.

'I can't see him here. I can't imagine it.' Our father on this deck, our father putting a few dollars on the dogs, our father wining and dining his internet date at the edge of the dark Pumicestone Passage. 'We're going to be stuck with some mysteries, and this looks like being one of them. So you have to tell me everything about *you*. In case you get hit by a bus or whatever. I don't want to find out about weird life memberships or your thing for the Russians once you're gone.'

He laughed, and leaned back in his chair. He took another look over his shoulder, back into the dining room. 'I thought when we came in that I'd look up and there he'd be in a commodore's cap in one of those photos. An old sea dog with a briar pipe. But that's not going to happen. Okay, me. Something about me.

Something that would be mysterious if I got hit by a bus.' He gave it some thought. 'Okay. In my flat you would find a couple of knitting needles and a pattern for a scarf. I have a friend who knits and he tells me it's very therapeutic.'

Mark laughed in a way I hadn't heard him laugh before, a big open – maybe even non-cynical – laugh that he didn't try to damp down. 'So this is our men's session? We get the Sunday roast and we talk about knitting? I don't think this is what my mother's expecting. Hilarious. When she goes out with her friends, they drink too much and talk about guys.'

'Well, obviously that's my life most of the time,' Patrick said, feigning offence, 'but I was trying to go a bit deeper. Okay, Chubs. Your turn. What's hiding in your cupboards that'd have me baffled?'

'Nothing.' Annaliese's clothes. Annaliese's clothes balled up, stuffed in a jumper and sealed in a bag. I'd answered too quickly, too twitchily. 'A story of Mark's. It could be interpreted as pornographic.'

'Jeez, it'd better be,' Mark said. 'If that's not porn, I'm taking money under false pretences.'

Our drinks arrived, two beers and a Coke.

Patrick waved his hands around. 'Back up a second. Porn? You write porn, and Curtis buys it from you? I thought you mowed his lawn.'

'No,' Mark said, as if Patrick wasn't too bright. '*Magazines* buy it from me. I just *gave* it to Curtis. One artist to another, you know?'

'All I'm saying is –' it was my turn to clarify – 'it would be an unexplained item in my house if I got hit by a bus. There being no other porn in the house.'

'Sure. That's what they all say. "It was just that one time . . ."' Patrick, his brush with the world of knitting now out in the open, was enjoying the game. 'Which leaves us with . . .' He turned dramatically to Mark. 'You. What's lurking in your room, waiting to be discovered?'

'Well . . .' Mark looked around the dining area, his crumpled collar buckling as he turned his head. 'There might be some fish.'

'Fish?' Patrick said, doing his best to sound inquisitorial. 'And what would be so confidential about fish?'

'Well, that's the big question, isn't it?' He took a large swig of his Coke, then battled to keep the gas down his oesophagus. He looked at me, then at Patrick again. 'You can't tell anyone this, right? No one else knows. And it's a bit bigger than knitting.'

'Secret men's business,' Patrick said, in a tone that sounded completely serious.

'My mother – I heard her talking to her friends. There's this uni course she wants to do. It's a teaching thing. And I think she'd be really good at that. But she can't do it while she's still got two lots of school fees to pay.' He paused, as if the next part wasn't easy to word.

'What about your father?' Patrick said. 'What about his contribution to your school fees? Doesn't that make a difference?'

'Yeah, well, that's not his thing. It's not how he wanted to allocate his resources. So, I have a couple of business ventures. There's the articles, which you now know about. And I'm about to breed Siamese fighting fish. So, that'll bring the money in big-time if it works out, and I can maybe pay one lot of school fees. Then she

267

can study. That's the plan.' He drank more Coke, and cleared his throat. It was clear we weren't to make too much of it. 'And Annaliese doesn't know, okay? She's got enough to deal with. She's the clean-cut high flyer and that's a full-time job, I reckon. I've got that whole oppositional defiant disorder thing working for me. It takes a lot of pressure off. Also, she likes to come across as worldly and experienced, but she's not.'

He was looking at me, as if he had tacked on his final point for my benefit. I hoped it was just his version of the message I'd got from Kate in the pool. He didn't mention the robe, the studio.

He coughed into his hand and gazed past me and towards the poker machines with a blank look on his face. There was no revelation coming.

'We've got to do something for this boy,' Patrick said as Mark shambled off in the direction of the gents. 'Oh my god, it's all for his mum. You'd just hug him if he wasn't so . . . sebaceous. And then there's that . . .' He waved his hand around near his ear. 'Carpentry accident.'

'It's silver, I think. The nail. It's not real. Jewellery for the oppositionally defiant. It's all about keeping your parents afraid of what you might do next. But, you know, don't judge a kid by his ear nail, as he's just demonstrated to us.'

Our meals arrived, plates loaded with roast beef and gravy, pumpkin and potatoes, with cutlery rolled tightly in thin white serviettes. Mark clumped his way back from the toilets, the poker machines pinged and rang raucously, the PA system kept the seventies rock coming. A zit on Mark's neck flared red from his unsuccessful attempt to squeeze it in front of the bath-room mirror.

'Hey, classic nanna style,' he said as he saw the food and fitted himself back down into his chair. 'Cool.' He picked up a piece of pumpkin with his fork, smeared it with gravy and shoved it into his mouth.

'Okay, I've got bigger things in my life than knitting,' Patrick said, his own knife and fork in his hands and hovering above his plate. 'Not so long ago my partner, Blaine, left me, and he had this . . .'

Mark coughed and gagged, swallowed hard, tried to stay cool. He put his cutlery down and blinked.

'Are you all right there?' Patrick said. 'Do we need to call for a Heimlich, or anything?' He was looking around, as if a Heimlich was genuinely something you called for.

'No, no. A bit of pumpkin went the wrong way. It's just . . .' He cleared his throat forcefully, moved some mucus around in his sinuses, drank a mouthful of his Coke. 'It's all okay now. Blaine. You don't get a lot of Blaines.' He said it, I was sure, because it sounded like an adult line. Patrick's sexuality had somehow taken him by surprise. He was young after all in some ways, plenty of ways.

'And that's a good thing, if you ask me,' Patrick said. 'If they're all like my ex. What can I tell you that's nice about Blaine, so that I don't seem like a complete bitch? He sequesters a few kilos of carbon, I suppose. Anyway, he used to work from home. He used the second bed-room as an office. And he smoked. Not in the rest of the flat since I wouldn't let him, but he smoked in there. I made him shut the door and open the window, but the room's ruined, of course. I can steam-clean the carpet, but the walls need painting and the quote I've got's twelve hundred dollars.'

'They sound like expensive painters.' I could see where he was heading.

'Is there any other kind?' He glanced my way before focusing his attention again on Mark, who was manoeuvring another implausibly large load onto his fork. 'I don't know if you do painting, but you can have the job if you can match the quote.'

Mark's eyes threatened to leave their sockets at the thought of so much money, and he nodded and made a frantic mmm noise through his mouthful of food.

'I'll buy the paint,' Patrick said, 'since I can't expect you to undercut the professionals on paint price and, besides, I'm likely to be very picky.'

Mark swallowed, driving the large bolus of food down towards his stomach with nowhere near enough chewing. His eyes bulged again. It was as if the deal might be off the table in seconds if he didn't grab it. He took a breath, and put on his most business-like face. 'I'd say all we'd have to do is sort out the transport, and I'd be in.'

🎧

THERE REMAINED NO TRACE of our father at the Powerboat Club, no sign that he'd ever been there. Some mysteries stay that way.

As we drove south on the highway, past pine plantations and mountains hidden by the dark, I pictured him in a commodore's cap in one of those photos from the seventies, and then as the skipper on the Minnow, the boat on Gilligan's Island. I saw him pulling up at the pier that ran from the deck of the Powerboat Club and stepping ashore, ruddy cheeked and wind-blown and ready for a beer. But that wasn't him. He had more the dark hangdog looks of Thurston Howell the third, the useless millionaire. No boat, no beer, not our father.

'Well, thanks for giving it a go,' Patrick said. He had been off in his own thoughts and gazing straight ahead at the glowing white lines on the road. 'I needed to do that, but I couldn't seem to do it by myself. I think I needed you to be there in case anything freaky turned up. Now I guess we hunt down the Russian bride and stage a really bad amateur production of the opera, and we're done.'

Mark, his transient caffeine high long gone, was asleep in the back and had been for much of the trip, his head lolling towards the middle of the car or bumping on the window. The wheel hummed in my hands as we cruised along the bitumen at a hundred and ten.

'I've been meaning to thank you.' As I started to speak, a semi-trailer surged past us over the speed limit, buffeting us with its wake. 'For organising the funeral, and all of that. Or, worse, I didn't mean to thank you because I didn't even think of it then. I was a bit of a wreck, but I was well propped up by a lot of people with vested interests. I should still have thanked you though. And done more. I've been meaning to say that.'

'I was fine to do it.' There was no rancour in his voice at all. 'Sometimes it's better being the one who

271

has things to do at a time like that. I had to *deal* with it. With him being gone, I mean. You had people who looked like they were helping you, but they were all about you *not* dealing with it. All about being supportive as hell and making sure you were back on the tour in a few days. I had a strong big-brotherly urge to kick their arses.' It was one of the best things he had said to me, I thought. 'Anyway, now's your chance to turn yourself into a decent human being, Chubs. You've fought your way off the golden treadmill, and here you are.'

There was more traffic as we approached the city and swept left onto the Gateway Arterial. Still Water came on the radio, and I changed stations. I couldn't listen to it, didn't want to hear the snide back-announce that might come after. Or might not. Even if it was complimentary, it was better not to think that my Butterfish job went on and on in radio stations around the world.

'You know I was shitty with you for years for dropping me from that band,' Patrick said. 'And now I'm not. As of lunch last week.' He kept looking straight ahead, at the brake lights of the cars in front of us, as if he wasn't saying much. 'So, you and Dad and the opera – it was kind of like being dropped again.' I went to speak, but he held up his hand. 'No, let me finish.' He looked around into the back. Mark's chin was still on his chest, his head nodding with the bumps in the road. 'I know it wasn't like that, but I don't think you could guess how many times my nose has been rubbed in your success. Butterfish, Butterfish, Butterfish. I've had years of people not shutting up about Butterfish. And I even came up with the name. Did you remember that?'

'Yeah.' It felt like a moment of reckoning that was

272

coming at us from a long way off, deep in the past. I was right back in Patrick's old sharehouse. I was twenty-two, he was twenty-six, I was dumping him from the band and I had nothing good to say.

'But, you know, all those times I got my nose rubbed in it, there was one thing I failed to notice. It was never you doing the rubbing. I just kept thinking back to you squirming around, trying to drop me, and then off you went to that crazy level of success in the end. But I could never have played in that band, the band that Butterfish became. Whatever talents I've got, they're not musical. You did the right thing. Okay?'

'Okay.'

'And I realised I don't actually want to be you, always bracing yourself for the next autograph, or hassle, or whatever. I don't want people to know a hundred things about me before I meet them. It's got to get in the way.'

'It does. More than I . . . Yeah, it gets in the way.' More than I wanted it to, more than I might have guessed. 'But I can get past it. That's what I'm thinking now. That's my plan.' I was full of things to tell him about Kate, all of a sudden. 'Thank you,' I said to him. It had been more of a weight on me than I had known. 'There was a lot I didn't get right with the band, and that was just the start of it.'

'Well, if you ever have a track that's begging for a clarinet solo, I'm your man. Actually, I'm not. I'm so out of practice, I'd hardly know which end of it to blow into now.' He laughed. 'As the actress said to the bishop. I'm out of practice with plenty of things. Bloody Blaine. I'm glad he's gone. I know I've said it before, but this

273

time I really am. And who knows what's ahead?' I noticed he had something in his hands. He turned it over and a streetlight, for a fraction of a second, caught its laminated surface. It was our father's Powerboat Club membership card. 'I think I'll put this away somewhere. I can't see myself – I can't see either of us – going back there.' He took his wallet from his pocket and slipped the card into it. 'Baby steps, Chubs,' he said. 'Baby steps towards the big mysterious future.'

'You and me both.'

The questions – most of them – about the past had been about the future after all. And I realised it was Kate who was on my mind, not Jess, or the band, or even Patrick and the few tame secrets our father had managed to keep his own. Kate and that moment in the pool, and some parts of my big mysterious future that had been neglected in the years when the present had been everything, coming at me from everywhere, and I made mistakes and didn't fix them.

Mark half woke when we pulled up at Patrick's flat at New Farm. He didn't stir enough to think about moving into the front seat. Patrick clicked the door shut as quietly as he could, waved through the window and headed for the gate, his unworn and possibly nautical jacket folded over his arm. Mark was asleep and dreaming as we merged with the Ann Street traffic. The lights of the Valley and the city towered above us and he saw none of it, nor the curve we took that put us on Coronation Drive, nor the CityCats sidling along, up and down the black water of the river.

Lives went on, packed into traffic, stacked high in the Auchenflower apartment blocks that faced the city

274

and on the wrought-iron balconies of the Regatta Hotel, where I had been a student once, back when beer had been cheap and the pub had been a scruffy, crowded, simple, well-loved place. The city buzzed this Sunday night, at exactly its usual wattage. Its citizens drank wine by the glass and debated the merits of one pinot over another, or ordered in pizza and made their night's choices from the TV guide, or saw a febrile child through a passing crisis, or drove a cab all night long, ferrying the drunk and the sad and the simply weary to their places of sleep.

Lives unpicked and restitched themselves, with wonder and hope and regret, or just with the calm banal rhythms that see us through and let us deal with existences in which we aren't all heroes every minute and aren't all in the midst of the love they make movies out of, and songs. I had written some of those songs, and I had not done it from life or memory, not enough anyway. I had done it from other songs, cribbed the hearts out of them, because I knew what songs were and how you made them.

It was not too late though. Never too late.

I took the CD from its case and slipped it into the slot. With the volume down, I listened to the Splades' Lost in Time. It was a fine song, a song that would catch people and hold them, with any luck. This was the single, no doubt. Their ride was about to begin.

I turned down Gap Creek Road as The Light that Guides You Home came on. Mark stirred at the sound of his sister's voice.

'Hey,' he said, still not fully awake. 'That's kind of wussy, but really not bad. Really.'

275

He was asleep again as the car crested the last hill and the lights of his house appeared in the distance through the trees.

'We're nearly there,' I told him.

🎧

ON MONDAY THE MAIL arrived later than usual. I was pulling it out of the box when I saw Annaliese on the road, walking towards me. She was on her way home from school, her heavy maroon pack on her back and her hat in her hand.

I closed the lid of the box and I stood with my two letters. My hands wanted to shuffle them like cards, like a pair of cards, just to be doing something. I looked at the envelopes as if I needed to. I read my address on each of them. A ute drove past with two mountain bikes on the back. There was a snatch of Led Zeppelin from the open driver's side window, warped by the doppler effect as the sound stretched out.

Next door, Mark chopped at a tree root with an axe. I could hear the axe head pounding without rhythm into the embedded root and Mark swearing at it, though the words didn't carry. He had made me drop him at the end of their driveway the night before to avoid waking Kate and Annaliese, and I had stayed with my headlights on him as he walked towards the house. He had tripped on the tree root that he was now obliterating, and ended up face first in the dirt.

'Hey,' Annaliese said when I looked up.

'The mail was late today.'

She stood facing me, her socks rolled down, her cheeks flushed in the heat. She seemed to smile. I had meant that I hadn't been standing there for hours on the off chance that she would walk by.

'I wouldn't have had sex with you,' she said. A four-wheel-drive swept past from behind her, blowing her skirt around.

'No.' She had put my hand on her breast. I could remember she had taken it that far. It wasn't for me to say where she might have drawn the line, had I handled it differently. 'Well that would have been a good idea. Not to.' I remembered the pull of her arms around my neck, her warm body and the smell of her hair – my shampoo but her hair. And the panic that kicked through me.

'I'm keeping the robe,' she said. 'Mark reckons it'll go for a lot on eBay.' She watched me, and then laughed. A dozen different horrors must have passed through my mind and shown themselves. 'I'm kidding. Mark doesn't know. Mum saw it, but I covered it. I told her it was the pay-off for some excellent singing. I think she might have been jealous.' She fanned air across her face with her hat. She was watching me closely. I was supposed to be caught off guard, to give up something about how Kate might feel, or how I might feel.

'I didn't know I could have got her in to do the job,' I said, playing dumb. Some things would get to stay my business for just a little longer. My business and Kate's, perhaps, with a little luck. 'I didn't know she could sing.'

'She can't.' Annaliese was still laughing at me, and I didn't mind it at all. 'She sings about as well as she cooks. I'll come over to get my . . . clothes. Sometime.'

She kept her voice low and secret, as though we were breaking the rules right now, right here at the road-side. 'Some time when Markie's not hanging around nearby, smashing something. I'll be . . . discreet.' She had thought about the word, I was sure of it.

'Good. Discreet would be good.' She had a way about her. Billy Joel was right. She made 'discreet' sound as sensual as it could be. She was messing with me, simply because she knew she could. 'And the clothes being gone would be good too. But you're right – now's probably not the time. Particularly when Mark's got an axe in his hand. He's more protective of you than you'd know.'

She laughed, in the one-syllable 'ha' kind of way that she had laughed on the day we first met over her miss-ing dog. She half turned and looked in Mark's direction, though we couldn't see him clearly from here. The axe thumped down into the ground again.

'I know,' she said. 'He just can't know I know. Some other time then. At least if I run low on underwear I know who to call.'

'I got an email from the Splades.' I wanted to move the conversation on from her underwear. 'They like your voice. Maybe not for the track I got you to do – though I still think I was right – but they've sent something new that's actually really promising and they thought you might be good for it.'

'Oh.' She moved her school hat from one hand to the other. There was an ink stain on the band, blue run dark into the maroon. 'Well. That's positive, isn't it?'

'Yeah, definitely.' I hoped we had found ourselves at the start of a normal conversation. 'And I think it's time you got to hear something close to a final version of that excellent singing you did too. I've burned the two tracks onto a CD and I've put the new Splades song on there as well so you can listen to it. See what you think. Then maybe we can work on something with it. Not that I'm saying a big career necessarily follows, and I don't even know if that's for you. But if it's something you've ever thought about, maybe this'd at least be a chance to stick your toe in the water.' She was looking at me, nodding. This was a very different Annaliese from a minute ago. 'I don't want to push you into this. If you have any interest in commerce/law.'

'Business/law. Or business *or* law. And, no, no real interest. Maybe I want to do this. If you think I can do it, maybe it's what I want to do.' There was a sense of resolve when she said it. 'I've been thinking about it for a while.'

'You could still do business/law – or business or law – as well and see what happens. It's a tough industry. And so much of it's down to luck. The odds are a thousand to one. Or high at least.'

'I'll take that. I might be okay at business at school but I do vegie maths, so don't try to put me off with numbers.'

'Sounds like you'd better have a listen to the new song then, and let me know what you think.'

'You've got a deal,' she said. She looked past me, towards her house, and flapped some more air across her face with her hat. Stray tendrils of hair wafted and settled. 'I'd better get home. I don't imagine you'll be inviting me in for a cold drink, since I'm probably on some kind of probation at your place in case I jump you.'

She laughed at her own joke and, before I could work out a thing to say, she took a step towards me and gave me a kiss that pressed firmly into my cheek and lingered for a moment more than it should have, her hand on my shirt front. And then she stepped away, still laughing at me privately, having claimed back any power she needed to. And she set off down the road, waving as she went, her bag a misshapen graffitied jumble of books on her back, her heavy clumpy black school shoes light on the gravel.

I had music in my head, and words, the start of another verse perhaps. I took my letters and I walked to the house wondering if it might be a bigger song after all, if there might be more than two minutes to The Light that Guides You Home.

ACKNOWLEDGEMENTS

The more I got to know Curtis Holland, the more I realised I had to have a better grasp of what he did in the studio. I'm very grateful to Adele Pickvance for taking me on a tour of the gizmos she uses to make, record and shape music. I'm particularly grateful for her going beyond the studio tour and working with me to write the song 'The Light that Guides You Home'.

Without the enormous success of Savage Garden, I'm not sure that I would have credited Butterfish with the sales I did. Savage Garden showed that it was possible to come from here and shift twenty-million units over two albums. It remains a huge accomplishment. And the only thing the two bands have in common. This novel is not, in any way, the story of Savage Garden.

I'd like to thank Dana the stripper, who souvenired my shopping list in Coles (for Loretta) at exactly the time when I was wondering what Curtis's life might be like when he left the house. I would not like to thank the guy who pissed on my shoes at around the same time, or the clown who took my watch.

I'm very appreciative of the support and wisdom I've received from the team I'm now working with at Random House Australia, particularly Meredith Curnow, Sophie Ambrose and Judy Jamieson-Green. I'm also grateful for the trouble-shooting and wise counsel of my agent, Pippa Masson, at Curtis Brown in Sydney, and to Leslie, Jill, Euan and Jennifer, who look after my interests in the other hemisphere.

The True Story of Butterfish is the first time I've written a story, in parallel, as a novel and a play. Each has fed into and lifted the other. I'd like to thank Sean Mee, Andrew Ross and Sarah Neal for pushing me to explore my characters further, and in new ways, and for provoking me to write new scenes and conversations that have then slipped into the novel as if they'd been there all along.

And as always, I'd like to thank Sarah for putting up with the hours of toil and the angst – and the late meals and lost weekends – that seem to be part of this process.